Teaching Social Studies in an Era of Divisiveness

Teaching Social Studies in an Era of Divisiveness

The Challenges of Discussing Social Issues in a Non-Partisan Way

Edited by
Wayne Journell

ROWMAN & LITTLEFIELD
Lanham • Boulder • New York • London

Published by Rowman & Littlefield
A wholly owned subsidiary of The Rowman & Littlefield Publishing Group, Inc.
4501 Forbes Boulevard, Suite 200, Lanham, Maryland 20706
www.rowman.com

Unit A, Whitacre Mews, 26-34 Stannary Street, London SE11 4AB

British Library Cataloguing in Publication Information Available

Library of Congress Cataloging-in-Publication Data Available

ISBN 978-1-4758-2135-2 (cloth : alk. paper)
ISBN 978-1-4758-2136-9 (pbk. : alk. paper)

♾™ The paper used in this publication meets the minimum requirements of American National Standard for Information Sciences—Permanence of Paper for Printed Library Materials, ANSI/NISO Z39.48-1992.

Printed in the United States of America

Contents

Foreword

Cinthia Salinas

Preparing citizens for our democracy is a vital yet daunting task for social studies educators. As Carole Hahn (2008) explains, there is a long history of citizenship education in which many have written about "the importance of educating young people for their role as citizens in a democracy" (p. 263). However, the conceptualization of what is a good citizen and how might we best help to prepare an enlightened and participatory citizenry highlights the demanding nature of the endeavor.

For instance, Westheimer and Kahne (2004) have described images of citizenship that include the personally responsible citizen, the participatory citizen, and the justice-oriented citizen. The justice-oriented citizen, they note, is the least often found in citizenship education, and yet "effective democratic citizens need opportunities to analyze and understand the interplay of social, economic and political forces" (p. 242). Relatedly, Knight Abowitz and Harnish (2006) identify two dominant contemporary discourses as civic republican and liberal citizenship in contrast to critical discourses that "raise issues of membership, identity, and engagement in creative, productive ways" (p. 666).

Finally, Parker (2003) notes that our efforts to prepare citizens is not a neutral project but instead an opportunity to engage in multicultural education and questions of access and inclusion within those linguistically and culturally diverse school settings that provide "extraordinary fertile soil for democratic education" (p. xviii). These scholars and others ask that social studies educators attend to more feminist/womanist, cultural citizenship, reconstructionist, and queer and transnational discourses so that citizenship education may examine, challenge, and rethink civic membership, identity, and preparation.

I applaud Wayne Journell and our other colleagues contributing to *Teaching Social Studies in an Era of Divisiveness*, for they have taken up the charge of interrogating and oftentimes disrupting the traditional practices of citizenship education that are "authorized by dominant cultures who seek the continuance of their members' social status, social vision, and self regard" (Parker, 2008, p. 66). Unequivocally, the scholars in this project argue on behalf of civic membership that acknowledges the significance of race, class, gender, language, sexuality, legal status, and so forth in asserting the rights of citizenship.

The thrust of their contentions recognize the ever-changing dynamics of our democracy and classrooms that has prompted others to consider how to best examine the civic identities of diverse youth (Rubin, 2007), notions of multicultural citizenship (Dilworth, 2004), civic multicultural competence (Miller-Lane, Howard, & Espiritu Halagao, 2007), contrasting ideals of communal citizenship (Knight & Watson, 2014), and the intersectionality of citizenship with gender and race (Bondy, 2014; Vickery, 2015).

The body of chapters assembled here highlights controversial issues as a pedagogical means by which social studies educators can highlight political conflict and controversy as "core and vital elements" of our democracy (Hess, 2004, p. 257). Without question, fostering discussions through and with controversial issues has extended our abilities as social studies educators to promote civic participation (Hess & Avery, 2008). Social studies classrooms serve to provide content-rich opportunities for young citizens to learn how to engage diverse views over the most compelling political, social, and economic questions of democracy.

However, I argue that this collection of chapters moves our practices surrounding controversial issues forward in particular ways. First and foremost, the influence of this project is the explicit and unambiguous attention to race, class, gender, religion, sexuality, and so forth as essential to our pluralist democracy. Unabashed consideration of the "isms" that have historically restricted citizenship in the United States provides social studies educators an opportunity to re-conceptualize citizenship education.

I concur with Journell and his colleagues that outright attention to civic identities embodied by race, immigration, gender, sexuality, language, class, religion, and so forth has become requisite to citizenship education. While conceding that the outward "mark" of belonging and not belonging is both a historical and contemporary reality for many is not a glorious admission for our democracy, the deliberate shift requires that the compelling questions and controversial issues that define the day-to-day lives of our students be at the forefront of civic engagement.

Second, Journell and others here remind us that the means by which each generation gathers, interprets, and applies knowledge is inherently influenced by technologies that offer the medium by which to participate as citizens of our democracy. The printing press, radio, and television are but a sampling of the methods by which perspectives are added to dialogue between families, neighbors, and communities. For centuries, these technologies have fed our yearning for frequent and inclusive discussions, seminars, deliberations, town hall meetings, and inquiry that "develop the habits of thinking and caring necessary for public life" (Parker, 2003, p. 78).

Today, in an undeniable and significant way, new technologies have fostered the digital citizen. The digital citizen of the 21st century has provided for herself/himself other spaces for democratic participation that are unique and not found without our current paradigm. As our colleagues explain in their work here, becoming civically engaged through online participatory media in deep political controversy and dialogue is a form of civic action that is both an exciting and yet relatively unknown advent for social studies educators (O'Brien, 2010).

Finally, with this project, categorical attention to contemporary contexts and realities emerges in the growing use of controversial issues practices. The current tone of civil intolerance provides countless examples of a zero-sum landscape that does not yield a public good. The knee-jerk reaction by social studies classroom teachers might be to stifle discussion and to follow a path of avoidance and silence.

Instead, Journell and our colleagues here have proposed a concerted effort to support and host discussions that are informed, robust, and ongoing. A measured understanding of controversy and those pedagogical skills needed to address a deeply divided nation is deliberately presented to social studies educators. To both sustain and further our democracy, these scholars rightly claim that we must remain relentless in the pursuit of genuine political issues, their inherent controversy, and the ways in which we can engage with young citizens in informed and generative discussions.

Amy Gutmann (2007), in her call for civic equality, toleration, and recognition, argues on behalf of those creative tensions that emerge when a multicultural democracy decides upon how to best prepare its young citizenry. Creative tensions, she argues, are those purposeful deliberations that lead us toward the "innumerable ways not only on the means to more civic equality but also the other valuable ends of education" (p. 74).

Gutmann pays particular attention to those "multicultural groups" whose histories, contributions, as well civic worth are often diminished by deliberations that promote destructive tensions. I link Gutmann's creative tension to what Journell and the others here have provided in *Teaching Social Studies in an Era of Divisiveness* as account of controversial issues and pedagogies that will advance civic equality.

REFERENCES

Bondy, J. (2014). "Why do I have to pledge the U.S. flag? It's not my country!": Latina youths rearticulating citizenship and national belonging. *Multicultural Perspectives, 16*, 193–202.

Dilworth, P. P. (2004). Multicultural citizenship education: Case studies from social studies classrooms. *Theory & Research in Social Education, 32*, 153–186.

Gutmann, A. (2007). Unity and diversity in democratic multicultural education. In J. Banks (Ed.), *Diversity and citizenship education: Global perspectives* (pp. 71–96). New York, NY: Jossey-Bass.

Hahn, C. (2008). Education for citizenship and democracy in the United States. In J. Arthur, I. Davies, & C. Hahn (Eds.), *The SAGE handbook of education for citizenship and democracy* (pp. 263–278). Los Angeles, CA: SAGE.

Hess, D. (2004). Controversies about controversial issues in democratic education. *Political Science and Politics, 37*, 257–261.

Hess, D. & Avery, P. (2008). Discussion of controversial issues as a form and goal of democratic education. In J. Arthur, I. Davies, & C. Hahn (Eds.), *The SAGE handbook of education for citizenship and democracy* (pp. 506–518). Los Angeles, CA: SAGE.

Knight, M. G. & Watson, V. (2014). Toward participatory communal citizenship: Rendering visible the civic teaching, learning, and actions of African immigrant youth and young adults. *American Educational Research Journal, 51*, 539–566.

Knight Abowitz, K., & Harnish, J. (2006). Contemporary discourse of citizenship. *Review of Educational Research, 76*, 653–690.

Miller-Lane, J., Howard, T., & Halagao, P. E. (2007). Civic multicultural competence: Searching for common ground in democratic education. *Theory & Research in Social Education, 35*, 551–573.

O'Brien, J. (2010). Consumer or producers of democracy: Moving civic education from the information to the empowerment age. In R. Diem (Ed.), *Technology in retrospect: Social studies in the information age, 1984–2009* (pp. 195–238). Greenwich, CN: Information Age Publishing.

Parker, W. (2008). Knowing and doing in democratic citizenship education. In L. Levstik & C. Tyson (Eds.), *Handbook of research in social studies education* (pp. 65–80). New York, NY: Routledge.

Parker, W. (2003). *Teaching democracy: Unity and diversity in public life.* New York, NY: Teachers College Press.

Rubin, B. (2007). "There's still not justice": Youth civic identity development amid distinct school and community contexts. *Teachers College Record, 109*, 449–481.

Vickery, A. E. (2015). It was never meant for us: Towards a black feminist construct of citizenship in social studies. *Journal of Social Studies Research, 39*, 163–172.

Westheimer, J. & Kahne, J. (2004). What kind of citizen? The politics of educating for democracy. *American Educational Research Association, 41*, 237–269.

Cinthia Salinas is Professor and Chair of the Department of Curriculum and Instruction at the University of Texas at Austin. She also holds the Fellow in the Ruben E. Hinojosa Regents Professorship in Education. Her research interests include the construction of cultural citizenship notions within bilingual and immigrant school settings, critical multicultural education, and historical thinking practices that introduce critical/other historical narratives. In 2012, she received the Regents' Outstanding Teaching Award, which is the highest teaching honor bestowed by the University of Texas System, and in 2015, she received the Elizabeth Shatto Massey Award for Excellence in Teacher Education from the University of Texas at Austin.

Acknowledgments

I would first like to thank Tom Koerner and his staff at Rowman & Littlefield for all of their help and support in the process of publishing this book. It was Tom who initially saw the potential in creating two books after I had received so many quality proposals for my initial idea regarding a book on the social studies curriculum fifteen years after September 11. As a result, I have been able to edit two excellent books that serve distinctly different purposes for the field.

Putting together an edited book requires a lot of time and energy, but above all, it requires a great deal of faith in others. I once had a colleague tell me that putting together an edited book was akin to one of Dante's circles of hell. I would imagine that with the wrong set of authors, that could easily be the case; however, I was fortunate to work with a group of professionals who were thoughtful and passionate about their work. As a result, this process was painless, and I believe we have produced a book that will be of great use to practitioners and scholars alike. I will be forever appreciative for the opportunity to work with each of you.

I would also like to acknowledge the scholars who provided critical reviews of the chapters included in the book:

Cheryl Ayers	*University of Virginia*
Jennifer Bondy	*Virginia Polytechnic Institute and State University*
Chris Busy	*Texas State University*
Ken Carano	*Western Oregon University*
Christopher Clark	*University of Minnesota*
Robert Dahlgren	*State University of New York at Fredonia*
Kathryn Engebretson	*Indiana University*
Shakealia Finley	*University of Missouri*

Jason Harshman	*University of Iowa*
Dan Krutka	*Texas Woman's University*
Megan List	*Youngstown State University*
Sarah Mathews	*Florida International University*
Katherina Payne	*University of Texas*
Stephanie Serriere	*Indiana University-Purdue University Columbus*
Yonghee Suh	*Old Dominion University*
Dean Vesperman	*Luther College*
Ashley Woodson	*University of Pittsburgh*

I know I speak on behalf of each of the authors in saying that the final product is stronger due to your diligent reading and constructive feedback.

I will end by thanking my personal and professional support networks. My colleagues at the University of North Carolina at Greensboro have always supported me in my professional endeavors, and I am surrounded by loved ones—particularly my parents, Allen and Brenda, and my wife, Kitrina—who provide continual support and encouragement. Finally, as with all of my scholarly endeavors, I dedicate this book to my daughter, Hadleigh, who is the reason why I continually work to improve public education in my own small ways. It is my hope that she will have teachers who do not shy away from controversial issues and can teach such issues in ways that help her to become a tolerant and thoughtful citizen.

Introduction

Teaching Social Issues in the Social Studies Classroom

Wayne Journell

Within educational circles, it is commonly agreed upon that the primary mission of the K-12 social studies curriculum is to prepare students for active citizenship. This process involves both the transmission of knowledge and the development of skills and dispositions necessary for thoughtful civic participation. In a recent position statement, the National Council for the Social Studies (2013) argued for the inclusion of social issues into the curriculum as a way to achieve these goals, stating that "engaging students in civil dialogue about controversial issues provides opportunities to foster character and civic virtue[s] . . . [such as] civility, open-mindedness, compromise, and toleration of diversity" (para. 13).

This type of instruction, unfortunately, is rare in American social studies classrooms. Teachers often report covering current events with their students (Lipscomb & Doppen, 2013), but as Diana Hess (2008) noted in a review of the literature, "when researchers observe social studies classes they rarely find discussion of any sort and little attention to controversial issues" (p. 127). Many teachers, in fact, admit to purposefully avoiding controversial social issues in their instruction (Hess, 2004).

The reasons why teachers shy away from social issues are fairly straightforward. Although some list a perceived lack of instructional time or pressure to cover tested material (e.g., Journell, 2010; Kahne, Rodriguez, Smith, & Thiede, 2000), most cite fears related to either feeling unprepared to broach social issues in their classrooms or concerns that their instruction might incite adverse reactions from students, parents, administrators, or members of the local community (Hess, 2004; Journell, 2012, 2016b). Recent research also suggests that some teachers may not possess enough content knowledge of politics and current events to adequately address social issues in their classrooms (Journell, 2013).

Without question, broaching controversial social or political issues in one's classroom can be a frightening proposition, especially in this era of hyperpartisanship and 24-hour news cycles (McAvoy & Hess, 2013). Discussions of certain issues also have the potential to generate intolerant discourse that can offend, alienate, or intimidate students (Beck, 2013; McAvoy, Hess, & Kawashima-Ginsberg, 2011).

This type of inflammatory discourse can occur in any classroom and often depends on the diversity of ideological positions present, the issue being discussed, and the passion generated by a particular issue. Politically heterogeneous classrooms present a challenge due to the range of ideological positions that are represented, and politically homogeneous classrooms pose an inherent danger for those who dare speak out against the majority opinion (Hess & Ganzler, 2007; Journell, 2012; McAvoy & Hess, 2013).

Why, then, should teachers take the risk associated with discussing social issues as part of their instruction? Research on K-12 civic education has found that discussions of controversial public issues are an essential aspect of a quality civic education, one that creates space for students to practice the civic skills of deliberation and tolerance (e.g., Hess, 2009; Hess & McAvoy, 2015; Kahne & Middaugh, 2009). Moreover, depending on the issue being discussed and the student population engaged in the conversation, discussions of social issues have been found to increase student engagement with the curriculum (e.g., Hess & Posselt, 2002; Journell & Castro, 2011).

Perhaps more importantly, teachers should be willing to lead discussions of social issues in their classrooms because it allows for more democratic instruction. Social issues come with the territory of teaching social studies; students will introduce social issues into the curriculum whether teachers want them to or not. Once an issue is raised, the decision to silence or ignore a student's comment represents a break from neutrality or a departure from ambivalence (Callan, 2011; Reich, 2007). At that point, the teacher is exercising his or her power to limit discussion, which both affirms the status quo and prohibits deeper understanding of the issue.

Social issues provide a conduit between the static curriculum learned in schools and our democratic society. If the ideal social studies classroom adheres to Dewey's (1938) notion that schools are "laboratories of democracy," then students should be allowed to practice democratic discourse. As with any other type of skill, students' ability to engage with democratic discourse is improved over time, with practice, and under the guidance of well-trained mentors. When teachers avoid controversy in their classrooms, they have abandoned their responsibility in this process.

DEFINING SOCIAL ISSUES

For the purposes of this book, social issues are defined as issues of importance to society in which competing, rational viewpoints exist.[1] Social issues
typically hold political, socioeconomic, or moral implications that affect society at large. Whether the New England Patriots should have been penalized
for using deflated footballs prior to the 2015 Superbowl was an issue that was
hotly contested with rational arguments espoused from each side; however, it
could hardly be considered to have a social reach wider than fans of American
football. Thus, it would not meet our definition of a social issue.

Similarly, the question of whether the government should take measures to
ensure that the food Americans purchase is safe to be eaten is not a social issue
in the United States, although it was at one point in our nation's history (Regier,
1933). While there may exist a small number of Americans who believe that
the government should have no say in the regulation of commercially produced
food, most people would not consider that to be a rational viewpoint.

Yet, the question of *how* and *to what extent* the government should regulate the food industry remains a significant source of controversy (Nestle,
2013) and would be considered a social issue by our definition. This example
also illustrates the importance of context when determining social issues.
Although the question of whether the government should regulate commercially produced food is not a social issue in the United States, it is a controversial proposition in many parts of the world (Paarlberg, 2013).

On the surface, identifying a social issue may seem fairly straightforward.
However, several aspects of the definition require more nuanced discussion.
In particular, it is important that teachers can distinguish between topics and
issues, define rational disagreement, and recognize when issues are no longer
controversial.

Topics versus Issues

A topic is something that unto itself does not spark disagreement. Topics are
people, places, events, and items that can be researched and described. Issues
involve questions that have competing viewpoints. The Voting Rights Act
is an example of a topic. The question of whether voter identification laws
violate the Voting Rights Act is an issue that is currently being debated in
many states.

This distinction matters because topics and issues are often conflated. Take,
for example, the issue of police violence against African Americans, which
is the subject of chapter 6. At the heart of this issue is race, specifically how
Americans of a certain race are perceived to be treated unfairly by police in
the United States. Race, however, is not an issue unto itself; race is a topic.

It is impossible to separate the topic of race from the issue of whether police are disproportionately using violence against a certain demographic of the population based on the color of their skin. It is important, however, for teachers to be able to distinguish between topics and issues for the purposes of leading discussions. Without the distinction, students may choose to focus on the topic and not the issue, which ultimately is not productive. One cannot rationally deliberate a topic; therefore, the focus should be on the issue with related topics used as context for better understanding nuances of the issue.

Hess (2009) has also warned about the dangers of couching discussions of social issues within the guise of covering "current events." Many social issues are related to current events and vice versa, but current events themselves are topics. Simply having students describe what is going on in the world does not constitute broaching a social issue. Current events can be a great springboard to discussions of social issues, but there needs to be a deliberate focus on issues related to the current events and not just a description of the events themselves.

Defining Rational Disagreement

Issues, by definition, involve disagreement, but how much disagreement is necessary for a question to be considered what Hess (2009) has termed an "open" or controversial issue? Unfortunately, no simple answer to that question exists. Some scholars have advocated for framing issues as controversial if "numbers of people" disagree (Bailey, 1971, p. 69), but such an ambiguous measure creates a situation where almost *anything* could be considered controversial. What "number of people" would it take to deem an issue controversial? Two? Ten? A hundred?

Instead, most scholars agree that an issue should be taught as controversial if *rational* competing views exist, or what Dearden (1981) termed the "epistemic criterion." While useful, the epistemic criterion still requires teachers to use subjective judgment since what is deemed rational can vary from individual to individual. Michael Hand (2008, 2013), for example, has argued that same-sex marriage should not be taught as controversial since, in his opinion, arguments against same-sex marriage are not rational. Yet, surveys of K-12 social studies teachers suggest that this view is not universally shared among educators (Hess & McAvoy, 2015).

Teachers, therefore, must determine what they will consider to be open issues in their classrooms. Elizabeth Washington and Emma Humphries (2011) described the case of a White social studies teacher in a rural school district. This teacher found that many of her students disagreed with the idea of interracial marriage and positioned the issue as controversial. The teacher, however, did not view this disagreement as rational and used her authority to frame interracial marriage as a "closed," or noncontroversial, issue in her classroom.

The framing of issues as open or closed by teachers is itself controversial. When teachers use their authority in this way, it implicitly leads students toward a predetermined conclusion about a given issue.[2] Yet, it seems clear that teachers need some type of criterion for determining which issues are worthy of discussion and which should remain settled. Teachers should be mindful, however, that this criterion needs to extend beyond their personal belief systems or the beliefs held by the local community in which they teach.

Recognizing Changes in Controversy

Closely related to determining whether rational disagreement exists is recognizing that the controversial nature of an issue is subject to change. In some cases, an issue can remain controversial over time but aspects of the controversy may change. Immigration, which is the subject of chapter 3, is a perfect example. Immigration has been controversial throughout most of our nation's history, but the target of the controversy has changed. In the late nineteenth and early twentieth centuries, for example, Eastern European and Asian immigrants provoked the ire of anti-immigrant groups. Today, immigrants from Mexico, Latin America, and the Middle East are at the center of the controversy.

In other cases, an issue may move back and forth from controversial to noncontroversial and vice versa, a phenomenon that Hess (2009) calls "tipping." Take, for example, the aforementioned issue of interracial marriage. At one point in our nation's history, interracial marriage was a controversial issue. From a policy standpoint, the question of whether interracial couples should be allowed to marry was decided by the Supreme Court in *Loving v. Virginia* when the Court ruled that heterosexual couples of mixed races should legally be allowed to marry.

In the nearly fifty years since that decision, a common opinion has been formed that interracial marriages are acceptable in the United States. That is not to say, however, that *everyone* is in agreement. As Washington and Humphries's (2011) study shows, there remain pockets of the country where interracial marriage is still controversial.[3] A teacher, however, could easily make the case that those opposing interracial marriage do not hold rational viewpoints, and thus, it should be treated as a closed issue.

For comparison, consider the issue of same-sex marriage in the United States, the topic of chapter 5. Thirty years ago, it could easily be argued that the idea of same-sex marriage was a closed issue in that the overwhelming sentiment throughout the nation was that individuals should not be allowed to marry partners of the same sex. At some point in the last three decades, however, same-sex marriage tipped from a closed issue to one that was very much open. The public debate over the issue hit a fever pitch in 2003 when Massachusetts, via a court order, became the first state to legalize same-sex marriage.

In the decade that followed, it became clear that public opinion had begun to tip toward acceptance of marriage equality. President Obama publicly endorsed marriage equality in 2012, and in that same year, Maine, Maryland, and Washington became the first states to legalize same-sex marriage through popular vote. By the start of 2015, same-sex marriage was legal in 37 states and the District of Columbia.

However, in only 11 states and the District of Columbia did individuals receive that right through popular vote or legislative mandate. In many of the states where same-sex marriage was implemented via judicial decision, protests against the rulings and acts of civil disobedience by public officials charged with issuing marriage licenses made national headlines.

On June 26, 2015, the Supreme Court rendered a 5–4 verdict in *Obergefell v. Hodges* that legalized same-sex marriage throughout the nation. Although the decision was a landmark victory for lesbian, gay, bisexual, transgender, and queer (LGBTQ) rights, it is too early to determine whether it will be the final push that makes marriage equality a settled issue in the United States. In the meantime, teachers must decide how to frame marriage equality in their classrooms. Teachers could choose to frame it as open since public sentiment over the issue is still clearly divided, or as I have argued elsewhere (Journell, 2016b), teachers could decide that the *Obergefell* decision marks the point at which they should frame marriage equality as a closed issue.

All of the issues in this book are ones that fall "in the tip" (Hess, 2009, p. 124), which means they are clearly open issues. Where in the tip they fall varies from issue to issue. Some, like marriage equality, may be close to tipping toward a settled position. Most, however, represent issues in which public opinion is clearly divided and rational positions can be found on both sides. Regardless of where an issue lies, teaching in the tip is a challenging proposition for teachers.

PURPOSE OF THE BOOK

The purpose of this book is to help teachers delve into discussions of current social issues in their classrooms. Since the turn of the century, Americans have experienced the horrific attacks of September 11, 2001, that changed our society in fundamental ways; multiple foreign wars; and a devastating financial recession. Moreover, these events occurred during a time of rapid improvements in technology and communication. The rise of social media, in particular, has led to increased and far-reaching discourse about these events as well as domestic political issues related to civil rights, socioeconomic inequality, and the government's role in society.

This book covers many of the prominent social issues that have arisen since the start of the 21st century. The list of issues covered here is far from exhaustive; however, an effort was made to include issues that either have materialized as a result of the events listed above or have gained national prominence since the turn of the century. Abortion, for example, remains a hotly debated issue at both the state and national levels. It is not included here because educators have been grappling with how to teach about that issue since the Supreme Court's decision in *Roe v. Wade* over forty years ago.

The issues discussed in this book are both controversial and complex. The purpose in unpacking them here is not to proselytize or convince readers to adopt certain positions about any given issue. Rather, the authors have taken great care to problematize each issue and offer suggestions for how teachers can engage students with the issue in a nonpartisan way that encourages tolerant, democratic discussion.

STRUCTURE OF THE BOOK

The first two chapters of the book provide broad guidelines for teachers to follow when broaching controversial social issues in their classrooms. Although students of any age can engage with controversial issues, these discussions should be developmentally appropriate. Thus, discussions of social issues will be framed differently in elementary, middle, and high school classrooms.

In the first chapter, Andrea Libresco and Jeannette Balantic offer practical guidelines specifically tailored for the elementary classroom. They note that, even at such a young age, elementary students are political beings, and their teachers have a responsibility to start making them aware of the political world that surrounds them. Libresco and Balantic show how teachers can use traditional methods of elementary instruction, such as children's literature, to encourage their students to think more critically about issues of both personal and social importance.

By the time they reach middle and high school, students are ready to better understand the increasingly partisan political environment in which they live and engage with the difficult issues that are being debated within society. In her chapter, Paula McAvoy provides valuable advice for secondary teachers on how to successfully navigate the increasingly polarized political climate that too often permeates classroom walls. Although discussions of controversial social issues can be difficult, and sometimes risky, for middle and high school teachers, McAvoy offers research-based strategies for ensuring that these discussions are both productive and tolerant.

These two chapters serve to contextualize the chapters that follow. Each of the remaining chapters unpacks a prominent social issue in an attempt to provide a more nuanced understanding of that issue for teachers and students. Although many of the authors offer instructional suggestions for their respective issue, each teacher ultimately has to frame the issue in a way that is appropriate for his or her students, and referring back to these first two chapters can provide guidance on how best to achieve that goal.

Starting with chapter 3, individual issues are explored in depth. Jeremy Hilburn and Ashley Taylor Jaffee begin this conversation by looking at the divisive issue of immigration. They first contextualize contemporary immigration within a historical understanding of different waves of immigration to the United States. Then, they offer an asset-based approach for discussing the recent immigration of people from Mexico and Latin America to the United States, which, as they argue, is necessary, given that more states have become gateways for immigrant groups over the past decade.

The next chapter builds on Hilburn and Taylor Jaffee's work by looking at a specific subset of people—Arabs and Arab Americans. In this chapter, Paul Yoder, Aaron Johnson, and Fares Karam discuss popular misconceptions and stereotypes that have arisen about the Arab world since the September 11 attacks. The authors then offer several suggestions for how teachers can encourage a more holistic portrayal of Arabs and Arab Americans using tenets of global education.

In chapter 5, J. B. Mayo discusses perhaps the most prominent social movement in the United States over the past twenty years—the fight for marriage equality for gay and lesbian individuals. As previously noted, this issue was resolved legally in 2015 via a Supreme Court decision making same-sex marriage legal throughout the nation. Yet, the controversy over same-sex marriage still persists. In his chapter, Mayo explores the question of how teachers should discuss the issue of same-sex marriage in an era of legalized marriage equality and offers several resources that can help teachers effectively broach this issue in their classrooms.

Chapter 6 focuses on the #BlackLivesMatter movement, a social movement that was sparked in response to the slew of young African American men who have been killed by police officers over the past several years. LaGarrett King, Chezare Warren, Mariah Bender, and Shakealia Finley first situate #BlackLivesMatter within a historical context of Black violence at the hand of the state and then describe two deliberate attempts—one within a K-12 classroom and another on a university campus—to make sense of the shooting of Michael Brown in Ferguson, Missouri. Teachers can use the lessons learned from these two experiences to better facilitate issues of race and systemic power in their classes.

Bonnie Bittman and Will Russell address a related issue in chapter 7, the question of gun control in the United States. Beginning with the horrific shootings at Columbine High School in 1999, the start of the 21st century has seen an alarming number of mass shootings in K-12 schools, universities, churches, and other public places. These events have prompted calls for increased gun regulations at both the state and federal level; however, advocates for Second Amendment rights have largely stymied such legislation. In their chapter, Bittman and Russell offer suggestions for how teachers can discuss this volatile issue using congressional simulations.

In chapter 8, H. James Garrett addresses the collection of Big Data and the increased state of surveillance by the federal government since 9/11. The question of whether the U.S. government should collect and store private conversations was largely prompted by the release of classified material by Edward Snowden in 2013 that showed the reach of government surveillance and the role of major telecommunication companies in this process. Garrett discusses what teachers need to know about Big Data and the questions they need to ask in order to make their students think critically about the concession of privacy in exchange for public safety.

Given that Americans are spending an unprecedented amount of our time online and that our communication, search histories, and buying habits are being monitored and recorded, it is essential that students become more aware of their digital footprints. As Eric Moffa, Carolyn Brejwo, and Robert Waterson note in chapter 9, current K-12 students are the first generation of students who have lived almost their entire lives in a world interconnected by social media. The authors explore ways in which teachers can encourage a critical understanding of social media and how these relatively new forms of media can be used for political purposes.

The final chapter by Thomas Lucey, Mary Frances Agnello, and James Laney centers on the teaching of financial literacy in the wake of the 2008 Great Recession. Although slowly improving, the American economy is still feeling the effects of the Great Recession, and the authors believe that this experience should change social studies teachers' economics and personal finance instruction. They argue for a compassionate approach to financial literacy, one that frames financial decision-making within a justice-oriented disposition that seeks to recognize and combat the wealth disparity in the United States.

The issues discussed in this book are divisive, timely, and unlikely to be resolved anytime soon. As such, they remain a frightening proposition for teachers. Although no amount of preparation will ever completely alleviate the anxiety of broaching controversial social issues with students, the nuanced discussions presented in these chapters will help teachers ensure that these issues are addressed tolerantly and in a way that is consistent with the democratic mission of social studies education.

NOTES

1. This definition is presented for a basic understanding of social issues and is not necessarily meant to be all encompassing. Others have written more nuanced typologies and definitions of what constitutes an issue. Diana Hess and Paula McAvoy (2015), for example, separated issues into empirical questions and policy questions, which are often interrelated. They then delineated further by discussing open empirical and policy questions, which are subject to disagreement based on conflicting evidence or multiple viewpoints on policy decisions, and settled empirical and policy questions, which have been sufficiently answered by evidence or are not considered controversial.

2. Callan (2011), for example, argued that teachers should not silence any type of discourse as long as it is being conducted in a civil manner. Others have argued that it is the responsibility of teachers to guide students toward rational conclusions to controversial issues, especially when only one viewpoint is deemed rational using the epistemic criterion. For a nuanced discussion of this role of the teacher, refer to the ongoing discussion in *Educational Theory* among Hand (2008, 2013), Petrovic (2013), Warnick and Smith (2014), and Gregory (2014).

3. To further this point, a 2012 Public Policy Polling survey of likely Republican primary voters in Alabama and Mississippi (over 1,200 total) found that over 20 percent (21 percent for Alabama and 29 percent for Mississippi) believed interracial marriage should be illegal. Another 12 percent in Alabama and 17 percent in Mississippi indicated that they were "not sure."

REFERENCES

Bailey, C. (1971). Rationality, democracy and the neutral teacher. *Cambridge Journal of Education, 1*, 68–76.

Beck, T. A. (2013). Identity, discourse, and safety in a high school discussion of same-sex marriage. *Theory & Research in Social Education, 41*, 1–32.

Callan, E. (2011). When to shut students up: Civility, silencing, and free speech. *Theory and Research in Education, 9*, 3–22.

Dearden, R. F. (1981). Controversial issues in the curriculum. *Journal of Curriculum Studies, 13*, 37–44.

Dewey, J. (1938). *Experience and education*. New York, NY: Simon & Schuster.

Gregory, M. R. (2014). The procedurally directive approach to teaching controversial issues. *Educational Theory, 64*, 627–648.

Hand, M. (2008). What should we teach as controversial? A defense of the epistemic criterion. *Educational Theory, 58*, 213–228.

Hand, M. (2013). Framing classroom discussion of same-sex marriage. *Educational Theory*, *63*, 497–510.

Hess, D. (2008). Controversial issues and democratic discourse. In L. S. Levstik & C. A. Tyson (Eds.), *Handbook of research in social studies education* (pp. 124–136). New York, NY: Routledge.

Hess, D. & Ganzler, L. (2007). Patriotism and ideological diversity in the classroom. In J. Westheimer (Ed.), *Pledging allegiance: The politics of patriotism in America's schools*. New York, NY: Teachers College Press.

Hess, D. & Posselt, J. (2002). How high school students experience and learn from the discussion of controversial public issues. *Journal of Curriculum & Supervision*, *17*, 283–314.

Hess, D. E. (2004). Controversies about controversial issues in democratic education. *PS: Political Science & Politics*, *37*, 257–261.

Hess, D. E. (2009). *Controversy in the classroom: The democratic power of discussion*. New York, NY: Routledge.

Hess, D. E. & McAvoy, P. (2015). *The political classroom: Evidence and ethics in democratic education*. New York, NY: Routledge.

Journell, W. (2010). The influence of high-stakes testing on high school teachers' willingness to incorporate current political events into the curriculum. *The High School Journal*, *93*, 111–125.

Journell, W. (2012). Ideological homogeneity, school leadership, and political intolerance in secondary education: A study of three high schools during the 2008 Presidential Election. *Journal of School Leadership*, *22*, 569–599.

Journell, W. (2013). What preservice social studies teachers (don't) know about politics and current events—and why it matters. *Theory & Research in Social Education*, *41*, 316–351.

Journell, W. (2016a, April). *Should marriage equality be taught as controversial post-Obergefell v Hodges?* Paper presented at the annual meeting of the American Educational Research Association, Washington, DC.

Journell, W. (2016b). Teacher political disclosure as *parrhēsia. Teachers College Record*, *118(5)*, 1–36.

Journell, W. & Castro, E. L. (2011). Culturally relevant political education: Using immigration as a catalyst for civic understanding. *Multicultural Education*, *18*(4), 10–17.

Kahne, J. & Middaugh, E. (2009). Democracy for some: The civic opportunity gap in high school. In J. Youniss & P. Levine (Eds.), *Engaging young people in civic life* (pp. 29–58). Nashville, TN: Vanderbilt University Press.

Kahne, J., Rodriguez, M., Smith, B., & Thiede, K. (2000). Developing citizens for democracy? Assessing opportunities to learn in Chicago's social studies classrooms. *Theory & Research in Social Education*, *28*, 311–338.

Lipscomb, G. & Doppen, F. (2013). Finding one's place in the world: Current events in the K-12 social studies classroom. In J. Passe & P. G. Fitchett (Eds.), *The status of social studies: Views from the field* (pp. 247–256). Charlotte, NC: Information Age.

McAvoy, P. & Hess, D. (2013). Classroom deliberation in an era of political polarization. *Curriculum Inquiry*, *43*, 14–47.

McAvoy, P., Hess, D., & Kawashima-Ginsberg, K. (2011, April). *How do students experience and learn from high-quality discussions of political issues?* Paper presented at the annual meeting of the American Educational Research Association, New Orleans, LA.

National Council for the Social Studies. (2013). Revitalizing civic learning in our schools. Retrieved from http://www.socialstudies.org/positions/revitalizing_civic_learning

Nestle, M. (2013). *Food politics: How the food industry influences nutrition and health* (10th anniversary ed.). Berkley, CA: University of California Press.

Paarlberg, R. (2013). *Food politics: What everyone needs to know* (2nd ed.). Oxford, England: Oxford University Press.

Petrovic, J. E. (2013). Reason, liberalism, and democratic education: A Deweyean approach to teaching about homosexuality. *Educational Theory, 63*, 525–541.

Public Policy Polling. (2012, March 12). Very close race in both Alabama and Mississippi. Retrieved from http://www.publicpolicypolling.com/main/2012/03/very-close-race-in-both-alabama-and-mississippi.html

Regier, C. C. (1933). The struggle for federal food and drugs legislation. *Law and Contemporary Problems, 1*, 3–15.

Reich, W. (2007). Deliberative democracy in the classroom: A sociological view. *Educational Theory, 57*, 187–197.

Warnick, B. R. & Smith, D. S. (2014). The controversy over controversies: A plea for flexibility and "soft directive" teaching. *Educational Theory, 64*, 227–244.

Washington, E. Y. & Humphries, E. K. (2011). A social studies teacher's sense making of controversial issues discussions of race in a predominately white, rural high school classroom. *Theory & Research in Social Education, 39*, 92–114.

Chapter 1

Every Issue Is a Social Studies Issue

Strategies for Rich Discussion in the Upper Elementary Classroom

Andrea S. Libresco and Jeannette Balantic

In Jon Sceiscka's (1995) *Math Curse*, Mrs. Fibonnaci proclaims to her class, "YOU KNOW, you can think of almost everything as a math problem," and in the science class, Mr. Newton exclaims, "YOU KNOW, you can think of almost everything as a science experiment." In our elementary classes, from the first day, we engage students in activities that reveal that almost every issue is a social studies issue.

On the first day of school, our students keep a 24-hour record of the places they go, the people they see, and their interactions with others. The next day, when we go over the items in their 24-hour logs, we ask students how their experiences connect to social studies. Initially perplexed, students are unsure how to respond. So we select some of the items on their lists and help them to identify questions worthy of discussion.

For example, based on a conflict on the playground experienced by one student, we develop the following discussion question: "How should we decide what game to play at recess?" When one student recounts an argument with his father over his bedtime on a school night, we frame the question as: "How should decisions about family rules be made?" When two students report that they saw trees being cut down on their block, the question becomes: "Who should decide what the neighborhood looks like?" When another student relates that a classmate was unwilling to share the crayons she brought from home, the question arises: "Should individual supplies become class property?"

The seemingly simple questions generated from playgrounds, bedtimes, trees, and crayons raise social studies issues of fairness, rule-making, individual versus community rights, community values, and decision-making. Moreover, they are all "should" questions that raise issues about which smart, thoughtful people – like our students – might disagree. Over the course of students' lives, these questions will not be confined to crayons and playground squabbles but will extend to discussions of local, national, and global issues relevant in the 21st century.

Our goal as teachers of social studies is to nurture students to be wide awake in the world, noticing the little things (which are actually big things) and identifying social studies issues worthy of discussion on their own. This exercise in the first week of school begins our work toward that goal of fostering citizens of a democracy who will seek out and discuss controversial issues throughout their school careers and beyond. In so doing, we are adhering to the National Council for the Social Studies (NCSS) (2013) rationale for civic learning, whereby

> schools should incorporate discussion of current local, national, and international issues and events into the classroom, particularly those that young people view as important to their lives. Engaging students in civil dialogue about controversial issues provides opportunities to foster character and civic virtue – important civic dispositions that are the habits of the heart and mind conducive to the healthy functioning of the democratic system. Examples include civility, open-mindedness, compromise, and toleration of diversity, all of which are prerequisites of a civic life in which the American people can work out the meanings of their democratic principles and values. (para. 13)

In our society, discussion of controversial issues may be anything but civil, as positions on issues are often cast as black or white. This chapter is devoted to fostering civil discourse at the elementary level, scaffolding discussions that allow for a diversity of positions and acknowledge the gray areas in substantive, challenging topics. To that end, we provide strategies for teachers to identify issues for discussion, help their students seek reliable information, craft meaningful questions, facilitate successful discussion of complex issues, and collaborate with colleagues as they do so.

IDENTIFYING ISSUES FOR DISCUSSION

Topics for classroom discussions are everywhere. Some topics are selected for teachers, via state standards and district curriculum guides; some are generated by the news; and some just tumble into the classroom from the playground. Whatever the source, teachers, the curricular instructional gatekeepers of their classrooms (Thornton, 1991), have the power to inform themselves about a topic, tease out the controversial aspect of it, and formulate questions to nurture thoughtful discussion.

Official curricular documents outline the content to be taught at each grade level, but teachers can make conscious decisions to address the interesting and sometimes controversial issues embedded in the content. For example, most state standards specify that elementary-aged students should learn about the Bill of Rights; however, there is a difference between teaching what the amendments are and planning lessons that enable students to discuss and evaluate the varied interpretations given to the amendments by the different branches of government throughout U.S. history.

One of the advantages of teaching at the elementary level is that, even if a Supreme Court ruling is common knowledge to adults, elementary students are not likely to be aware of the ruling and may engage in a free-flowing discussion about the right and its limits prior to being taught about the outcome of a particular case. Even after the Supreme Court has issued a ruling, the controversy is not necessarily over; the societal discussion continues and is sometimes followed by new legislation and/or subsequent court cases.

Thus, students can fully explore the establishment clause of the First Amendment by reading scenarios based on the landmark prayer in school case (*Engel v. Vitale*, 1962) and more recent cases that address prayers at public school events (*Lee v. Weisman*, 1992; *Santa Fe v. Doe*, 2000) and engage in nuanced discussions based on questions that address the ongoing controversy:

- *Is it constitutional for a public school to encourage recitation of a state-composed prayer?*
- *Is it constitutional for a public school to invite a cleric to deliver a nondenominational prayer at graduation?*
- *Is it constitutional for a student to recite a prayer over a loudspeaker before a public school football game?*

The news provides many possible topics for classroom discussion, some that are obvious, some that are less obvious, and some that teachers may decide are not appropriate at the elementary level. With any current events topic, when teachers purposefully select an article for all students to read or a broadcast for all students to view, all students will be prepared to discuss the questions that the teacher has crafted. This approach runs counter to typical "current events Fridays," where all students bring in summaries of often-unrelated articles, negating the possibility of an informed full-class discussion on any single issue.

Obvious current events topics that land in elementary classrooms are weather-related catastrophes. Understandably, these events can lend themselves to science lessons and well-intentioned fund-raising efforts. However, these topics can also prompt the exploration of social studies–related, sometimes controversial issues. For example, in the case of Hurricane Katrina, students probably noticed that the great majority of those adversely affected by the hurricane were African American (Whoriskey, 2007), making the issue a great opportunity to discuss the connections between race and poverty as well as other issues that are reflected in the questions below (Crocco, 2007):

- *Why did many poor and African American residents live in the lowest-lying parts of the city?*
- *Were the financial resources devoted to building and maintaining the levee system adequate?*
- *What accounts for the government's sluggish response to the devastation of Katrina?*
- *Do citizens expect too much of their government in times of crisis, or does an emphasis on individual responsibility place an undue burden on people least able to take of themselves, such as the poor, disabled, and elderly?*

Current events issues that captivate students' attention may seem less obviously related to social studies; however, a perceptive teacher can tease out underlying controversial issues. The 2015 New England Patriots "deflategate" controversy may have yielded heated arguments in classrooms over how the footballs in the playoff game with the Indianapolis Colts came to have less air pressure, but those arguments didn't necessarily address larger ethical issues about the role of sports in society:

- *How should honesty and winning be reconciled? (Is all fair in love and war ... and sports?)*
- *What price should the Patriots pay for "deflategate"? Who should bear the responsibility – the individual, the team, the owner?*
- *How important is this infraction compared to others committed by athletes (doping, betting on games, abuse of a family member, hazing of a teammate, carrying concealed weapons, etc.)? What should the consequences for each be?*

Some issues that teachers might think are not appropriate for discussion at the elementary level find their way into the classroom via the news. For example, while some teachers may not be inclined to raise the topic of same-sex marriage, students may certainly do so, given the fanfare around recent Supreme Court decisions and gay pride parades. The fact that the issue is a hot topic in the news and/or that students have brought it up begs that it be addressed in a thoughtful and deliberative manner, with questions that facilitate discussion:

- *What is meant by "equal protection of the law"? How does it relate to the Supreme Court finding for same-sex marriage? For interracial marriage?*

- *Should people who object to same-sex marriage on religious grounds be allowed to deny services (e.g., a wedding cake) to same-sex couples?*
- *Should there be a national law banning discrimination based on sexual orientation?*

Incidents on the playground, the cafeteria, and the bus may all provide topics for classroom discussion. As children charge into the classroom, they may bring with them disputes that arose in noninstructional settings. Teachers can choose to explore these conflicts that often involve contested issues around fairness, equality, and equity; these are teachable moments to talk about the application of important concepts to real-world situations.

Rather than getting mired in the "he said – she said" of exactly what occurred in the conflict outside the classroom, the larger issues inherent in the conflict can be the basis for full-class discussion. Teachers often start the year by making rules for the classroom with their students; however, students encounter places where there are predetermined rules that may be worthy of investigation and possible re-thinking:

- *Is it fair that some kids don't get to play on a team at recess? What is the most equitable way to allocate the available resources (balls, hopscotch court, jungle gym, etc.) at recess?*
- *Are the peanut-free tables in the cafeteria established in a fair way? What's the most equitable way to balance the needs of kids with allergies with the desire of friends to sit together?*
- *Should there be assigned seats on the school bus? What's the most equitable way to deal with seating on the bus?*
- *If the rules break down and a dispute emerges, what is the most effective way to resolve the problem?*

SEEKING RELIABLE INFORMATION

We also use the beginning of the school year to advance our goal of nurturing students – future citizens of our democracy – to seek reliable knowledge as they prepare for discussion of complex issues. Within the first two weeks of school, we read Ed Young's *Seven Blind Mice* (2002) aloud. Young retells the famous Indian fable of the seven blind men who individually investigate the different parts of an elephant and argue about what they each have found. In this story, seven blind mice replace the seven blind men.

Upon encountering an elephant, six of the seven mice each believe that they have found something different – a snake, a fan, a cliff, etc. because they "see" from their own vantage point. The seventh mouse, however, goes all the way up, down, and around the "Something," and she discovers the truth – that all of the parts together make up an elephant. Questions[1] guide students to grapple with issues of perspective and how to determine reliable knowledge:

- *In what color does each mouse "see" the part of the elephant it encounters? Why do you think the author does this?*
- *To what extent do you think people see things through their own eyes?*
- *Why do the mice change their views about what they have "seen"?*
- *How did the white mouse help the other mice reconsider their initial impressions?*
- *What is the moral of the story?*

We value this book because it provides us with the opportunity to lay the foundation for what is essential in our classes – that students consider perspective and seek out reliable information before engaging in discussion and drawing conclusions.

Thus, when we are preparing to discuss a current issue, students examine how the issue is reported in a variety of sources including newspapers and news broadcasts (selected by the teacher) and consider the following questions:

- *What differences did you discover in the way each source covered the same story?*
- *Which source do you think is the most reliable and why?*
- *What is the value in consulting multiple sources?*
- *To what extent did the place of publication or the broadcast of the source affect its coverage?*
- *What questions does the coverage of this story raise in your mind?*
- *To what extent does this comparison affect what papers you might read and news channels you might watch in the future?*

There is a temptation to get drawn into a large, unwieldy issue instead of planning for a focused discussion. For example, taking on the entire presidential election as a topic for meaningful discussion is neither desirable nor feasible. It makes more sense to plan for a series of smaller discussions that address candidates' positions on health care, student loans, voting rights, gun control, and others.

To have a rich discussion on any of these issues requires that it be grounded in data. Teachers can choose excerpts from candidates' speeches and party platforms, graphs that trace the effects of an economic policy, photographs of supporters (and protesters) and their signs at campaign rallies, campaign advertisements, commentators' reporting on candidates' positions, and other sources. The discussion must include an interrogation of the data and its reliability:

- *What does the data/graph tell us about ___(issue)___?*
- *What questions does the data raise for you?*
- *What does the speech/platform tell us about the candidate's views on the issue?*
- *To what extent does what the candidate is saying match what the data reveals?*
- *What values are revealed in the candidates' positions?*
- *Which candidate's position on this issue most closely matches your own?*
- *How reliable are the sources that we have examined?*
- *What other sources should be investigated to provide a fuller picture of the candidates and their positions on this issue?*

CRAFTING QUESTIONS AS THE BASIS FOR DISCUSSION

The most important aspect of conducting good discussions is, in advance, to formulate good questions that are worthy of discussion. Jay McTighe and Grant Wiggins (2013) advocate for the use of essential questions across the curriculum. The key attributes of such questions are that they are open ended, thought provoking, and intellectually engaging; they call for higher-order thinking, raise additional questions, encourage further inquiry, require support and justification, and are often revisited over time.

Inquiry is at the heart of the *College, Career, and Civic Life (C3) Framework for Social Studies State Standards*, created by NCSS and aligned with the Common Core. The *C3* is designed to strengthen the critical thinking, problem solving, and participatory skills of engaged citizens. At the heart of inquiry are good questions, which the *C3* refers to as "compelling questions" (NCSS, 2013, p. 24). Essential or compelling questions do not have a single, correct answer; their open enededness promotes multifaceted discussions that uncover the complexity and shades of gray in a topic – even for elementary students.

In fact, some of the most engaging picture books lend themselves to deep discussions around compelling questions. For example, Dr. Seuss (Geisel, 1958) wrote *Yertle the Turtle* in the wake of World War II to raise questions about a public's willingness to go along with a fascist dictator. Of course, World War II and fascism are not primary-grade topics; however, the issue of whether to speak up when someone is doing something that you know is not right may well be a primary-grade issue. Thus, we frame our discussion with a compelling question: "Is it ever okay for good citizens to question and defy those in authority?"

In *Yertle the Turtle*, the dictator, Yertle, attempts to build a bigger and bigger throne on the backs of his loyal subjects (literally). The turtles continue to join the ever-growing stack of turtles until the bottom turtle, "a plain little turtle whose name was just Mack," decides he's had enough: "That plain little turtle did a plain little thing. He burped, and his burp shook the throne of a king" (Geisel [Seuss], 1958, n.p.).

We ask students to look for good and bad citizens in the story and give reasons for their classifications. The students are quick to identify Yertle as a bad citizen and Mack as a good one; however, when we pose the following questions, and students begin to grapple with the relationship of citizenship to questioning authority, they become less certain:

- *May good citizens suggest new ideas to – or disobey – someone in power?*
- *Should citizens counteract the power of someone, like Yertle, who sets himself up as a dictator?*
- *Are the turtles who get in the stack "innocent bystanders"?*
- *Is there such a thing as an innocent bystander?*
- *To what extent is Mack's burp an act of civil disobedience? Is it appropriate?*
- *Is Mack a good citizen?*
- *Are the other turtles in the stack good citizens?*

Picture books such as this provide an entry point for teachers to raise questions about issues of citizenship and authority in real life:

- *May good citizens suggest new ideas to someone in power (like the principal)?*
- *Can it ever be a sign of good citizenship to break the law, if you believe the law is wrong? What if you believe the law discriminates against certain people?*
- *Was Martin Luther King Jr. a good citizen?*
- *When the Black Lives Matter protesters blocked traffic, were they being good citizens?*
- *Do good citizens always obey authority or are there times when they may question authority?*

Picture books can also be a vehicle for raising questions that hit closer to home for students. For example, *The Araboolies of Liberty Street* by Sam Swope (2001) explores the balance between people retaining their individuality and living together peacefully with others in a community. General Pinch and his wife rule the residents of Liberty Street, preventing all laughter and nonconformity.

When the Araboolies move in, with their colorful sense of individuality and gaiety, all of this begins to change. As the General tries to force the family out, the children of the town come to their defense in a creative show of support; they paint all of their homes in the Araboolie style. In an ironic twist of fate, the General's own order to remove the different-looking house results in his own eviction from the town.

Knowing that we want students to consider the balance between freedom and conformity, individual rights and community welfare, we scaffold our questions accordingly:

- *Throughout the book, how much freedom is there on Liberty Street?*
- *What are the positives and negatives of the conformity on Liberty Street?*
- *Why do you think the townsfolk go along with every house looking the same?*
- *What does it mean to express yourself?*
- *How do we express ourselves (e.g., clothes, hairstyle, cars, houses, jewelry, etc.)?*
- *Can self-expression ever lead to problems for others?*
- *How would you feel if the Araboolies lived next door to you?*
- *How do you respond to people who look or act different from you?*
- *How can people retain their individuality and live together peacefully with others in a community?*
- *How could the Araboolies of Liberty Street have had a better outcome for all of its residents?*
- *Can community rules allow the Araboolies and the Pinches to be who they are and to live on the same block together happily?*
- *Who should develop community rules that govern behavior?*

In addition to having a discussion, guided by the questions above, activities can allow students to consider the points of view of both the Araboolies and the Pinches and, thus, negotiate the balance between self-expression and community needs. Students can act out a skit of the discussion that might ensue between the Araboolies and the Pinches as they try to arrive at a consensus regarding the balance between individuality and community rules. They can re-write the story so that it reflects the Araboolies' and the Pinches' efforts to arrive at a consensus regarding the balance between individuality and community rules.

These are not idle questions or exercises. Neighbors and zoning boards confront these issues frequently. This is an opportunity for students to attend a zoning board meeting or invite a member of a zoning board into the classroom to discuss the real-life controversies that have been brought before the board. Students can also read about the controversy that ensued when author Sandra Cisneros painted her house purple and came into conflict with the San Antonio Historic Design and Review Commission (Rimer, 1998); they can then weigh in during a "four corners" activity.

Each corner of the room is labeled with a sign: strongly agree, agree, disagree, strongly disagree. Students react to the statement, "Sandra Cisneros should have to re-paint her house a color more acceptable to the community," by moving to the corner of the room that reflects their view. Students have the opportunity to change their opinion, based on the discussion; if they do so, they move to the corner of the room that reflects their new position. Engaging in this type of activity demonstrates that students are considering different points of view and re-thinking their initial positions on an issue that, it turns out, defies simple answers.

Kinesthetic activities can entice students to participate in a discussion. Keith Barton (2015) offers other techniques to get people to talk about ideas they might be reluctant to discuss. While he offers these techniques in the context of conducting interviews with research subjects, they are also worthy of consideration in the discussion of controversial issues in elementary classrooms. Drawing pictures or filling in thought bubbles on pictures, photographs, or cartoons may help students address issues of perspective prior to the actual discussion of an issue. Similarly, sentence completion activities may help to refine students' thinking as they approach a controversial issue.

FACILITATING A SUCCESSFUL DISCUSSION

Crafting questions for a discussion on a controversial issue can feel daunting. Happily, the National Issues Forum Institute (NIFI) provides an excellent model for deliberation of specific issues for middle and high school students as well as for citizen forums. They publish booklets on a variety of topics that provide at least three detailed approaches or options for dealing with a contemporary issue. Through deliberation, students (NIFI, 2014)

- explore the underlying perspectives of multiple stakeholders,
- identify the basic things people value such as security, liberty, fairness, order, and care for the vulnerable,
- analyze the trade-offs associated with different options for addressing a problem, and
- seek common ground among stakeholders before deciding on an action plan.

While NIFI is currently developing booklets for the elementary level, the format that they provide for structured deliberative discussion and the questions in their moderator's guide are a valuable resource for elementary teachers who want to engage their students in a thoughtful and thorough discussion of any social issue.

The class rules that most elementary teachers work with their students to create at the beginning of the year (e.g., "Listen to your classmates. Let your classmates finish their thoughts before speaking, yourself.") may provide the basis for civil discussion. Prior to discussing sensitive issues, these rules may need to be revisited and expanded. For example, students and teachers may want to add "We have the right to pass" to the list so that students will not have to discuss an aspect of the topic that makes them uncomfortable.

Elementary teacher Lori McGarry (2015) lays out a process by which teachers can apply the NIFI principles to their own issues discussions:

- Obtain guidebook from NIFI/Kettering: "Developing Materials for Deliberative Forums" by Brad Rourke (2014).
- Identify and *name* a current classroom, school, or community issue of concern to students (i.e., a school rule, such as recess, lunchroom, etc.).
- Research background information/gather data on the issue to identify multiple stakeholders, concerns, and constraints.
- *Frame* the issue by identifying three possible options for addressing the problem.
- Prepare an issue guide that contains background information on the issue and descriptions of Option 1, Option 2, and Option 3; each option should contain a summary of the possible action and several advantages/disadvantages.
- Conduct and/or host a deliberative forum; student writers can act as participants in their own forum and/or facilitators for another group of students.
- Create/enact an action plan for addressing current issues, based on the results of the forum.

Forums typically begin with a question that gets at the participants' connection to the issue at hand (the questions that follow are a slightly modified version of those from the NIFI Moderator's Guide):

- *How does this issue affect you personally?*

Then, each of the three options for dealing with the issue is explored individually. The questions below help ensure a thorough exploration of each option:

- *What is appealing about this option?*
- *What makes this option a good idea – or a bad one?*
- *What things are most valuable to people who support this option?*
- *What could result from doing what this option proposes?*
- *Can you give an example of what you think would happen?*

Once all three options have been explored, it is time to ask questions that invite comparisons among the options and consider whose views might not have been represented:

- *Why is this issue so difficult to decide?*
- *What do you see as the tension between the options?*
- *What are the "gray areas"?*
- *Who is not in the room, having this discussion with us? If this person WERE here, how might the tenor of the conversation change?*
- *What might someone who is (gender, race, class, age, religion, occupation, region, etc.) say?*

The NIFI booklets are designed to prompt students to consider fairly a variety of perspectives other than their own. However, students may still make statements that reflect stereotypical views of certain groups. Rather than having to deal with their comments off the cuff, we have found that being prepared with a mini-lesson on the problematic nature of stereotypes is important.

When a student makes a stereotypical comment, we pause in our lesson. In order for students to understand how it feels to be stereotyped, we put a list of statements about "all kids" on the board (e.g., "You have to watch kids in stores because they steal stuff." "Kids today don't take school seriously and don't do their homework."). We ask our students:

- *Are the statements true?*
- *How do the statements make you feel?*
- *How do you want to react when people make statements such as these?*
- *What would be a more accurate way to phrase comments that do not apply to an entire group?*

Seizing this teachable moment yields great benefits. Instead of chastising students who may unknowingly utter stereotypes, this short exercise drives home the damaging nature of stereotyping and shows students that by choosing their words carefully ("some" vs. "all" – or the implied "all"), they can avoid it.

During a discussion, students may be curious about their teacher's position on the issue and ask a direct question to that effect. As is the case with the stereotyping example above, it is worthwhile for teachers to consider in advance whether or not they want to share their views. Although many teachers may decide to keep their own points of view out of the classroom entirely, if teachers deem it appropriate to share theirs, they generally wait until the end of the discussion to do so.

If the question comes during an election year, teachers who decide to share their voting preferences with their students generally wait to do so until after the election. By waiting until after the discussion or the election is over, teachers are not exerting undue influence on students' positions. They are modeling the behaviors of informed, active citizens who research candidates' positions and weigh evidence in accordance with their values to make thoughtful, selections.

Toward the end of an issues forum, the teacher-moderator tries to determine whether the students in the class can find common ground for action on the issue:

- *What direction seems best for taking action on the issue?*
- *What trade-offs are we willing to accept?*
- *What trade-offs are we unwilling to accept?*
- *What are we willing to do as individuals or as a class to solve this problem?*

After the discussion is over, invite students to reflect both individually and as a class on the process and what has been accomplished:

- *How has your thinking about the issue changed?*
- *How has your thinking about other people's views changed?*
- *How has your perspective changed as a result of what you heard in this forum?*
- *What perspective might have been absent from our discussion?*
- *What do we still need to talk about?*

All students need not be official participants in a discussion. Teachers can designate some students to be "inside the fishbowl" as active participants and others to be "outside the fishbowl" as observers who take notes and provide feedback on both the process ("I liked it when Johnny said, 'I kind of agree and I kind of disagree with Keesha's point' because he was respectfully disagreeing") and the content ("The point that convinced me was the one about how many people were actually helped by Option 3.") of the discussion. Whether inside or outside of the fishbowl, students are living John Dewey's (1916) maxim that "a democracy is more than a form of government; it is primarily a mode of associated living, of conjoint communicated experience" (p. 87).

STRIVING FOR COMPLEXITY

As important as it is to plan for meaningful discussions of controversial issues in our elementary classrooms, it is equally vital to anticipate some of the pitfalls. In this chapter, we talk a lot about discussion, as opposed to debate, because discussion allows students to explore a range of positions and options with respect to an issue. Debate, however, has, by its nature, two sides and rewards sticking to a black-and-white position in an effort to win.

Unlike discussion, debate tends to preclude students from discussing the gray, more nuanced aspects of a topic. Also, unlike discussion, the tone of a debate may be adversarial, as opposed to deliberative, which is likely contrary to the way we would like students to interact in our classroom and in life.

Although it may be tempting to pull away from an issue too soon or try to reach for a tenuous connection to students' lives, it is important to ensure that the issue gets the weight and attention that it deserves. For example, focusing solely on Martin Luther King Jr.'s "I have a dream" speech and concluding the lesson by asking students to identify their own dreams takes valuable time away from the exploration of King's lesser known and more provocative positions (opposition to the war in Vietnam, solidarity with poor people). The "What's *your* dream?" exercise also does not ask students to examine the challenges that King and others faced, or evaluate the choices they made in the struggle to achieve the dream of an equal, just, and peaceful society.

Sometimes, in an effort to relate an issue to students' lives, teachers try to connect weighty historical injustices to much less consequential challenges that students might have faced in their lives. Introducing a lesson about segregation by asking students to recall a time when they were treated unfairly may be a bridge too far, particularly if their responses include disappointments like not getting the lead in the school play or having too early a bedtime.

It is more effective and relevant to provide students with a primary source document that details an actual description of someone's experiences of living in a segregated society. The use of appropriate sources helps students to consider alternative perspectives and develop a sense of empathy while avoiding the trap of applying false equivalencies.

COLLABORATING WITH COLLEAGUES

Generating questions worthy of discussion is a skill that takes practice and doesn't have to be done alone. We advocate that professional meeting time be spent honing this skill. Almost any topic can be used toward this end.

For example, at a grade-level meeting, we used an excerpt from a pop-culture television show seemingly unrelated to social studies that some of the teachers had been watching, "Chopped," to model how to formulate and generate questions. The episode that we used (Food Network, 2011) spotlighted four female school cafeteria chefs competing to raise awareness about the importance of healthful meals for kids. White House chef, Sam Kass, served as a guest judge.

Some of the mystery ingredients with which they had to cook included dill pickles and canned tuna, staples of many school lunch programs. After showing the first ten minutes of the episode, we asked teachers to brainstorm the questions worthy of discussion that the excerpt raised. It is interesting to note how the questions evolved throughout the brainstorming session, from the more factually based "what" questions to the more evaluative "should" questions:

- *How do the cafeteria chefs feel about their jobs?*
- *What challenges did the chefs have preparing the meals on "Chopped"?*
- *How did the judges react to their food?*
- *What was their goal as school cafeteria chefs?*
- *What were the obstacles to them achieving their goals?*
- *For how many kids is school lunch the only full meal of the day?*
- *Was there any controversy when the free and reduced lunch and breakfast programs were put into place?*
- *How does poverty influence what kids eat outside of school?*
- *What's a "food desert"?*
- *Should the government decide what goes into school lunches?*
- *Should "junk food" be banned from lunches?*
- *Should deep-fried food (chicken nuggets, French fries) be banned from school cafeterias?*
- *Should vending machines selling junk food be banned from schools?*
- *Should class parties be limited to only "healthful" food?*
- *How do school menus in different places compare? Who sets the school menu? Who should set the menu? The chefs? The community? The principal? The school board? The state government? The federal government?*
- *Who supplies food to schools?*
- *Who selects the suppliers? Who should select the suppliers?*
- *What kinds of trays, plates, and utensils do students use during lunch? Is there a recycling program? Whose responsibility should it be to start one?*
- *Why only lunch "ladies"? What do they get paid? How does their pay compare to custodians' pay? To secretaries' pay? Should secretaries and food preparers get paid less than custodians?*

Our goal for this activity was to help teachers broaden their conception of the multifaceted nature of *any* issue and develop the skill of writing meaningful questions, which are at the heart of any worthwhile discussion. As Grant Wiggins and Denise Wilbur (2015) point out, "Creating [webs of related questions] usually points to a deeper and more powerful direction for inquiry" (p. 15).

Participating in this type of activity can increase the possibility that teachers will collaborate with their colleagues to formulate and ask better questions in their respective classrooms. Moreover, it can increase the possibility that teachers will share this responsibility with students and scaffold *their* ability to ask multiple, meaningful questions.

In the debriefing, teachers were enthusiastic about collaborating with their colleagues and impressed with the quantity and quality of the questions they developed. However, they also expressed concern about the amount of time they would have to devote were they to engage their students in a similar activity. They are right. These question-generating sessions *do* take time, but they promote student inquiry, the backbone of the *C3 Framework* and social studies education, in general.

Just as devoting faculty meeting time aimed at developing a questioning frame of mind is time well spent, so too is designating grade-level meetings at which teachers can grapple with how to teach controversial issues. Questions for consideration at grade-level meetings may include:

- *To what extent do we use literature as a vehicle for activating students' empathy about challenging issues?*
- *How can we use our class meeting time as a place to discuss challenging issues?*
- *How can we provide students with a variety of perspectives to emphasize the complex nature of many issues, past and present?*
- *To what extent are we able to foster informed discussion, rather than "I win/you lose" debates?*
- *To what extent can we involve family members in our discussions?*
- *At what ages do we think students are prepared to discuss ____(various issues)___?*
- *How should we respond when students make statements that are rooted in stereotypes?*

MOVING BEYOND DISCUSSION

When time has been spent planning with colleagues – identifying issues for discussion, seeking reliable information to support informed positions, crafting meaningful questions, setting ground rules for civil conversation, exploring multiple perspectives (of those present and not present), considering the ramifications of different positions – rich, meaningful discussion of complex, controversial issues can take place. Elementary teachers with whom we work, however, sometimes express anxiety about facilitating discussions of controversial issues, fearing that they will "mess up" in some way.

Advance planning, as detailed in this chapter, can alleviate many of these concerns; it is also the case that unpredictable comments can be made in any given discussion and revisited at any point. However, avoiding discussion of controversial issues in our classrooms is akin to malpractice, as it prevents us from fulfilling our responsibility to foster democratic discourse among our students – future voters and active citizens.

At the elementary level, such democratic discourse may move from controversial issues that involve fictional characters (Yertle the Turtle) to real-life controversial topics (civil disobedience in past and present civil rights movements) or from the personal (equitable distribution of equipment on the playground) to the political (equitable distribution of resources in education or health care).

Delving deeply into controversial topics can enable students to tackle issues at the school, local, national, or even global level. Wherever the conversation begins, informed, thoughtful discussion is not the end; rather, it is the beginning of a process to nurture students who will be eager and able to take informed, thoughtful action.

NOTE

1. Questions for picture books throughout this chapter are adapted from Libresco, Balantic, and Kipling (2011).

REFERENCES

Barton, K. (2015). Elicitation techniques: Getting people to talk about ideas they don't usually talk about. *Theory & Research in Social Education 43*, 179–205.

Crocco, M. S. (Ed.). (2007). *Teaching the levees: A curriculum for democratic dialogue and civic engagement.* New York, NY: Teachers College, Columbia University.

Dewey, J. (1916). *Democracy and education: An introduction to the philosophy of education.* New York, NY: The Macmillan Co.

Engel v. Vitale, 370 U.S. 421 (1962).

Food Network. (2011, November 22). Class acts. *Chopped 9(13)*. Retrieved from http://www.tv.com/shows/chopped/class-acts-1404249/

Geisel, T. S. [Dr. Seuss, pseud.] (1958). *Yertle the turtle and other stories.* New York, NY: Random House Books for Young Readers.

Lee v. Weisman, 505 U.S. 577 (1992).

Libresco, A. S., Balantic, J., & Kipling, J. (2011). *Every book is a social studies book: How to meet standards with picture books, K-6.* Santa Barbara, CA: ABC-CLIO.

McGarry, L. S. & Stoicovy, D. M. (2015). Deliberation and democracy: How living history equips students for democratic participation today. *Social Studies and the Young Learner 28*(2), 9–13.

McTighe, J. & Wiggins, G. (2013). *Essential questions: Opening doors to student understanding*. Alexandria, VA: ASCD.

National Council for the Social Studies. (2013). *The college, career, and civic life (C3) framework for social studies state standards*. Silver Spring, MD: National Council for the Social Studies

National Council for the Social Studies. (2013). Revitalizing civic learning in our schools: A position statement of the National Council for the Social Studies. Retrieved from http://www.socialstudies.org/positions/revitalizing_civic_learning

National Issues Forums Institute. (2014). Deliberation. Retrieved from https://www.nifi.org/en/deliberation

National Issues Forums Institute. (2014). Guide to organizing and moderating forums. Retrieved from https://www.nifi.org/sites/default/files/product-downloads/NIF%2520Energy_14_gd_forums_0.pdf

Rimer, S. (1998, July 13). Novelist's purple palette is not to everyone's taste. *The San Antonio Journal*. Retrieved from http://www.nytimes.com/1998/07/13/us/san-antonio-journal-novelist-s-purple-palette-is-not-to-everyone-s-taste.html

Rourke, B. (2014). Developing materials for deliberative forums. *The Kettering Foundation*. Retrieved from https://www.google.com/url?sa=t&rct=j&q=&esrc=s&source=web&cd=1&ved=0ahUKEwjz5v-CuLbLAhXKGD4KHUXFBjgQFggcMAA&url=https%3A%2F%2Fwww.kettering.org%2Fwp-content%2Fuploads%2FDeveloping-Materials-guide.pdf&usg=AFQjCNE5iRMpUKCnHFy11pBLUzmFQtMfxQ&bvm=bv.116573086,d.cWw&cad=rja

Santa Fe Independent School Dist. v. Doe, 530 U.S. 290 (2000).

Sciescka, J. (1995). *Math curse*. New York, NY: Viking.

Swope, S. (2001). *The Araboolies of liberty street*. New York, NY: Farrar, Strauss, and Giroux.

Thornton, S. J. (1991). Teacher as curricular-instructional gatekeeper in social studies. In J. P. Shaver (Ed.), *Handbook of research on social studies teaching and learning* (pp. 237–248). New York, NY: Macmillan.

Whoriskey, P. (2007, May 10). Katrina hit Blacks harder than Whites, study finds. *The Washington Post*. Retrieved from http://www.washingtonpost.com/wp-dyn/content/article/2007/05/09/AR2007050902556.html

Wiggins, G. & Wilbur, D. (2015). How to make your questions essential. *Educational Leadership 73*(1), 10–15.

Young, E. (2002). *Seven blind mice*. New York, NY: Penguin Putnam Books.

Chapter 2

Preparing Young Adults for Polarized America

Paula McAvoy

In the summer of 2004, a little-known state senator from Illinois named Barack Obama delivered the keynote address at the Democratic National Convention. In his speech, Obama (2004) took aim at "pundits" and "spin masters," who "like to slice and dice our country into red states and blue states" (para. 49). Pushing back on a public discourse of divisiveness, Obama declared, "Well, I say to them tonight, there's not a liberal America and a conservative America; there's the United States of America. There's not a Black America and White America and Latino America and Asian America; there's the United States of America" (para. 47).

The senator's words struck a chord with the audience, which erupted with enthusiastic applause. Yet, the sentiment that there is a united America can only be understood as aspirational; it is rhetorically effective precisely because Americans are acutely aware of our many divides. Today, as President Obama is nearing the end of his time in the Oval Office, social science research shows that we are, in fact, a red America and a blue America, a White America and a Black America, a rich America and a poor America.

The chapters in this volume encourage social studies teachers to investigate and discuss "21st-century social issues" with their students. To do this effectively, teachers must keep in mind that these social issues are embedded within a (relatively new) fractured context—politically polarized and deeply divided along lines of race and social class. Further, this is the only political context that today's middle and high school students have ever known, and the divisiveness does not appear to be abating.

Together, these two realities make engaging students in deliberations about controversial political issues essential and challenging. In this chapter, I provide background about the social forces dividing the U.S. public and offer guidance about how, given this reality, social studies teachers might best engage middle and high school students in discussions of controversial issues.

HOW DID WE GET HERE?

There is no single cause for how the United States came to be as socially and politically divided as it is today. Elsewhere, Diana Hess and I have reviewed the political science literature on the factors contributing to political polarization (McAvoy & Hess, 2013). Within that literature, researchers define political polarization as the forces pulling the two major parties away from the political center and toward more ideological extremes.

This trend began when the centrist "purple" parties of the 1950s and 1960s began to ideologically realign and transform into what we now know as the liberal Democratic Party and the conservative Republican Party. This "sorting" of the parties began in the 1960s and was complete by the early 1990s. Since then, the parties have continued to pull further apart, with the Republican Party moving furthest away from the center (Hare, McCarty, Poole, & Rosenthal, 2012; Theriault, 2013).

The ideological sorting of the political parties is matched by the ideological sorting of the American public. Most adults, even if they identify as independents, now hold views on public issues that primarily line up on one side of the political spectrum (Abramowitz, 2010; Levendusky, 2009). Contributing to this trend is the fact that more Americans are now living and working with people who hold similar political views (Bishop, 2008).

When we socialize with people who think like we do, our views tend to become more extreme, and we become less able to believe that people who disagree with us are reasonable (Mutz, 2006; Schkade, Sunstein, & Hastie, 2007). Further, social scientists find that those who have the strongest identification with a particular party are most likely to experience "affective polarization," meaning they feel that their partisan opponents are not just unreasonable but also dangerous for the country (Iyengar & Westwood, 2015; Pew Research Center, 2014b).

Finally, changes in technology and journalism make it possible for people to access information from news and news-like sources on the Internet and cable television that are often more one sided than traditional newspapers and network broadcasts (Sunstein, 2001). This trend has happened alongside an increase in what Mutz (2015) labels "in your face politics," in which television broadcasts use tighter camera angles and heated commentary to intensify the viewer's emotional response to what is being said.

The result is that viewers experience more negative feelings about commentators with whom they disagree, while simultaneously becoming more interested in current events. In sum, the trends from the last 35 years show that the ideological positions of the two parties and the American public have become more extreme. The political center has disappeared and we are left with two dominant political positions—a conservative America and a liberal America.

Undergirding the divides between these two Americas are ideological differences about race. Prior to 1965, Democrats and Republicans were both moderate parties that had liberal and conservative members (Levendusky, 2009; Pildes, 2011). The Democrats were truly, in today's parlance, a "purple" party that held together a coalition between conservative, pro-segregation "Dixiecrats" from the South and northern liberals. This relationship began to fray when the northern Democrats supported using federal power to advance the cause of civil rights by, for example, sending in troops to desegregate southern schools and integrate interstate busses.

The Democratic coalition was set on the path toward full disintegration following the passage of the Civil Rights Act of 1964 and the Voting Rights Act of 1965 (Levendusky, 2009; Pildes, 2011). Together, these acts gave the federal government new authority to override discriminatory state-level policies. While both pieces of legislation passed with large majorities from both parties, southern White legislators and their southern White constituents were vehemently opposed.

In the years following, some Dixiecrats moved to the Republican Party, and others were voted out of office and replaced by Republicans (Pildes, 2011). As the Dixiecrats defected, they left behind a more solidly liberal Democratic Party and contributed to the creation of a more socially conservative Republican Party (McCarty, Poole, & Rosenthal, 2006; Pildes, 2011). While many issues have contributed to the continued polarization of the parties, it is important to remember that the ideological realignment has at its origin disagreements about the role of the federal government and responses to racial injustice.

We also see divisions between White and non-White America that exist independent of our partisan disagreements. The millennial generation (those born after 1980), for example, is the most liberal generation in recent history and is also the most ethnically and racially diverse, with 43% identifying as non-White (Pew Research Center, 2014a). The millennials are in agreement about many social issues—there is, for example, wide support for marriage equality and the legalization of marijuana.

Yet, on other issues there are clear racial divides. Seventy-one percent of non-White millennials would like the federal government to provide more social services, compared with thirty-nine percent of White millennials. A similar divide exists with generation X (those born between 1960 and 1980) and boomers (those born between 1946 and 1960). For example, 71% of non-White generation Xers support more government services, compared to 27% of Whites, and 60% of non-White boomers support more government services, compared to 23% of Whites. Non-Whites across these three generations are also much more supportive of President Obama, and they approve of his policies at about double the rate of White Americans (Pew Research Center, 2014a).

Lastly, the polarization of America is related to the emergence of a rich America and a poor America. In the past century, polarization and income inequality have been rising and falling together, and the United States is currently experiencing historic highs in both (McCarty, Poole, & Rosenthal, 2006). One reason that these two trends seem to "dance" with one another is that as income inequality rises, redistribution becomes a major point of contention between the parties (McCarty et al., 2006; Voorheis, McCarty, & Shor, 2015).

As one illustration of this phenomenon, recent Gallup (2015a) polling shows that 63% of Americans believe that income should be more evenly distributed. However, when we look at those views along party lines, 86% of Democrats favor a more even distribution compared to 34% of Republicans. Additionally, Schlozman, Verba, and Brady (2012) show that as income inequality rises, the most affluent and most educated members of society are able to exert significantly more influence on public officials. As a result, redistributive policies that might decrease inequality, such as increasing inheritance taxes or increasing the minimum wage, are less likely to be passed because they are not in the interests of the wealthy.

When we look at the aggregate effects of polarization, there is good news and bad news. The bad news is that our ideological-partisan divides have created groups who greatly distrust each other. A Pew Research Center (2014b) poll of the American public found that 38% of Democrats and 43% of Republicans have a "very unfavorable view" of the other party, numbers that have roughly doubled since 1994. Gallup (2015b) polls show that between 2013 and 2015, the views of non-Hispanic Whites and Blacks who believe race relations are "good" or "somewhat good" both dropped 20%, the lowest they have been since 2001.

Allen (2004) argues that the ability to trust our fellow citizens is an essential feature of democracy. Everyone will experience political losses, but losing is tolerable only when citizens can trust that the winners will still govern with a spirit of goodwill. When distrust takes hold, Allen (2004) notes, it "paralyzes democracy; it means that citizens no longer think it sensible or feel secure enough to place their fates in the hands of democratic strangers" (p. xvi).

The good news is that polarization has increased overall interest and engagement in the political system. Abramowitz (2010) finds that since the

1980s, the number of people who count as "the engaged public" (those who, in addition to voting, pay attention to political contests, discuss politics with friends, and donate to political campaigns) has steadily increased. He also finds that the people who are most likely to engage in these activities are also the people with the strongest ideological and partisan views.

Abramowitz (2010) argues that the ideological sorting of the two major parties has made choices more clear for the voting public, and this has increased the public's interest in politics. As evidence of this, Greg McAvoy (2015) uses an aggregate analysis of public opinion polls over time to show that partisanship helps the American public make sense of the issues of the day. He finds that even though information is often distorted in the current political sphere, in the aggregate, polarization still helps the public become more informed about issues than they would be in less-polarized times.

WHAT DOES THIS MEAN FOR TEACHERS?

Scholars of democratic education have long promoted engaging young people in discussions of the controversial issues of the day as a way to prepare young people for democratic life (i.e., Dewey, 1916/2004; Gutmann, 1999; Hess, 2009; Hess & McAvoy, 2015; Kunzman, 2006; Parker, 2003). Ideally, discussion should help young people learn to think democratically by teaching them to listen and respond to views that span a range of political, but also religious and cultural, differences.

Diana Hess and I (2015) have captured the democratic aims of discussion under the label "political classroom," by which we mean classes that engage students in questions that ask, "How should we live together?" Public policy issues such as "Should undocumented workers be given amnesty?" and "Should public money be used to fund Planned Parenthood?" are questions that both inform students about the issues of the day and require them to think about the values that shape society.

When thinking about the aims of classroom discussion, it is essential to keep in mind that discussion is a social activity. As Laden (2014) argues, reasoning *together* about an issue—be it two people deciding where to go for dinner or a class discussing whether there should be stricter regulations for gun ownership—requires a different set of skills and dispositions than when we simply make a decision for ourselves. When we reason together, it requires us to listen and be responsive to the views of others; our thinking changes from "What do I want for myself?" to "What do I think is fair for all concerned?"

When teachers ask students to deliberate an issue (versus listening to a lecture or doing independent research about an issue), they are asking students to reason socially and think about the needs and interests of others. The challenge for teachers in the United States today is that the democratic "we" is fractured, and this makes teaching young people to consider competing points of view, evaluate evidence, and reevaluate their political positions in light of new arguments particularly challenging.

These challenges do not mean that discussion should be avoided in the classroom. Indeed, it is more important than ever to engage students in discussions of controversial political issues, because the classroom is an unusual forum in which young people encounter differences of opinion and have the opportunity to practice social reasoning in a setting that is more deliberative than what is often seen in the public sphere (Hess, 2009).

At the same time, the realities of polarization and divisiveness mean that teachers need to think carefully about how to present issues so that young people are able to productively discuss by using good information and being willing to listen to competing views. In what follows, I offer suggestions for how teachers should think about engaging students in classroom deliberations, given the realities of polarization.

Discussions Need Structure

One common concern that teachers have when they consider including controversial political issues in the classroom is that discussions will get too heated and out of control. In other words, they worry that they are inviting the divisiveness of the political climate into their classrooms. It is true that students can get emotionally invested in classroom discussions (this is also what makes discussion engaging), but teachers can help set the tone of the discussion and make sure that all voices are being heard by using discussion strategies that provide students with a set of norms for productive participation.

In the Discussion of Controversial Issues study that provides the research base for *The Political Classroom* (Hess & McAvoy, 2015), Hess and our research team observed, surveyed, and interviewed 35 high school social studies teachers and 1,001 of their students, collecting data from 2005 to 2009.[1] Using this data, we sorted teachers into "Discussion" and "Lecture" teachers. Discussion teachers were those who used discussion of controversial issues about 20% of the time, or roughly one hour of class time per week. Lecture teachers were those whose primary teaching strategy was to lecture to the class, though they may have occasionally used class time for films, research, or discussion.

We further sorted the Discussion teachers into those who were particularly skilled at facilitating and structuring discussion, a practice we labeled "Best Practice," and those who used discussion but, in practice, that discussion fell short in some way. When observing a Best Practice teacher, an observer would see:

- Students preparing in advance for the discussion
- Students drawing upon common sources of information as they make their comments (e.g., readings, a film they watched, lecture notes)
- Students directing most of their comments to each other and not to the teacher
- All, or nearly all, of the students participating and engaging in the discussion.

The teachers in the Best Practice classrooms had also prepared in advance for the discussion by identifying readings and resources that would push students to consider new evidence and competing points of view and by thinking about how best to structure the discussion so that students could engage productively with each other and the material. To that end, we observed teachers using a variety of discussion strategies, including[2]:

- Fishbowl discussions
- Moot courts
- Structured academic controversies
- Socratic seminars
- Town hall meetings
- Legislative simulations
- Roundtable discussions.

What these teachers did not do was throw out a controversial political issue and say to a class, "So, what do you think?" When nonbest practice teachers did this, we observed that the discussion often involved a handful of students who directed their comments to the teacher. The rest of the class was left to watch from the sidelines.

Typically, those who participate in this situation are students who already pay some attention to the news, and often they are also those who are growing up in middle and upper class households. In fact, our findings show that students from lower social class backgrounds and those with less political knowledge were significantly more likely to report that they hesitate to speak in discussion, because they worry about the judgment of their peers and the teacher (Hess & McAvoy, 2015).

This finding is an educational problem—teachers want all students to feel comfortable participating—but it is also a democratic problem. Under conditions of polarization, income inequality, and racial division, students need to consider how policies differently affect various groups. If some students are silenced in class discussion, important voices are missing, and the discussion may end up reinforcing, rather than disrupting, inequalities.

Conversely, when the teacher provides a structure for the discussion, more students have an opportunity to engage because they have been given background information, sometimes they have been assigned a role, and the structure gives them a much clearer sense about how, when, and in what way they should participate. Importantly, discussion structures also put some limitations on students who are likely to dominate the discussion, as turn taking and listening are typically built into structured discussions.

As one case in point, consider a lesson observed in Ms. Ingles's twelfth-grade government course in which the class was considering the question, "Should the death penalty be used in the United States?" For this lesson, Ms. Ingles asked students to prepare in advance by reading competing points of view about the issue and arriving to class with some idea about where they stood. During the class session, Ms. Ingles facilitated a structured group debate in which students were first put into like-minded teams (those in favor of the death penalty sat together and faced off against those opposed). On this particular day, the class was split down the middle with eleven in favor and ten against.

The two groups were then given time to confer and develop their strongest arguments, and then each side presented an opening statement. The teams listened to each other and then reconvened to rebut the arguments presented. During the activity, students could switch groups if they changed their opinions. Ms. Ingles facilitated by keeping a record of the views presented on the board, and she would occasionally step in to ask probing questions of both teams to push them to sharpen their reasoning or clarify a point. For the most part students directed their comments to each other.

In addition to promoting engagement by having students rely on each other to develop new arguments, this discussion format models important democratic values. First, students were consulting materials vetted by the teacher, which allowed them to draw upon credible evidence as they discussed. Second, the design of the activity encouraged students to listen and respond to opposing points of views. Third, the discussion encouraged changing one's mind in light of better arguments and evidence. On this last point, traditional debate formats encourage students to defend a view at all cost, and while this can be a valuable critical thinking exercise, it does not model intellectual humility and the virtue of being willing to change one's mind.

Given that students see very little mind changing in the public sphere—indeed, those who do are often derisively labeled "flip floppers"—it is important for teachers to build into the structure of the class moments for students to reflect on the question, "How have my views changed?" Finally, the structure of the discussion diminishes the possibility that things will get "out of hand" because the teacher has provided students with the sources and procedures to discuss productively.

Teach for Ideological Understanding

Recall that the ideological sorting of the two major parties is a key feature of polarization. Also, recall Abramowitz's (2010) findings that the citizens most engaged in electoral politics (and associated activities) are people who have strong ideological and partisan views.[3] Given these realities and given that one important aim of social studies education is to develop "enlightened" citizens who are engaged in public decision-making (Parker, 2003), teachers should help students to understand not just the evidence but also the underlying ideological values embedded within an issue.

A simplified framing for the concept of political ideology is: Our ideological commitments reflect our answers to the questions: What is a good society? How should we get it? While liberals and conservatives within the American context generally agree that a good society is democratic and we should achieve it through the democratic structures outlined in state and federal constitutions, they nevertheless disagree about what a *good* democracy looks like. That is, they disagree about core issues such as:

• How much (if at all) should the federal government regulate the economy?
• To what extent should a state or the federal government provide a social safety net for the least advantaged in society?
• How should our society rectify social injustice?

Helping students understand how and why a liberal and a conservative have different answers to these questions (as do libertarians, radicals, and reactionaries) is essential for understanding our partisan divides.

Government and civics teachers often introduce students to the political spectrum, but when Hess and I (2015) studied classroom discussion, we found only one school where teachers consistently connected the issues being discussed with ideological and partisan positions.[4] More typical were discussions like the one that Ms. Ingles had, in which students were primarily encouraged to rely on evidence as they discussed a particular issue.

Drawing upon evidence is clearly one important component of reasoning well, but it is also possible to make a perfectly reasonable argument without using any evidence. One might, for example, make the liberal argument that, in a democracy, it is an overreach of state power (and violation of civil liberties) to take someone's life—regardless of whether there is evidence that the death penalty deters crime or that it is fairly or unfairly implemented. Conversely, one might argue for the conservative view that justice requires that the death penalty is the only appropriate response to murder. Such a position needs argumentation but not necessarily evidence.

Arguments like these often come out in a death penalty discussion, but it is important for teachers to help students see these as competing ideological positions that reflect differing beliefs about the role of government, what justice requires, and views about personal responsibility. For example, Ms. Ingles could follow up the death penalty discussion with the question, "Which of the arguments that we generated fall within liberal ideology and which are conservative? Why?"

Even better is to go one step further and connect this to partisanship by asking, "Both the Democratic Party Platform (2012) and the Republican Party Platform (2012) are supportive of some use of the death penalty. Given that the Democrats are more liberal, why would they be in favor?" This discussion would help students understand that political parties are not beholden to ideology and often bend toward public opinion.

Political ideology is a complex concept and one that students (and adults) struggle to understand. Teachers who include political controversy in their curriculum will help students to interpret the current political climate when they encourage students to interrogate not just the evidence but also the ideological values that support a particular view.

Recognize Structural Inequalities

As noted earlier, the United States is not just ideologically divided but also divided by race, ethnicity, and income. Further, issues related to race and income inequality are particularly polarizing in the current political context because they are emotionally charged and deeply personal to most students.

In the past few years, our racial divides have become front-page news in ways not seen since the 1992 Rodney King verdict (Gallup, 2014). Since Michael Brown was shot and killed in 2014, the United States has witnessed many high-profile cases of unarmed Black men being shot by the police. Such events have resulted in the creation of the Black Lives Matter movement. This grassroots organization is committed to keeping the public's attention on the issue of police violence and other ways in which African American lives are devalued.

In addition, the findings of the Department of Justice's investigation into the Ferguson Police Department show "a pattern of unconstitutional policing" and expose the many ways in which the city of Ferguson was pillaging the Black community through excessive fines as a way of increasing revenue—a practice happening in many cities through the United States (U.S. Department of Justice, 2015, p. 2; Rakia, 2015). In 2015, the mass shooting of Black parishioners at Emanuel African Methodist Episcopal Church in downtown Charleston spurred a national debate about flying the Confederate flag over South Carolina's statehouse.

These cases raise a number of important policy issues, such as: How should police officers be monitored and/or held accountable to the public?

Should the Confederate flag be allowed to fly over a statehouse? Should a student be allowed to wear a Confederate flag shirt to school? There are, of course, many other issues that require students to consider policies that address structural inequalities, such as: Should universities consider race and ethnicity when making admissions decisions? How should the United States respond to increases in undocumented workers? Should the minimum wage be increased?

The first challenge for bringing these issues into the classroom is that school demographics are increasingly unequal. Eighty-four percent of teachers in the United States are White, and about 50% of students are non-White (Feistritzer, 2011; National Center for Education Statistics, 2015). Further, 45% of Black and Hispanic students are in schools that are labeled "high poverty" (Snyder & Musu-Gillette, 2015).[5]

Given these disparities, the odds are that discussions of race and social class will take place in one of two conditions. The first is a White teacher in front of a class of nearly all Black and Hispanic students, most of whom have low socioeconomic status. The second condition is a White teacher in front of a class that is majority White with a small number of non-White students. Both situations are nonideal for having discussions about race and social class.

One purpose of deliberation is to have participants reason together so that they consider how people are differently affected by particular policies. This helps people move from self-interested thinking to considering which policy is most fair, given competing points of view. In the first situation, a racially segregated class does not get the benefit of being heard by White students. As a result, all students miss out on the opportunity to broaden their perspectives on important current issues. This is particularly troubling for White students who, in classes without many students of color, often fail to fully recognize racial injustice (Swalwell, 2013).

Hess and I (2015) found that the second situation, the majority White class, is particularly difficult for teachers to navigate. There is a danger that middle class White students will dominate the discussion and, in so doing, may dismiss the views expressed by their non-White peers. Students of color often found these discussions frustrating. Though, it is important to note, both White and non-White students reported that they saw value in the discussion, even if the discussion was emotionally charged (Hess & McAvoy, 2015).

Despite these limitations, these discussions are necessary for democratic education. As with other discussions, students need preparation and a structure designed to make sure that different views are fairly considered. To that end, discussions that address structural inequalities need to be begin with a firm understanding of the empirical reality of structural inequalities.

Imagine that a teacher wants to have students discuss whether Congress should pass a law to increase the minimum wage. In order to have an informed discussion about this, students would need to understand that income inequality is real and at a historic high. However, because the political discourse around this issue is filled with divisive language that pits the "99%" against the "job creators," and appeals to stop "corporate welfare" get attacked for being "class warfare," to teach students the empirical reality will appear to some students that the teacher is being unfairly partisan. Yet, not teaching students the truth about income inequality leaves students misinformed.

Similarly, discussions of affirmative action are not productive, and possibly hurtful, when privileged students are not aware of the many inequalities in the American public school system, how these inequalities map onto race, and the ways that racism plays out in society today. These are also empirical realities that need to be taught prior to productive discussions about college admissions.

Laying this empirical groundwork prior to a discussion may also appear biased to those who believe that the system is basically fair; however, if teachers want students to be "informed citizens," then they need be honest about these political realities. *What to do* about structural inequalities are open questions and are the type of questions that students should be deliberating in the classroom.

Establish a Climate of Mutual Respect

When teachers decide to include discussions of controversial political issues in the curriculum, they must also decide whether they will share their views with the class. Hess and I (2015) have argued that teachers should think about sharing views with students as a "pedagogical tool." That is, rather than taking a firm stand that "I will never share my view" or "I will always share my view," a teacher should use professional judgment to decide whether sharing in a particular moment will promote the aims of democratic education.

A teacher might, for example, decide that sharing an opinion would shut down a discussion and so withholds from sharing, even if students ask to hear her views. That same teacher might in a different moment decide that sharing a view would encourage students who are hesitating to speak to enter into a discussion. This is not to say that whatever a teacher decides is the correct decision; instead, we argue teachers will make better judgments about this issue if they are thinking about their educational aims and the needs of their students.

That said, it is also true that in today's polarized climate there is more public scrutiny of teachers and how they treat political issues. In communities that are politically divided or where the teacher's views are not aligned with the majority view in the community, a teacher may want to withhold his views, simply because sharing could invite outside pressure that would make it more difficult to engage students in discussions of controversial political issues.

Finally, in the Discussing Controversial Issues study, we found that most high school students were supportive of teachers who occasionally shared a view. When interviewing students, it became clear to us that what students want most is to learn in a culture of fairness and mutual respect. To that end, teachers need to provide students with resources that introduce them to a variety of competing views and then help them to see how people reason differently about political issues.

Most importantly, teachers need to ensure that students are learning how to listen to each other and how to respectfully disagree. The norms of civility are not often seen in today's public sphere, but they must be established and maintained in the classroom if we want students to experience productive political discussions.

CONCLUSION

An important goal for most social studies teachers is to prepare their students to engage in public decision-making. In a politically, economically, and socially divided United States, this is a difficult task. If the country is ideologically fractured, should teachers prepare young people to engage with the world as it is and become ideological partisans? Or should teachers prepare students to have a more idealistic view of democracy and embrace deliberative values that are rarely seen on the national stage? Stanley (2010) describes this as a perennial tension for social studies teachers between teaching to "transmit" the social order and teaching to "transform" it.

When it comes to political polarization, income inequality, and structural inequalities, social studies teachers should certainly avoid transmitting these social problems, but it is unrealistic to believe that teachers can "transform" society through the way they teach. This is especially true for political polarization, which by all indicators appears to be the new normal for American politics. However, meaningful work can be done if teachers aim to *prepare* students for the world as it is while helping them to develop a conception of what a better democracy might look like.

To that end, teachers should inform students about the empirical truths of our many "Americas" and about the social forces that have contributed to these fault lines. Students need to understand that the United States is currently experiencing historical levels of polarization and income inequality, and the combination of the two puts democracy at risk and exacerbates structural inequalities that create our racial and ethnic divides.

At the same time, students should understand that their opinions about how best to address these issues subsume ideological values that reflect a particular understanding of democracy. An important aim for social studies educators is to support students as they discuss not just the issues but also how their political views express their vision of a better society.

ACKNOWLEDGMENTS

I'd like to thank Abby Beneke, Rebecca Fine, and Amato Nocera for their help with this chapter. Thanks also to the reviewers and Wayne Journell for their very insightful comments. Finally, a thank you to Diana Hess for her support of this work.

NOTES

1. Diana Hess is the principal investigator on the Discussing Controversial Issues study. The study was funded by grants from the McCormick Foundation, the Carnegie Corporation of New York, the Center for Information and Research on Civic Learning and Engagement (CIRCLE), the Choices for the 21st Century Education Program at Brown University, and the Spencer Foundation. The study was housed in the Wisconsin Center for Educational Research at UW-Madison.

2. There are many sites on the Internet that provide resources for each of these strategies. Diana Hess and I have created a list of many that we find particularly helpful. See http://thepoliticalclassroom.com/resources.php. We also describe teachers using these strategies in *The Political Classroom*. Hess (2009) also provides descriptions of teachers using a variety of these discussion strategies.

3. Elsewhere, Hess, and I (2014) have explored the question of whether, given this reality, social studies teachers should, as one of their educational aims, encourage students to develop partisan identities. This is a controversial pedagogical issue for teachers that I will set aside.

4. For a detailed discussion of this school, see Hess and McAvoy (2015), Chapter 5, "Adams High."

5. Only 8% of White students are in high-poverty schools.

REFERENCES

Abramowitz, A. (2010). *The disappearing center: Engaged citizens, polarization, and American democracy.* New Haven, CT: Yale University Press.
Allen, D. S. (2004). *Talking to strangers: Anxieties of citizenship since Brown v. Board of Education.* Chicago, IL: University of Chicago Press.

Bishop, B. (2008). *The big sort: Why the clustering of like-minded America is tearing us apart.* New York, NY: Houghton Mifflin.

Democratic Platform (2012). Ensuring safety and quality of life. Retrieved from: www.democrats.org/party-platform#ensuring-safety

Dewey, J. (1916/2004). *Democracy and education.* Mineola, NY: Dover Publications.

Feistritzer, E. (2011). *Profile of teachers in the U.S. 2011.* National Center for Education Information. Retrieved from http://www.edweek.org/media/pot2011final-blog.pdf

Gallup (2014). As a major U.S. problem, race relations sharply rise. Retrieved from http://www.gallup.com/poll/180257/major-problem-race-relations-sharply-rises.aspx.

Gallup (2015a). Americans continue to say U.S. wealth distribution is unfair. Retrieved from www.gallup.com/poll/182987/american-continu-say-wealth-distribution-unfair.aspx.

Gallup (2015b). Race relations. Retrieved from www.gallup.com/poll/1687/race-relations.aspx.

Gutmann, A. (1999). *Democratic education.* Princeton, NJ: Princeton University Press.

Hare, C., McCarty, N., Poole, K., & Rosenthal, H. (2012). Polarization is real (and asymmetric). *Voteview Blog.* Retrieved from: http://voteview.com/blog/?p=494

Hess, D. (2009). *Controversy in the classroom: The democratic power of discussion.* New York, NY: Routledge Press.

Hess, D. & McAvoy, P. (2014). Should teachers help students develop partisan identities? *Social Education, 78,* 293–297.

Hess, D. & McAvoy, P. (2015). *The political classroom: Evidence and ethics in democratic education.* New York, NY: Routledge Press.

Iyengar, S. & Westwood, S. J. (2015). Fear and loathing across party lines: New evidence on group polarization. *American Journal of Political Science, 59,* 690–707.

Kunzman, R. (2006). *Grappling with the good: Talking about religion and morality in public schools.* New York, NY: State University of New York Press.

Laden, T. (2014). *Reasoning: A social picture.* Oxford, England: Oxford University Press.

Levendusky, M. (2009). *The partisan sort: How liberals became Democrats and conservatives became Republicans.* University of Chicago Press.

McAvoy, G. E. (2015). *Collective political rationality: Partisan thinking and why it's not all bad.* New York, NY: Routledge Press.

McAvoy, P. & Hess, D. (2013). Classroom deliberation in an era of political polarization. *Curriculum Inquiry, 43,* 14-47.

McCarty, N. M., Poole, K. T., & Rosenthal, H. (2006). *Polarized America: The dance of ideology and unequal riches.* Cambridge, MA: MIT Press.

Mutz, D. C. (2006). *Hearing the other side: Deliberative versus participatory democracy.* New York, NY: Cambridge University Press.

Mutz, D. C. (2015). *In-your-face politics: The consequences of uncivil media.* Princeton, NJ: Princeton University Press.

National Center for Education Statistics (2015). *Racial/ethnic enrollment in public schools.* Retrieved from http://nces.ed.gov/programs/coe/indicator_cge.asp.

Obama, B. (2004, July 27). Transcript: Illinois senate candidate Barack Obama. *Washington Post.* Retrieved from http://www.washingtonpost.com/wp-dyn/articles/A19751-2004Jul27.html.

Parker, W. (2003). *Teaching democracy: Unity and diversity in public life.* New York, NY: Teachers College Press.

Pew Research Center. (2014a). Millennials in adulthood: Detached from institutions, networked with friends. Retrieved from http://www.pewsocialtrends.org/files/2014/03/2014-03-07_generations-report-version-for-web.pdf

Pew Research Center. (2014b). Political polarization in the American public. Retrieved from http://www.people-press.org/2014/06/12/political-polarization-in-the-american-public/.

Pildes, R. H. (2011). Why the center does not hold: the causes of hyperpolarized democracy in America. *California Law Review, 99,* 273–333.

Rakia, R. (March, 2015). It's not just Ferguson: Cities nationwide are criminalizing black people to pay the bills. *The Nation.* Retrieved from http://www.thenation.com/article/its-not-just-ferguson/.

Republican Platform (2012). Renewing American values. Retrieved from: www.gop.com/platform/renewing-American-values.

Schlozman, K. L., Verba, S., & Brady, H. E. (2012). *The unheavenly chorus: Unequal political voice and the broken promise of American democracy.* Princeton, NJ: Princeton University Press.

Schkade, D., Sunstein, C. R., & Hastie, R. (2007). What happened on deliberation day? *California Law Review, 95,* 915–940.

Snyder, T. & Musu-Gillette (2015). *Free or reduced price lunch: A proxy for poverty?* National Center for Education Statistics. Retrieved from http://nces.ed.gov/blogs/nces/post/free-or-reduced-price-lunch-a-proxy-for-poverty.

Sunstein, C. R. (2001). *Republic.com.* Princeton, NJ: Princeton University Press.

Stanley, W. (2010). Social studies and the social order: Transmission or transformation? In W. Parker (Ed.), *Social studies today: Research and practice* (pp. 17–24). New York, NY: Routledge Press.

Swalwell, K. M. (2013). *Educating activist allies: Social justice pedagogy with the suburban and urban elite.* New York, NY: Routledge Press.

Theriault, S. M. (2013). *The Gingrich senators: The roots of partisan warfare in Congress.* New York, NY: Oxford University Press.

United States Department of Justice (2015). *Investigation of the Ferguson Police Department:* https://www.justice.gov/sites/default/files/opa/press-releases/attachments/2015/03/04/ferguson_police_department_report.pdf

Voorheis, J., McCarty, N., & Shor, B. (2015). Unequal incomes, ideology and gridlock: How rising inequality increases political polarization. Retrieved from http://ssrn.com/abstract=2649215

Chapter 3

Teaching Immigration as a Social Issue in 21st-Century Social Studies Classrooms

Jeremy Hilburn and Ashley Taylor Jaffee

While immigration is not unique to the 21st century, the turn of the century has seen changes in immigration around the world and in the United States particularly. In the first section of this chapter, we explain why immigration should be a priority in 21st-century social studies classrooms by focusing on three factors:

- Demographics
- Policy and political discourse
- The unique characteristics of recent immigration when compared to 18th-, 19th-, and, to some degree, even 20th-century immigration.

We focus our discussion on the United States, but readers in other nations may also be able to apply some of our guidelines, teaching methods, and implications to different contexts.

The first reason teachers should embrace teaching immigration as a social issue is the often reported numbers argument. Based on 2010 census data, 13.1% of the U.S. population is foreign born. This is not the highest proportion of immigrants in U.S. history—immigration as a proportion of the population peaked in 1910 at about 15%—yet this proportion is near historic levels. In terms of overall numbers, that proportion represents over 40 million people (U.S. Bureau of the Census, 2012a).

Immigration has slowed since the Great Recession but is projected to accelerate again as the U.S. economy improves (U.S. Bureau of the Census, 2014). One result of these recent trends is that U.S. schools are educating increasing numbers of first- and second-generation immigrant students. For instance, almost 2 million immigrant students were in U.S. schools in 2013, and over 11 million students have at least one foreign-born parent (Migration Policy Institute, 2013).

Put simply, there is a demographic imperative to teach this issue. In some ways, education researchers have responded to this imperative as there is a growing body of scholarship on immigration and education (e.g., Bartlett & García, 2011; Fránquiz & Salinas, 2013; Hilburn, 2014; Kao, Vaquera, & Goyette, 2013; Olneck, 2004; Suárez-Orozco, Suárez-Orozco, & Todorova, 2009; Taylor Jaffee, Watson, & Knight, 2014). This line of inquiry focuses in particular on how schools, teachers, and communities are addressing the social, cultural, linguistic, and academic needs of immigrant students, English language learners, emergent bilinguals, and newcomer youth.

Scholars have discussed integrating community interests/experiences, highlighting school-wide changes, integrating teaching methods, and drawing on youth's civic assets and skills. Yet little research has been conducted about teachers' perceptions of immigration as a *social issue* (Sox, 2009).

The second reason this issue is critical for 21st-century social studies educators relates to the policies and political discourse surrounding immigration. Immigration is a well-reported and contested policy area, especially during presidential election cycles. Most recently, immigration has been prominently featured in the run-up to the 2016 presidential election during debates and policy statements.

As recent election campaigns have shown, increased anti-immigrant/immigration sentiments have become a regular aspect of American political discourse. These sentiments have been framed as related to the rising number of immigrants/movement of migrants in the United States (and around the world) as well as the economic turmoil due to the 2008 Great Recession. The following quotations pointedly illustrate this type of sentiment:

"I would build a fence on America's southern border on every mile, on every yard, on every foot, on every inch of the southern border. I think that's what we have to do, not only build it, but then also have sufficient border security and enforce the laws that are on the books with the ICE agents, with our border security. And here's the other thing I would do. I would not allow taxpayer-funded benefits for illegal aliens or for their children [interrupted by applause]. That's a madness. End the madness for illegal aliens to come into the United States of America." Michelle Bachmann, GOP primary debate in Orlando, FL, Sept. 22, 2011. (FoxNews.com, 2011)

"What you need to do is attack their benefits: no free education, no free subsidies, no citizenship, no birthright citizenship." Ron Paul, GOP primary debate in Orlando, FL, Sept. 22, 2011 (FoxNews.com, 2011)

"Mexico's leaders have been taking advantage of the United States by using illegal immigration to export the crime and poverty in their own country." Donald Trump, excerpt from Trump's Immigration Reform Plan, 2015. (DonaldJTrump.com, 2016)

From a policy perspective, immigration has also been positioned as a national security issue. Post-9/11 political discourse about immigration has often focused more on border security than on economic, social, and/or legal issues. As Kim (2011) said in an insightful article ten years after 9/11, "The concept of immigration was suddenly viewed through the lens of 'homeland security', a newly ubiquitous term, and the debate swung heavily toward enforcement and prevention, accompanied by a heightened rhetoric of fear."

Perhaps most telling about the government's conceptualization of immigration after 9/11, the Department of Citizenship and Immigration Services was removed from the Department of Justice and folded into the new Department of Homeland Security. The department's own webpage describes its mission as "to secure the nation from the many threats we face" (U.S. Department of Homeland Security, 2015); thus, housing immigration services in the Department of Homeland Security speaks volumes about the national sentiment/rhetoric around immigration/immigrants in the United States.

Furthermore, in terms of policy at the federal level, comprehensive immigration reform has been all but impossible to achieve. In place of a comprehensive approach, there has been an "asymmetry in the immigration debate: enforcement as the default immigration policy" (Rosenblum, 2011, p. 11). The "secure borders" discourse associated with immigration can make it difficult for social studies teachers to teach immigration holistically. Likewise, teachers are confronted with how to navigate this discourse in their classrooms between students who might have negative, deeply rooted conceptions, assumptions, and ideas about immigration in the United States, on the one hand, and newcomers and children of newcomers on the other.

There are other policies and civil rights issues to consider when teaching immigration. The Development, Relief, and Education for Alien Minors (DREAM) Act at the federal level—as well as its variants at the state level—is a highly contested and timely issue for the nation, for higher education, and for the future of many K-12 students. Likewise, rights of citizenship, states' rights, and federalism are topics of interest in the media and directly impact the lives of many immigrants in numerous states.

For instance, recent immigration policies in Arizona (S.B. 1070) and Alabama (H.B. 56),[1] as well as the 287g program (which delegates immigration law enforcement to local jurisdictions) (U.S. Immigration and Customs Enforcement, 2011), all raise issues of states' rights, citizenship, and the Fourteenth Amendment. Each of these topics represents social issues of public import and can be studied in social studies classrooms across and within content areas.

The last justification to study immigration as a social issue is due to the unique nature of 21st-century immigration. Although U.S. history and civics standards are still stranded in a past-oriented approach to immigration (Hilburn, Journell, & Buchanan, 2016), six characteristics separate contemporary immigration from past immigration (Rong & Preissle, 2009). For the sake of brevity, we highlight two characteristics here.

First, there are new disbursement and settlement patterns for immigrant families. Although traditional gateway states such as New York, Texas, and California still receive the largest number of immigrants, the fastest growth *rate* for immigrants are southern states (e.g., North Carolina, Georgia) and inter-mountain states (e.g., Iowa, Nebraska), areas that have historically not been the preferred settlement locales for newcomers. These new gateway states[2] (Rong & Preissle, 2009) have "limited experience and infrastructure" (Terrazas & Fix, 2008, p. 8) for settling newcomers.

This challenge is particularly acute in new gateway state schools, which have yet to develop infrastructure and expertise in K-12 education and teacher education to prepare teachers to work with new immigrant students (Sox, 2009; Hilburn, 2014). The end result is that a greater number of teachers in a wider range of areas are teaching immigrant students, and many of these teachers have not received appropriate preparation to work with these students.

A second characteristic of 21st-century immigration has been a major shift in the national origins of immigrants. The first three waves of immigrants migrated in large part from Europe. Most 21st-century immigrants, however, have arrived to the United States from Asia and Latin America (U.S. Bureau of the Census, 2012b). There are several reasons for this shift, including the United States Civil Rights Movement and economic restructuring related to globalization, but the 1965 Immigration Act was the major catalyst.

Whereas previous immigration policies prioritized European immigration and implicitly or explicitly prevented individuals from other regions from moving to the United States, the 1965 Act prioritized family reunification and filling high-need jobs. The Act was also intended to more equitably distribute the number of immigrants admitted to the United States from different nations (Rong & Preissle, 2009).

This population shift has broad implications for the demographic makeup of the United States as well as for K-12 classrooms. Teachers who focus only on the first three waves of historical immigration are likely to remain metaphorically "stranded" at Ellis Island (Journell, 2009). A European-focused immigrant narrative—rather than a geographically diverse portrayal of contemporary immigration—is unlikely to accurately reflect the changing and nuanced nature of the immigration experience in the United States today.

Each of these reasons—demographics, policy and political discourse, and the unique characteristics of recent immigration—suggests that immigration as a *social issue* should be a priority in social studies classrooms. Teaching immigration as a social issue can help teachers and students better understand this complex phenomenon and the relationship between immigration and politics, both historically and contemporarily. Perhaps most importantly, it can help social studies teachers better understand their students and the students better understand each other as well.

Yet, precisely because immigration is complex, contentious, nuanced, and politicized, many teachers may be hesitant to broach this topic. Thus, two of our goals for this chapter are to promote the importance of teaching immigration as a social issue and to alleviate the hesitation that teachers may feel in addressing this difficult issue by suggesting two forward-thinking teaching strategies. In the remainder of this chapter, we will discuss four helpful "guidelines" for teaching immigration, describe two teaching methods about immigration as a social issue, and end with a discussion about the pedagogical implications of teaching immigration in the social studies classroom.

GUIDELINES FOR TEACHING IMMIGRATION

One key guideline when teaching about immigration in the social studies classroom is for teachers to establish a safe environment and a classroom culture of respect. Classroom safety is absolutely critical when discussing controversial issues such as contemporary immigration, as students need to feel as though their comments are treated with respect. Oftentimes it can be difficult to listen to and engage with a comment that one might disagree with, perpetuates stereotypes, or is blatantly incorrect. However, intellectual growth—and ultimately challenging student thinking—cannot happen without offering students the classroom space to do so (Adams, Bell, & Griffin, 2007).

In order to establish a foundation for thoughtful, empathetic, and respectful comments, social studies teachers might consider establishing guidelines for discussion, also known as *contracting*, so that students feel as though their comments are important. Likewise, it is important to forefront discussion by having a conversation with students about using appropriate and respectful language. For instance, teachers could inform students that they can critique other students' ideas, but not other students personally.

Another key guideline is to include both historical and contemporary perspectives of immigration as well as civic perspectives. When teaching immigration, it can be tempting to fall into the past-oriented trope. Several factors contribute to this approach. First, contemporary immigration is a controversial issue that many teachers may avoid (Hess, 2009). Teachers may also feel that discussing contemporary immigration may initiate conversations that include nativist, anti-immigrant statements that could cause tension in the classroom (Hilburn, 2014).

It seems that while contemporary immigration can be a touchy subject for many teachers, teachers often feel far enough removed from earlier waves of immigration that those iterations are no longer considered controversial and more likely to be taught (Rong, 1998). In actuality, earlier iterations of immigration, particularly at the turn of the twentieth century, were very controversial. Overtly recognizing the controversial nature of immigration over time may help students understand that anti-immigrant sentiment is not unique to 21st-century immigration, that resentment directed at specific groups (e.g., Irish, German immigrants) can wane over time, and that harmful rhetoric is unproductive in working toward the best immigration policies.

Formal curriculum materials such as standards and textbooks also promote past-oriented approaches. Journell (2009) found that U.S. history standards are stranded in nineteenth-century perspectives of immigration that implicitly ended at Ellis Island. Hilburn et al. (2016) confirmed this finding in states with long histories of immigration and high rates of contemporary immigration *and* even in states with limited historical orientations to immigration other than contemporary immigration.

Furthermore, this past-oriented approach extended to civics standards, which, given contemporary political discourse on this topic, should emphasize contemporary perspectives. Other studies identified specific teaching practices that reify this past-oriented narrative, especially when teachers are unaware of their own biases (Rong, 1998). Thus, our guideline is to use materials beyond the textbook and to move beyond the gaps in U.S. history and civics standards to teach immigration as a dynamic and ongoing cultural and political phenomenon, rather than a static phenomenon relegated to the past.

Our third guideline is for teachers to debunk myths associated with immigration. There is a great deal of misinformation related to immigrants and immigration policy that can interfere with students' understanding of this complex topic. For instance, in the book, *They Take Our Jobs! And 20 Other Myths about Immigration,* Chomsky (2007) teases out the myths associated with immigration such as the Horatio Alger narrative (that hard work alone directly leads to upward social mobility) and the myth of migrating to a new country is exclusively an individual's decision (rather than at least partially attributable to structural or historical factors).

While teachers should not feel obligated to overtly or systematically tackle myths like Chomsky, they should feel comfortable correcting some of the more common misconceptions about immigration, such as the following:

- Gaining citizenship is a simple and fairly easy process.
- Since most Americans are descendants of immigrants, all Americans start on equal footing.
- Most immigrants are motivated to come to the United States only for employment.

Our final guideline is to use an asset-based approach when teaching immigration. Asset-based approaches draw on the strengths, life experiences, skills, knowledge, and perspectives of immigrant students to enrich learning for immigrant and native-born youth. Scholars have advocated several ways to do this, with three major benefits for immigrant youth:

- Utilizing linguistic assets (e.g., Orellana, 2001)
- Leveraging assets to achieve individual academic attainment (e.g., Yoon, 2012)
- Maintaining and honoring heritage cultures (Qin, 2006; Yosso, 2005).

These asset-based approaches stand in contrast to deficit and subtractive approaches that can lead to academic and socialization problems (Lee, 2001; Levinson, 2012; Valenzuela, 1999). Furthermore, highlighting immigrant communities' culture and experiential knowledge also works to challenge racial and linguistic subordination in U.S. society (Yosso, 2005).

While these approaches are general to education, there are also positive implications for using asset-based approaches in social studies specifically. Hilburn (2015), for instance, identified three advantages to using an asset-based approach in civics classrooms: adding comparative and international perspectives, initiating critical civic discourse, and challenging native-born students' assumptions. Doing so resulted in a "reciprocal process in which both immigrant and native-born students accrued academic benefits" (p. 384).

Teachers who wish to use asset-based approaches must adopt dispositions that recognize the strengths, in addition to the needs, of immigrant youth. Pedagogically, asset-based approaches include seeking participation from immigrant students during class discussions to create an opportunity for students to share and engage with their "community['s] cultural wealth" or knowledge, experiences, histories, languages (Yosso, 2005, p. 75) in the classroom. Opening up a space for immigrants to compare and contrast their experiences in multiple cultures and countries, and using resources beyond textbooks (and other traditional modes of teaching) in order to initiate these conversations, are also important elements of asset-based teaching.[3]

TEACHING METHOD 1: IMMIGRATION POLICY SIMULATION[4]

For our first teaching method, we describe a simulation[5] designed to teach students how U.S. immigration policy has changed over time. This teaching method aligns with several of the characteristics we described in the previous section, as it includes historical, contemporary, and civic perspectives as well as disproves myths associated with immigration.

As the case with all simulations, each student has a role to play (Wright-Maley, 2014). For this simulation, students take one of two general roles: students simulate an immigration officer or they simulate an immigrant who is trying to enter the United States. Students simulating immigration officers are organized into "waves" of immigration. That is, one or two officers will handle all immigrants seeking admission during the first wave (before 1820), another one or two officers will handle the second wave (1820–1860), and so on. In order to prepare for the simulation, officers are provided with information about the immigration policy specific to the era.[6]

Students simulating immigrants are not organized by wave; rather, they are given individualized index cards that describe their circumstances. These circumstances include: name, year of attempted entry, gender, heritage nation, job training, health, and literacy.

What does this look like in practice? A few days before the simulation, teachers can assign (or have students volunteer) which students will be immigration officers. Then she provides those students with policy contexts according to different time periods. On the day of the simulation, the teacher organizes the classroom so that there are four stations at the front of the room. She should allow space in front of each station so that students can form lines—one line in front of each station.

Students simulating immigration officers will sit at the stations (one station for first wave, one station for second wave, etc.). Students who are simulating immigrants will receive their index cards. After reading their index cards, they will go to the appropriate station (e.g., a student attempting to enter the United States in 1980 will go to the fourth wave station).

These students will hand their card to the appropriate immigration officer, and that officer will make a decision to admit or deny based on the U.S. immigration policy in place at that time. The officer will explain his or her decision. The students simulating immigrants will return to their seats, where they will read a timeline of U.S. immigration policy.

Based on their experience during the simulation, and on the reading, students will write a description of why or why not they were admitted, as well as a description of if their character would have been admitted or denied entry during a different wave. The class will then debrief the simulation as a class discussion.[7] Finally, students will respond to a prompt that compares and contrasts contemporary immigration policy with previous iterations of immigration policy. The specific prompt is worded as: describe at least three similarities and three differences between immigration policy today with policy in the past.

There are two main limitations to this teaching method: Teachers rely on students (those simulating immigration officers) to interpret policies correctly and possible unproductive downtime with students waiting in line. The former can be somewhat mediated by providing these students with the handout several days in advance and building assessment into the simulation—either assessing their accuracy as "officers" during the simulation or providing some sort of quiz to add an additional encouragement to understand the content before the simulation. The latter can be somewhat mediated by having four lines and by using two "officers" per station rather than one.

Simulations and the use of role-play are great strategies to consider for English language learners' (ELLs) content and language needs in the social studies classroom. Additional modifications teachers might consider for ELLs might be to offer a pre-written script of their role for students on index cards. These cards should be given to ELL students prior to the simulation, so they can read, translate, and paraphrase their role.

Additionally, any context-setting information (e.g., texts, directions, questions for discussion, etc.) should also be given in advance so ELL students feel well prepared for the simulation. Lastly, teachers might consider organizing students into small groups of two or three for the postsimulation activity; therefore, ELLs can work together to discuss and write (or create an image of) their reflection to the prompt. With these slight modifications, students are more likely to fully experience and engage in the simulation.

TEACHING METHOD 2: THE NEW IMMIGRANT EXPERIENCE: EXPLORING CASE STUDIES FROM 21st-CENTURY IMMIGRATION

The second teaching method is a scaffolded, multi-stage project moving from knowledge acquisition to community action. The stages of this method include presenting background information, gathering family histories, exploring case studies, conducting oral histories, and delivering a community presentation. This method is aimed at unearthing stories and experiences as well as making connections with recent immigrants in the United States.

Prior to beginning this method, students need to have a clear understanding of what immigration is, who immigrants are (e.g., national/linguistic backgrounds, documented/undocumented, refugees, and asylum-seekers), and what are the reasons or purposes of immigration to and from the United States. These are necessary historical and contemporary contexts to consider prior to implementing this method. With this foundation, students will be more aware and knowledgeable of contemporary immigration and, therefore, will likely have a foundation for exploring the experiences of 21st-century immigrants in the United States.

This method supports the goals of both multicultural education (Banks, 2008) and social justice education (Adams et al., 2007) as the aim is to support students in their understanding of the experiences of diverse racial, cultural, linguistic, and ethnic groups as well as use their new knowledge of these experiences to combat issues of racism, linguicism, and other forms of immigrant oppression, and take action on these issues in their daily lives (either personally, locally, nationally, or globally).

Students will begin their journey of learning about the 21st-century immigrant experience by conducting some research about their family history. Questions they might ask their family members include:

- If and when did your family migrate to the United States?
- Where did your family originally settle in the United States?
- What are the migration patterns (if there are any) of your family in the United States?
- Did members of your family move back to their home country(ies)?
- What were the occupations of your family members when they arrived to the United States?

Teachers are encouraged to create questions of their own and ask students to also create questions they might want to ask regarding their family's histories and experiences in the United States. Once students have collected this information, teachers can have them share their personal/familial immigrant stories with the class.

The next part of this method is a case study exploration. Students will spend some time researching 21st-century immigrant stories. An excellent resource for this research is the PBS program and website titled "The New Americans."[8] Teachers can have students spend time reading the "Meet the New Americans" narratives and learn about the journeys and experiences of "new Americans" from India, Nigeria, and other countries to the United States.

Another idea is for students to investigate a particular immigrant group, for example, Latino/a or Asian immigrants of the 21st century. A useful resource to examine Latino/a immigrant stories and experiences is from the National Museum of American History "Americans on the Move" exhibit on *Immigration and Migration*.[9] Another resource that explores Asian immigrant experiences can be found at the Library of Congress's presentations on "Immigration"[10] and "Interviews with Today's Immigrants." The interview with immigrants' resource provides students with a drop-down menu where they can explore narratives of immigrants from regions all over the world.[11]

The goal of the case study exploration is for students to analyze and examine the nuances and complexities of the immigrant experience. The political discourse, as well as numerous state social studies standards on immigration, often cluster all newcomers into one category (Hilburn et al., 2016). By investigating a number of new immigrant stories, students will be able to see (and feel) how different each immigrant journey is and how diverse each person's experience has been.

In order to move this method from knowledge acquisition to taking action toward combating issues of injustice involving immigrants and immigration, students must share their new knowledge with others and develop an action project to challenge injustice and oppressive systems in the United States (Banks, 2008). One way students can take action to share their new knowledge of diverse immigrant experiences and combat anti-immigration sentiments around racism and linguicism is to conduct oral histories of recent immigrants in their community.

The oral history project should focus not only on the experiences of new immigrants but also on a current issue (or issues) facing the participant. The student, acting as an oral historian, should consider asking questions about:

• The immigrant participants' journey
• Experiences in the United States
• Issues they currently face
• How they are challenging this issue or hope others will challenge the issue(s) in their community, nation, and/or world.

Students should be encouraged and supported in conducting their oral histories in participants' native languages.

If students do not have access to immigrants in their communities, perhaps reaching out to an organization that supports new arrivals (e.g., Church World Service) and discussing these items with a leader of the organization could be an alternative assignment. Additionally, students who are monolingual English speakers should be encouraged to find a bilingual community member, teacher, or peer who could help facilitate the interview and translation of the oral history. Translating the narrative will not only help students understand and interpret the oral history but also facilitate sharing the narrative with the teacher (for assessment purposes) as well as the larger community.

Lastly, a critical piece of this project is to share these narratives with others in the school and/or surrounding community. For example, students could display their projects in a school-wide fair or present their narratives at a local community event. Students might also consider holding a digital event, such as using social media to share their narratives. This approach would require audio- or videotaping their oral histories; however, it would be a great way to showcase student work as well as the voices of recent immigrants. The goal is that these narratives will ignite and spur discussion (and hopefully action-taking) around current issues facing new immigrants in their communities.

This teaching method supports ELLs in numerous ways. Interviewing family members and becoming oral historians draw on students' cultural and linguistic assets by offering students a chance to conduct interviews in their native language as well as share their historical narratives in their home language as well as English. This strategy might further support ELLs by opening up the possibility for ELL students to explore case studies in their own communities or perhaps research narratives/stories using sources in their native language.

Translating the interviews and case study narratives is an important task; however, offering ELL students support from other teachers, peers, and/or family/community members to complete this task is necessary. Lastly, the final piece of this method should offer ELL students a choice for how they would like to share their narrative (e.g., oral presentation, guest speakers, poster display, video creation, audio representation, etc.). Giving ELLs a choice for their final presentation provides the space for students to showcase their academic and linguistic assets, and decide how best to highlight their knowledge of the content.

PEDAGOGICAL IMPLICATIONS

The pedagogical implications of teaching immigration as a social issue are threefold. First, students will have the foundational content knowledge for understanding the current discourse involving immigration in the United States. Teachers should consider teaching the three factors for why teaching immigration should be a priority in 21st-century social studies classrooms: demographics, policy and political discourse, and the unique characteristics of 21st-century immigration.

If social studies teachers spend time contextualizing classroom discussions about immigration (using these factors as supporting evidence), students might become better informed about the issues surrounding immigration and immigrants in the United States. With this foundational knowledge and context, students could be better equipped to filter political discourse about immigration and better equipped to consider taking action in their communities.

Second, students learn to challenge their misconceptions, assumptions, and stereotypes when discussing immigration as a social issue, particularly when including both historical and contemporary perspectives. Offering a safe space for youth to feel open to being uncomfortable is important when discussing contemporary issues related to immigration.

By offering a safe and open classroom climate, students are provided with an environment to participate, discuss, and work toward challenging their preconceived notions and beliefs (Adams et al., 2007). Furthermore, creating this classroom space promotes respect, tolerance, and most importantly an environment to engage in questions and discussion of possible actions one might take when challenging oppressive systems and engaging in societal change-making.

Lastly, we encourage teachers to adopt forward-thinking teaching strategies when teaching immigration beyond traditional methods of lecture, textbooks, and worksheets. We provided two exemplars for doing this, but these strategies are not exhaustive. Using the four guidelines that we describe here, teachers should develop the forward-thinking strategies most appropriate to the students in their classrooms.

These methods offer students a chance to experience issues related to immigration by engaging in simulations, case studies, or face-to-face interactions with new immigrants. We hope that teachers will employ asset-based approaches in their middle and secondary social studies classrooms with the primary goal of highlighting the strengths and diversity of immigrant journeys, experiences, and successes in the United States.

NOTES

1. Arizona SB 1070 requires police to determine the immigration status of someone arrested or detained when there is "reasonable suspicion" they are not in the United States legally. Alabama H.B. 56, among other things, called for school officials to determine if newly enrolled students are documented or undocumented immigrants. Although aspects of these laws have been deemed unconstitutional in higher courts, they passed with widespread legislative support in their respective states.

2. These have also been termed "new destination states" or "new growth states."

3. When using these strategies, it is important to prompt students to speak only about their own experiences. It would be unethical to ask students to speak on behalf of others.

4. These teaching methods align with NCSS Disciplinary Standards 1: *History* and 3: *Civics and Government*. They also align with NCSS Thematic Standards I: *Culture and Cultural Diversity*, II: *Time, Continuity, and Change*, III: *People, Places, and Environments*, and IV. *Individual Development and Identity*. Teachers who use or modify these approaches should also align with their state and/or local standards.

5. For recent research on using simulations in social studies, see Wright-Maley (2014, 2015) as well as Dack, van Hover, and Hicks (2016).

6. For a concise but thorough timeline of U.S. immigration policy, see Chomsky (2007). For a more detailed timeline, see Migration Policy Institute (2013) Fact Sheet

7. Sample discussion questions include: For what reasons were you denied or accepted entry into the United States? Do these reasons seem fair and sensible? Based on this simulation, what would you like to see changed about immigration policy, if anything?

8. The "New Americans" program can be found at http://www.pbs.org/independentlens/newamericans/index.html

9. The "Americans on the Move" exhibit can be found at http://amhistory.si.edu/onthemove/themes/story_51_2.html

10. The "Immigration" presentation can be found at http://www.loc.gov/teachers/classroommaterials/presentationsandactivities/presentations/immigration/

11. The "Interviews with Today's Immigrants" program can be found at http://www.loc.gov/teachers/classroommaterials/presentationsandactivities/presentations/immigration/interv/toc.php

REFERENCES

Adams, M., Bell, L. A., & Griffin, P. (Eds) (2007). *Teaching for diversity and social justice: A sourcebook* (2nd ed.). New York, NY: Taylor & Francis.

Banks, J. (2008). *An introduction to multicultural education* (4th ed.). Boston, MA: Pearson.

Bartlett, L. & García, O. (2011). *Additive schooling in subtractive times*. Nashville, TN: Vanderbilt University Press.

Chomsky, A. (2007). *"They take our jobs!" And 20 other myths about immigration*. Boston, MA: Beacon Press.

Dack, H., van Hover, S., & Hicks, D. (2016). "Try not to giggle if you can help it": The implementation of experiential instructional techniques in social studies classrooms. *Journal of Social Studies Research, 40*, 39–52.

DonaldJTrump.com. (2016). Immigration reform that will make America great again. Retrieved from https://www.donaldjtrump.com/positions/immigration-reform

FoxNews.com. (2011, September 22). Transcript: Fox News-Google GOP debate. Retrieved from http://www.foxnews.com/politics/2011/09/22/fox-news-google-gop-2012-presidential-debate.html

Fránquiz, M. & Salinas, C. (2013). Knowing English is not enough! Cultivating academic literacies among high school newcomers. *The High School Journal, 96*, 339–367.

Hess, D. E. (2009). *Controversy in the classroom: The democratic power of discussion*. New York, NY: Routledge.

Hilburn, J. (2014). Challenges facing immigrant students beyond the linguistic domain in a new gateway state. *The Urban Review, 46*, 654–680.

Hilburn, J. (2015). Asset-based Civics for, with, and by immigrant students: Three sites of enriched teaching and learning for immigrant and native-born students. *Theory & Research in Social Education, 43*, 372–404.

Hilburn, J., Journell, W., & Buchanan, L.B. (2016). A content analysis of immigration in traditional, new, and non-gateway state standards for U.S. History and Civics. *The High School Journal, 99*, 234–251.

Journell, W. (2009). Setting out the (un)welcome mat: A portrayal of immigration in American history standards. *The Social Studies, 100*, 160–168.

Kao, G., Vaquera, E., & Goyette, K. (2013). *Education and immigration.* Malden, MA: Polity Press.

Kim, M. J. (2011). After 9/11, immigration became about homeland security. *US News and World Report.* Retrieved from: http://www.usnews.com/news/articles/2011/09/08/after-911-immigration-became-about-homeland-security-attacks-shifted-the-conversation-heavily-toward-terrorism-and-enforcement?page=2

Lee, S. J. (2001). More than "model minority" or "delinquents:" A look at Hmong American high school students. *Harvard Educational Review, 71*, 505–528.

Levinson, M. (2012). *No citizen left behind.* Cambridge, MA: Harvard University Press.

Library of Congress. (2015). *Interviews with today's immigrants.* Washington, DC: Author. Retrieved from: http://www.loc.gov/teachers/classroommaterials/presentationsandactivities/presentations/immigration/interv/toc.php

Migration Policy Institute. (2013). *Major U.S. immigration laws, 1790-present.* Washington, DC: Author. Retrieved from: http://www.migrationpolicy.org/research/timeline-1790

National Museum of American History, Smithsonian Institution. (2015). *American on the move.* Washington, DC: Author. Retrieved from: http://amhistory.si.edu/onthemove/themes/story_51_2.html

Olneck, M. (2004). Immigrants and education in the United States. In J. Banks (Ed.), *Handbook of research on multicultural education* (pp. 381–404). San Francisco, CA: Jossey-Bass.

Orellana, M. F. (2001). The work kids do: Mexican and Central American immigrant children's contributions to households and schools in California. *Harvard Educational Review, 71*, 366–389.

Qin, D. B. (2006). The role of gender in immigrant students' educational adaptation. *Current Issues in Comparative Education, 9*, 8–19.

Rong, X. L. (1998). The new immigration: Challenges facing social studies professionals. *Social Education, 62*, 393–399.

Rong, X. L. & Preissle, J. (2009). *Educating immigrants in the 21st century: What educators need to know* (2nd ed.). Thousand Oaks, CA: Corwin Press.

Rosenblum, M. R. (2011). *U.S. immigration policy since 9/11: Understanding the stalemate over immigration reform.* Washington, DC: Migration Policy Institute.

Sox, A. K. (2009). Latino immigrant students in southern schools: What we know and still need to learn. *Theory into Practice, 48*, 312–318.

Suárez-Orozco, C., Suárez-Orozco, M. M., & Todorova, T. (2008). *Learning a new land: immigrant students in American society.* Cambridge, MA: Harvard University Press.

Taylor Jaffee, A., Watson, V.W., & Knight, M. (2014). Toward enacted cosmopolitan citizenship: New conceptualizations of African immigrants' civic learning and action. *Journal of Global Citizenship & Equity Education, 4*(1). Retrieved from http://journals.sfu.ca/jgcee

Terrazas, A. & Fix, M. (2008). *Gambling on the future: Managing the educational challenges of rapid growth in Nevada.* Washington, DC: Migration Policy Institute.

U.S. Bureau of the Census. (2012a). *Foreign-born current population survey: 2012 data tables*. Washington, DC: Author. Retrieved from: http://www.census.gov/population/foreign/data/cps2012.html

U.S. Bureau of the Census. (2012b). *Foreign-born population in the United States: 2010*. Washington, DC: Author. Retrieved from: http://www.census.gov/prod/2012pubs/acs-19.pdf

U.S. Bureau of the Census. (2014). *National population projections*. Washington, DC: Author. Retrieved from: http://www.census.gov/population/projections/data/national/2014.html

U.S. Department of Homeland Security. (2015). *About DHS*. Washington, DC: Author. Retrieved from: http://www.dhs.gov/about-dhs

U.S. Immigration and Customs Enforcement. (2011). *Delegation of immigration authority section 287(g) Immigration and Nationality Act*. Washington, DC: Author. Retrieved from: http://www.ice.gov/287g

Valenzuela, A. (1999). *Subtractive schooling: US-Mexican youth and the politics of caring*. Albany, NY: State University of New York Press.

Wright-Maley, C. (2014). Beyond the "Babel Problem": Defining simulations for social studies. *Journal of Social Studies Research, 39*, 63–77.

Wright-Maley, C. (2015). On stepping back and letting go: The role of control in the success or failure of social studies simulations. *Theory & Research in Social Education, 43*, 206–243.

Yoon, B. (2012). Junsuk and Junhyuck: Adolescent immigrants' educational journey to success and identity negotiation. *American Educational Research Journal, 49*, 971–1002.

Yosso, T. J. (2005). Whose culture has capital? A critical race theory discussion of community cultural wealth. *Race, Ethnicity, and Education, 8*, 69–91.

Chapter 4

(Mis)perceptions of Arabs and Arab Americans

How Can Social Studies Teachers Disrupt the Stereotypes?

Paul J. Yoder, Aaron P. Johnson, and Fares J. Karam

A social issue that has leapt onto the front page of newspapers and Facebook news feeds in recent years is the stereotypical depiction of Arabs and Arab Americans. In short, within the United States, Arabs are viewed as terrorists and extremists (Altwaiji, 2014; Gerhauser, 2014; Klepper, 2014). The voice of the moderate Arab is silenced within media portrayals and general discourse in favor of the minority of Arabs who advocate for and commit terrorist acts (el-Aswad, 2013).

Arab American communities, in turn, have often faced discrimination (Abu El-Haj, 2006; Merskin, 2004; Wingfield, 2006) or been largely omitted from discussions of American society (Eraqi, 2015b; Naber, 2000; M. Suleiman, 2000). On the international stage, the face of the Arab is that of the Islamic State of Iraq and Syria (ISIS) and Al-Qaeda.

The stereotype of the Arab as terrorist is not limited to news headlines. Morgan (2012) and others argue that an array of popular cultural outlets, including Western media (Elbih, 2015), video games (Šisler, 2008), and political discourse (Merskin, 2004; Nimer, 2007) perpetuate this depiction. Unfortunately, research suggests that social studies curricular materials do little to combat this image.

For example, in a recent study of five secondary U.S. history textbooks, Eraqi (2015b) found that Arabs and Arab Americans were either omitted or primarily "mentioned during times of tension, violence and conflict" (p. 71). Recent analyses of world history (Hantzopoulos, Zakharia, Shirazi, Bajaj, & Ghaffar-Kucher, 2015; Morgan & Walker, 2008) and other social studies textbooks (Morgan, 2008) have found similar results, suggesting that the social studies curriculum too often reinforces common misrepresentations, presenting stereotypical portrayals of Arabs as violent and ignoring the inherent linguistic, religious, social, and cultural diversity found in the Arab world.

In the face of this pervasive caricature—the Arab as terrorist—an important question arises: How can social studies teachers address public portrayals of Arabs and Arab Americans? The question cuts across disciplines within the field of social studies, encompassing a range of topics including the role of government, foreign policy, media studies, terrorism, race, gender, and equality. In this chapter we begin by asking the deceptively simple question: Who are Arabs? We then present a global education framework, which we use to organize suggestions for social studies teachers regarding practices and resources that can contribute to the disruption of stereotypical portrayals of Arabs and add depth to classroom instruction and dialogue.

COMMON (MIS)PERCEPTIONS OF ARABS

Who are Arabs? According to the 22 member states of the Arab League, an Arab is "someone who speaks Arabic, lives in an Arabic-speaking country, and upholds Arabic culture" (Elbih, 2015, pp. 113–114). The Arab American Institute (2015) and scholars (e.g., Abbudabeh, 1996; Lewis, 1995) similarly identify Arabs as having a shared language and geographic origin. Yet we also acknowledge the limitations of the term "Arab" given the fluid nature of identity and the ways in which labels are often used to assert power over others (Norton, 2013).

We recognize that scholars such as Salameh (2010) problematize the idea of a cohesive "Arab world" and "Arab people," critiquing such terms as Western projections of the concept of national identity that do not truly reflect the region's linguistic, ethnic, and religious diversity. Thus, while the Arab League definition above provides a working definition for the purposes of this chapter, we seek to address the fact that our conceptual understanding of "Arab" has been shaped by caricatures that are prevalent in popular culture, the media, and even scholarly literature.

In this section we identify some of the common (mis)perceptions of Arabs. We do not attempt to provide a comprehensive review of the literature on this topic, nor an exclusive list of (mis)representations; rather, we aim to highlight three of the common (mis)perceptions of Arabs and present alternate perspectives that run counter to these dominant and often biased representations (see also Elbih, 2015). We argue that it is essential for social studies teachers to be cognizant of such biased portrayals of Arabs and thus offer practical suggestions to help teachers provide contexts for students to learn about the Arab world and Arab Americans from multiple perspectives.

Linguistic (Mis)Perceptions

Although Arabic is the official language in most Arab countries, observers are unlikely to hear the same Arabic dialect spoken in the streets across the different Arab countries. Thus, while some may think that Arabic is a uniform language, Suleiman (2003) noted the existence of different dialects of Arabic beyond Modern Standard Arabic (MSA), which is mainly used in academic settings, newspapers, and legal documents. Salameh (2010) argued that MSA is a colonial language, representing "an elitist view of language, memory, and identity in the Middle East—more specifically an Arab nationalist and Muslim traditionalist view—and one not reflecting the Middle East's cultural and ethnic diversity" (p. 1).

This Arab nationalist perspective holds MSA as an essential and sometimes prerequisite identity marker of being Arab and perceives the Arab world as a cohesive nation with a unified language, ignoring the linguistic diversity that exists among the various countries. As an example, Salameh (2010) described the "compulsory Arabness" views espoused by Syrian writer Sati' al-Husri. Al-Husri believed that all Arab speakers are Arabs even if they do not think of themselves as such and that Arabic speakers who do not believe that they are Arabs should be educated out of their ignorance and led to embrace their Arab identity (as cited in Salameh, 2010).

In resisting such hegemonic views, modern "Arab" thinkers such as the Lebanese poet Said Akl have claimed that the Lebanese language is not even an Arab dialect, but rather an indigenous language that has Phoenician roots (as cited in Salameh, 2010). Thus, while the United Nations views Arabic as a common language that can be used to further advance cooperation among Arab countries (Fergany, El Hamed, & Hunaidi, 2002), others view "the Arabic language, in its Classical and Modern Standard forms, [a]s a key factor in the Middle East's turbulence, authoritarianism, intellectual torpor, cultural rigidity, and lack of freedoms" (Salameh, 2010, p. xvii). In short, the definition and role of "Arabic" should both be considered contested concepts in the face of the linguistic diversity found within Arab countries.

Religious (Mis)Perceptions

Another common myth is that the terms "Arab" and "Muslim" can be used interchangeably (Elbih, 2015). While it is true that most citizens of Arab countries are Muslim, not all Arabs are Muslims, and certainly not all Muslims are Arabs. In fact, only 20.1% of Muslims live in the Middle East-North Africa region where the Arab countries are located (Pew Research Center, 2009). In a poignant example of the relevance of Islam outside of the Middle East, Indonesia—a non-Arab country in the Asia-Pacific region—is the country with the largest population of Muslims (approximately 13% of the global Muslim population).

While the majority of Arabs are Muslims, the religious diversity within the Arab world must not be overlooked. For example, Telhami (2013) argued that while the concept of a "Christian Arab" might sound "foreign" in Morocco (p. 21), such would not be the case in Egypt and the Levant. Lebanon has the most religious diversity in the Arab world with 54% of Lebanese identifying as Sunni or Shia Muslims (Central Intelligence Agency, 2015). The rest of the Lebanese population is divided among mainly Christian dominations such as Maronites and Orthodox sects. As such, it is important not to conflate the terms "Arab" and "Muslim."

Finally, to the extent that Arabs are associated with Islam—and Islam as a religion has been associated with terror—Arabs have been termed "radicals" and "terrorists" (Elbih, 2015). Much has been written on this topic (e.g., Asani, 2011; Huntington, 1996), but it is important to note that while twisted versions of Islam have been used to recruit and radicalize terrorists, scholars such as Yahya (2015) have argued that Islam as a religion denounces terror.

As Yahya (2015) noted, "The religion of Islam can by no means countenance terrorism. On the contrary, terror (i.e., murder of innocent people) in Islam is a great sin, and Muslims are responsible for preventing these acts and bringing peace and justice to the world" (p. 17). Among Muslim Americans, a clear majority (78%) are opposed to using terror and attacking civilians in defense of Islam (Pew Research Center, 2009).

Gendered (Mis)Perceptions

While marginalization of women in Arab countries cannot be dismissed as a mere myth, a monolithic portrayal of the role of women in the region should be avoided. In discussing women's rights, the United Nations Development Program (UNDP, 2012) concluded that "gender inequality across the region [among Arab countries] is prevalent" (para. 4). The UNDP continued, "Statistics show that only 25% of Arab women participate in the labor force, half the average for developing nations. Because of the male-centric culture in many Arab societies, many women experience limited roles outside the home" (para. 4).

One of the well-known limitations on women's rights is the prohibition of female drivers in Saudi Arabia. However, not all Arab countries have similar bans, and Saudi Arabia's example represents only one end of the spectrum of the status of women's rights. Notable counter-examples in other Arab countries include Mariam al-Mansouri, the Emirati fighter jet pilot who participated in flying missions as part of the U.S.-led war against ISIS, and Tawakkol Karman, the Yemeni activist who was one of three women to receive the 2011 Nobel Peace Prize (Telhami, 2013).

Such examples do not take away from the harsh reality of gender inequality and the marginalization of women in some Arab countries; however, it is important not to further dehumanize women in the region by adhering to a stereotypical portrayal of disempowered and oppressed Arab women.

Gender inequality in Arab countries is often attributed to Islam. A common myth is that Islam is a religion that oppresses and marginalizes women—with the hijab (the veil) being a symbol of women's oppression. It is a commonly held misperception that women "have to" wear the veil and cover their faces in all Arab countries. Again, this is true in some Arab countries, but certainly not in others. For example, Christian and Muslim women in Jordan, Lebanon, and Syria have traditionally had the freedom to choose whether or not to wear the hijab. A walk in the streets of Beirut will quickly reveal that most women are not veiled even though more than half of the population is Muslim.

Crocco, Pervez, and Katz (2009) have contested that the "the purportedly 'religiously grounded' restrictions placed on women within certain societies have little or nothing to do with the teachings of Islam" (p. 110). They further explain that there is a discrepancy between the religious texts in Islam and patriarchal practices aimed at limiting women's access to power. Similarly, Bubtana (2000) argued that Islam "gives great importance to the role of women in developing and shaping society as a whole" (p. 49).

Thus, Islam is not the sole determiner of gender norms in Arab countries; other factors such as culture, family, and society also contribute to gender roles. Crocco and colleagues concluded that "women from the nations of the Middle East are just as much a product of their culture as of religion, even if the distinction is difficult to make" (p. 111). Moreover, it is important to avoid faulty generalizations about the status of women's rights in the Arab world where women (and men) continue to fight for achieving more equitable societies.

INSTRUCTIONAL SUGGESTIONS FOR
SOCIAL STUDIES TEACHERS

In light of the (mis)perceptions described above, social studies teachers have a unique opportunity to break down stereotypes in classroom portrayals and discussions of Arabs and Arab Americans. Merryfield and Kasai (2010) identified the potential of global education in preparing students for the realities of globalization, particularly in the areas of multiple perspectives, global interconnectedness, global issues, and cross-cultural experiences (see also Gaudelli, 2003; Merryfield, 2002; Noddings, 2005).

Kirkwood-Tucker (2009) articulated five tenets that serve as an accessible framework with the potential to create rich, pedagogical space in which teachers can disrupt commonly held assumptions (see also A. P. Johnson, 2015). According to Kirkwood-Tucker (2009), the basic principles of global education comprise the abilities (pp. 137–138)

- To see one's world from multiple perspectives, recognizing that others may have views of the world profoundly different from one's own
- To see the causes and effects of globalization as they affect the lives of communities and people, of students and schools
- To be able to analyze cross-cultural commonalities and differences and appreciate the contributions made by nations and cultures to civilization
- To perceive the interconnectedness of cultural, economic, geographic, political, and technical phenomena with their often-numerous unanticipated consequences
- To perceive the ramifications of decisions made by individuals, groups, and entire nations and how they affect the future of the world.

In this section, we present examples of instructional strategies and resources that map onto each of these five values.

Multiple Perspectives: Employing Visuals in Depicting Diversity

The names given to places and landforms provide a treasure trove of information for social studies teachers and students to discover. Yet Segall and Helfenbein (2008) have concluded that geography receives too little attention in the social studies. In studying the Middle East or Arab world, the names of places can play a particularly important role in denoting multiple perspectives over specific contested areas.

The case of the body of water that lies between Saudi Arabia and Iran serves as a prime example. A wide angle on Google maps provides the name Persian Gulf, as most other English-language maps do. However, zooming in reveals the contested nature of this body of water with two labels—"Persian Gulf and (Arabian Gulf)"—coming into view. Google's decision to use the term "Arabian Gulf" has drawn criticism in Iran (see, for example, X, 2012).

On the other side of the debate, some sources from a clearly Arab perspective provide only the term "Arabian Gulf" (see, for example, Rehren, 2011). Social studies teachers can provide students with opportunities to analyze these and other historical and primary sources as a case study of the ethnic and linguistic complexities in what is often referred to as the Middle East or Arab world.

The Effects of Globalization: Analyzing
Depictions of Daily Life in Trade Books

In conceiving how students of all ages may best grasp tangible aspects of a complex phenomenon such as globalization, trade books provide social studies teachers with a unique resource for examining the impacts of migration and change on the lived experiences of Arabs and Arab Americans. Schwebel (2011) and Johnson (2009) described ways in which the careful analysis of children's literature can provide an important source for engaging students in the social studies classroom. In research specific to students' views on Arabs, Johnson and colleagues (2013) found that reading narrative fiction that includes Arabs and Muslims can counter stereotypes and increase "empathy and perspective-taking" (p. 578).

In one such book, *Lailah's Lunchbox*, Reem Faruqi (2015) tells the fictional story of a little girl whose family moves from Abu Dhabi to Peachtree City, Georgia. The titular lunchbox takes center stage as young Lailah's mother announces that Lailah has come of age and will not need her lunchbox while she participates in Ramadan, the Muslim month of fasting. Lailah is excited, but is also worried about what her elementary school classmates might say. When Lailah's teacher and the school librarian support her decision to spend the lunch period in the library instead of the cafeteria, Lailah interprets their smiles and notes of encouragement as support for her cultural identity.

The beautiful watercolor illustrations in this book bring young Lailah to life through expressive and lively images. The strategic illustrations include humanizing depictions of everyday activities, such as Lailah dancing with her schoolyard friends, as well as contextualizing content, including Lailah tracing the journey from the Middle East to the United States on a map. An author's note reveals that *Lailah's Lunchbox* is based on Faruqi's own life.

Through telling Lailah's story—her own story—Faruqi uses the account of one Arab American's experience to provide the reader with a child's perspective on what it might be like to feel like an outsider, lending nuance and voice to a viewpoint that is too often marginalized. This is only one example of a trade book that teachers can use for this purpose. A list of other works can be found in Appendix A.

Cross-Cultural Commonalities and Difference: Comparing Arabs and Muslims

The Inquiry Design Model (IDM) provides a powerful and structured learning format to address the common assumption that all Arabs and Arab Americans are Muslim. The IDM's basic components and structure support the *College, Career, and Civic Life (C3) Framework* (National Council for the Social Studies, 2013) inquiry arc and include the use of both compelling and supporting questions.

Compelling questions, which serve to frame the overall learning experience, address an enduring social studies issue, appeal to student curiosity, and are worthy of instruction time. Supporting questions by contrast are intended to scaffold student investigations as they navigate issues and ideas behind a compelling question and begin to develop a response to the compelling question (Grant, 2013).

In Appendix B we present an IDM lesson plan built around the two compelling questions: "Are all Arabs Muslim?" and "Are all Muslims Arab?" During the lesson, students participate in a series of formative performance tasks. Each task guides students as they respond to three supporting questions. At the conclusion of the lesson, students are prepared to return to the underlying compelling questions and are encouraged to share their responses as part of a class discussion.

Interconnectedness: Examining Freedom and the Hijab

Kirkwood-Tucker (2009) has argued that global education serves to expose the interconnected nature of forces (i.e., cultural, economic, geographic, political) in our world and the often unanticipated consequences that arise as part of the shared and lived experience. Within unanticipated consequences emerge the opportunity for teachers to address controversial and complex issues that may ultimately serve to underscore the extent to which our world is interconnected. Structured Academic Controversy (SAC) represents an accessible instructional strategy intended to facilitate this process.

The SAC strategy builds on a compelling and controversial question that lends itself to opposing viewpoints and authentic discussion (see Stanford History Education Group, 2015). The strategy places students in teams of four embedded with two dyads; each dyad is assigned an opposing side of the debate that stems from the question. In dyads, students grapple with two to three sources provided by the teacher and through analysis craft a substantiated opinion, after which they deliberate with the other dyad—which has been assigned the opposing side of the debate.

Following the deliberation, students switch sides and craft an argument based on the sources that support the opposing view and then deliberate again. Through the process of SAC, students investigate both sides of the issue and ultimately attempt to develop a consensus opinion based on their analyses of both viewpoints.

This particular SAC centers on the hijab and how the garment itself may provide students with a perspective on the complex and changing role of gender in the Arab world. Before introducing the SAC to students, we suggest providing them with contextual and historical information about the hijab. For example, students can visit the UNC Center for Global Initiatives' website on "Arabs in America" (Amer, 2016) and explore the history of the hijab and its many forms, including the niqab and burqa. The site also addresses why some

Arab women choose to wear the garment and others do not—information particularly germane to this SAC.

After learning about the history and nuances of the hijab, students are then presented with the following question: Does banning the hijab from the public square advance women's rights? This question stems from efforts in Europe and parts of Asia to ban veiling in the public square. Interestingly, these efforts have fostered both support and disdain from Arab communities and women around the world, two perspectives that are interwoven into this activity.

Students can be introduced to this SAC by first viewing the BBC's (2014) report "European Court Upholds French Full Veil Ban," which establishes a necessary context for student analysis. After viewing the news report students can then be assigned a side of the controversy to begin exploring. Given the SAC format, much of the success of this activity lies in the selection of resources for students to analyze. For this reason, we suggest resources that effectively serve to capture the lived experiences of Arab women and their stances on this issue (e.g., Ali, 2015; Alvi, 2014; Nusrat, 2012; Tremblay, 2014).

After exploring both sides of the issue presented in these sources, students may begin to craft their own opinions regarding the compelling question: Does banning the hijab from the public square advance women's rights? To conclude this SAC, the teacher can pose another question to students: How does the hijab represent complex gender roles within the Arab world? Such a question may launch further inquiries into issues of gender and how they are changing within Arab communities and other cultures (e.g., Gorney, 2016).

Decisions Made in a Global Society: Integrating Current Events

Recent conflicts in the Arab world have resulted in the displacement of millions of individuals and families. Many refugees from war-torn Syria and Iraq have, for example, flocked to nearby locations including Lebanon, Jordan, and Turkey. Others have journeyed toward Europe, often risking their lives to find asylum in countries such as Germany or Sweden.

Syria in particular has captured the world's attention as more than half of its population has either fled or been killed since its civil war erupted in 2011. The recent migration crisis foregrounds the notion that decisions made by governments (e.g., the Assad regime in Syria) in a global society often have ramifications that extend beyond national borders and affect the world.

With this realization in mind, social studies teachers should consider avenues for keeping students abreast of situations occurring within the Arab world—such as those unfolding in Syria—and lead students in investigating how they affect the rest of the world. One approach for teachers to consider is the regular incorporation of current events into class discussions and other learning activities. "The Learning Network: Teaching and Learning with the *New York Times*" (2016) is a resource that offers "50 Ways to Teach with Current Events" that are accessible by theme including "Reading and Writing," "Speaking and Listening," and "Making Connections." All articles linked within the site are free for teachers and can be accessed without a subscription.

Teachers may also create a webquest as a way of guiding the learning sequence and the content students encounter. A webquest focused on the Syrian refugee crisis, for example, could visit a timeline of articles including the growing opposition of the Assad regime in the context of the Arab Spring, tactics employed by the Assad regime to squelch the revolt, and the international response to these events, including statements made by the United States, Russia, and Iran.

Free online resources (i.e., "zunal.com," 2001) allow teachers to upload selected news articles and other media and prompt students with specific questions to guide their reading. For further help with what questions to ask students as they examine news articles, PBS NOW Classroom (2016) offers teachers a graphic organizer that features supporting questions that aid students in seeing how events are connected. Webquests that curate recent publications can provide students with a strong framework for working with current events and demonstrate how local and national decisions can have effects on a global scale.

CONCLUSION

While unfair and stereotypical portrayal of Arabs and Arab Americans is most prevalent in popular media outlets (Elbih, 2015; Morgan, 2012), analysis of history and social studies textbooks suggests that the images and narratives students encounter in the classroom have also reinforced the image of Arabs as violent (e.g., Eraqi, 2015b; Hantzopoulos et al., 2015). In order to disrupt the many (mis)perceptions of Arabs and Arab Americans that persist, social studies teachers should provide students with alternative narratives and opportunities to analyze multiple perspectives through a global education lens.

While the suggestions and resources we have presented above represent only the tip of the proverbial iceberg, our intent is to identify the problem and spark the conversation. As long as the ongoing war with ISIS persists, the images and discussions of Arabs and Arab Americans that social studies teachers privilege will only grow in importance. In as much as "the limited inclusion of positive contributions by these groups within the social studies curriculum" (Eraqi, 2015a, p. 93) serves to perpetuate stereotypes, we offer this chapter in order to help social studies teachers engage in fairer, more representative, and academically rigorous instruction.

REFERENCES

Abu El-Haj, T. R. (2006). Race, politics, and Arab American youth: Shifting frameworks for conceptualizing educational equity. *Educational Policy, 20*, 13–34.

Abbudabbeh, N. (1996). Arab families. In M. McGoldrick, J. Giordano, & N. Garcia-Preto (Eds), *Ethnicity and family therapy* (2nd edn., pp. 333–346). New York, NY: Guilford Press.

Ali, H. (2015, September 18). Egyptian women urged to 'put on your dress'. *Al-Monitor.* Retrieved from http://www.al-monitor.com/pulse/originals/2015/09/egypt-put-on-your-dress-campaign-sexual-harassment.html

Altwaiji, M. (2014). Neo-orientalism and the neo-imperialism thesis: Post-9/11 U.S. and Arab world relationship. *Arab Studies Quarterly, 36*, 313–323.

Alvi, B. (2014, June 14). What I wear is my choice. *Huffington Post.* Retrieved from http://www.huffingtonpost.com/bushra-alvi/what-i-wear-is-my-choice_b_5142943.html

Amer, S. (2016) What is the hijab and why do women wear it? *Arabs in America.* Retrieved from http://arabsinamerica.unc.edu/identity/veiling/hijab

Arab American Institute. (2015). Who are Arab Americans? Retrieved from http://www.aaiusa.org/who-are-arab-americans

Asani, A. S. (2011). Enhancing religious literacy in a liberal arts education through the study of Islam and Muslim societies. *The Harvard Sampler: Liberal Education for the Twenty-first Century*, 1–31.

Aswad, E. el- (2013). Images of Muslims in western scholarship and media after 9/11. *DOMES: Digest of Middle East Studies, 22*, 39–56.

Bubtana, S. (2000). Women, culture and power sharing: The case of the Arab region. In M.-L. Kearney (Ed.), *Women, power and the academy: From rhetoric to reality* (pp. 43–52). New York, NY: Berghan Books.

Central Intelligence Agency. (2015). Lebanon. *The World Factbook.* Retrieved from https://www.cia.gov/library/publications/the-world-factbook/geos/le.html

Crocco, M. S., Pervez, N., & Katz, M. (2009). At the crossroads of the world: Women of the Middle East. *The Social Studies, 100*, 107–114.

Elbih, R. (2015). Teaching about Islam and Muslims while countering cultural misrepresentations. *The Social Studies, 106*, 112–116.

Eraqi, M. M. (2015a). Arab-American and Muslim-American contributions: Resources for secondary social studies teachers. *Multicultural Perspectives, 17*, 93–98.

Eraqi, M. M. (2015b). Inclusion of Arab-Americans and Muslim-Americans within secondary U.S. history textbooks. *Journal of International Social Studies, 5*, 64–80.

European court upholds French full veil ban. (2014, July 1). Retrieved from http://www.bbc.com/news/world-europe-28106900

Faruqi, R. (2015). *Lailah's lunchbox: A Ramadan story.* Thomaston, ME: Tilbury House.

Fergany, N., El Hamed, A. L. Y., & Hunaidi, R. K. (2002). *Arab human development report 2002: Creating opportunities for future generations.* Cairo, Egypt: Government of Egypt, Institute of National Planning.

Gaudelli, W. (2003). *World class: Teaching and learning in global times.* Mahwah, NJ: Erlbaum.

Gerhauser, P. T. (2014). Framing Arab-Americans and Muslims in U.S. Media. *Sociological Viewpoints, 30,* 7–35.

Grant, S. G. (2013). From inquiry arc to instructional practice: The potential of the C3 framework. *Social Education, 77,* 322–326, 351.

Gorney, C. (2016, January 13). The changing face of Saudi women. *National Geographic.* Retrieved from http://ngm.nationalgeographic.com/2016/02/saudi-arabia-women-text

Hantzopoulos, M., Zakharia, Z., Shirazi, R., Bajaj, M., & Ghaffar-Kucher, A. (2015). New curricular approaches to teaching about the Middle East and North Africa. *Social Studies Research and Practice, 10,* 84–93.

Huntington, S. P. (1996). *The clash of civilizations and the remaking of world order.* New York, NY: Touchstone.

Johnson, A. P. (2015). Chasing them number nine: Five practical strategies for making global connections. *Social Studies Research and Practice, 10,* 84–95.

Johnson, D. (2009). *The joy of children's literature* (2nd ed.). Boston, MA: Harcourt.

Johnson, D. R., Jasper, D. M., Griffin, S., & Huffman, B. L. (2013). Reading narrative fiction reduces Arab-Muslim prejudice and offers a safe haven from intergroup anxiety. *Social Cognition, 31,* 578–598.

Kirkwood-Tucker, T. F. (Ed.). (2009). *Visions in global education: The globalization of curriculum and pedagogy in teacher education and schools: Perspectives from Canada, Russia, and the United States.* New York, NY: Peter Lang.

Klepper, A. (2014). High school students' attitudes toward Islam and Muslims: Can a social studies course make a difference? *The Social Studies, 105,* 113–123.

Lewis, B. (1995). *The Middle East: A brief history of the last 2,000 years.* New York, NY: Scribner.

Merryfield, M. M. (2002). The difference a global educator can make. *Educational Leadership, 60,* 18–21.

Merryfield, M. M. & Kasai, M. (2010). How are teachers responding to globalization. In W. C. Parker (Ed.), *Social studies today: Research & practice* (pp. 165–173). New York, NY: Routledge.

Merskin, D. (2004). The construction of Arabs as enemies: Post-September 11 discourse of George W. Bush. *Mass Communication and Society, 7,* 157–175.

Morgan, H. (2008). American school textbooks: How they portrayed the Middle East from 1898 to 1994. *American Educational History Journal, 35,* 315–330.

Morgan, H. (2012). Counteracting misconceptions about the Arab world from the popular media with culturally-authentic teaching. *Journal of International Social Studies, 2,* 70–83.

Morgan, H. & Walker, D. (2008). The portrayal of the Middle East in four current school textbooks. *Middle East Studies Association Bulletin, 42,* 86–96.

Mvondo, N. (2015). We're the people: Summer reading 2015. Retrieved from http://multiculturalism.rocks/2015/05/21/were-the-people-summer-reading-2015/

Naber, N. (2000). Ambiguous insiders: an investigation of Arab American invisibility. *Ethnic and Racial Studies, 23,* 37–61.

National Council for the Social Studies. (2013). *The college, career, and civic life (C3) framework for social studies state standards: Guidance for enhancing the rigor of K-12 civics, economics, geography, and history*. Silver Spring, MD: NCSS.

Nimer, M. (Ed.). (2007). *Islamophobia and anti-Americanism: Causes and remedies*. Beltsville, MD: Amana.

Noddings, N. (2005). *Educating citizens for global awareness*. New York, NY: Teachers College Press.

Norton, B. (2013). *Identity and language learning: Extending the conversation* (2nd ed.). Bristol, UK: Multilingual Matters.

Nusrat, A. (2012, July 13). The freedom of the hijab. *New York Times*. Retrieved from http://www.nytimes.com/2012/07/14/opinion/the-freedom-of-the-hijab.html?_r=0

PBS NOW Classroom. (2016). Current events affect everyone. Retrieved from http://www.pbs.org/now/classroom/acrobat/lesson03.pdf

Pew Research Center. (2009). Mapping the global Muslim population. Retrieved from http://www.pewforum.org/2009/10/07/mapping-the-global-muslim-population/

Rehren, T. (2011). The UCL Institute of Archaeology and Qatar. *Archaeology International, 13/14*, 28–29. Retrieved from http://www.ai-journal.com/articles/10.5334/ai.1308

Salameh, F. (2010). *Language, memory, and identity in the Middle East: The case for Lebanon*. Lanham, MD: Lexington Books.

Schwebel, S. L. (2011). *Child-sized history: Fictions of the past in U.S. classrooms*. Nashville, TN: Vanderbilt University Press.

Segall, A. & Helfenbein, R. J. (2008). Research on K-12 geography education. In L. S. Levstik & C. A. Tyson (Eds.), *Handbook of research in social studies education* (pp. 259–283). New York, NY: Routledge.

Šisler, V. (2008). Digital Arabs: Representation in video games. *European Journal of Cultural Studies, 11*, 203–220.

Stanford History Education Group. (2015). Abraham Lincoln SAC. Retrieved from http://sheg.stanford.edu/lincoln

Suleiman, M. (2000). *Teaching about Arab Americans: What social studies teachers should know*. Paper presented at the meeting of the National Social Science Association, Las Vegas, NV. (ERIC Document Reproduction Service No. ED442714).

Suleiman, Y. (2003). *The Arabic language and national identity: A study in ideology*. Baltimore, MD: Georgetown University.

Teaching for Change Books. (2016). Arab and Arab Americans. Retrieved from http://www.tfcbooks.org/best-recommended/arabandarabamericans

Telhami, S. (2013). *The world through Arab eyes: Arab public opinion and the reshaping of the Middle East*. New York, NY: Basic Books.

The New York Times. (2016). The learning network: Teaching and learning with the *New York Times*. Retrieved from http://learning.blogs.nytimes.com/

Tremblay, P. (2014, September 16). Headscarf protests resume in Turkey. *Al-Monitor*. Retrieved from http://www.al-monitor.com/pulse/originals/2014/09/turkey-headscarves-protestes-resumes-education.html#

United Nations Development Program. (2012). About Arab states. Retrieved from http://www.arabstates.undp.org/content/rbas/en/home/regioninfo/

Wingfield, M. (2006). Arab Americans: Into the multicultural mainstream. *Equity & Excellence in Education, 39*, 253–266.

X, A. (2012, May 30). Google: Persian Gulf controversy cartoons. Retrieved from http://iranpoliticsclub.net/cartoons/persian-gulf/index.htm

Yahya, H. (2015). *Islam denounces terrorism* (5th edn.). New Delhi, India: Adam Publishers.

Zunal.com. (2001). Retrieved from http://zunal.com/

APPENDIX A—RECOMMENDED TRADE BOOKS

Primary (Grades K-2)
Bunting, E., & Lewin, T. (2006). *One green apple*. New York, NY: Clarion Books.
Ellabbad, M. (2006). *The illustrator's notebook*. Toronto, Canada: Groundwood Books.
Faruqi, R., & Lyon, L. (2015). *Lailah's lunchbox*. Thomaston, ME: Tilbury House.
Heidi, F.P., Gillian, J. H., & Lewin, T. (1992). *Sami and the time of troubles*. New York, NY: Clarion.
Heidi, F.P., Parry, F. H., & Lewin, T. (1995). *Day of Ahmed's secret*. New York, NY: HarperCollins.
Lewin, T. (1998). *The storytellers*. New York, NY: Lothrop, Lee & Shepard.
Nye, N. S., & Carpenter, N. (1997). *Sitti's secrets*. New York, NY: Aladdin Paperbacks.
Winter, J. (2005). *Librarian of Basra: A true story from Iraq*. New York, NY: Harcourt.
Intermediate (Grades 3-5)
Laird, E. (2008). *Oranges in no man's land*. Chicago, IL: Haymarket Books.
Laird, E., Neal, B., & Nimr, S. (2006). *A little piece of ground*. Chicago, IL: Haymarket Books.
Kimmel, E. A., & Rayyan, O. (2013). *Joha makes a wish: A Middle Eastern tale*. Las Vegas, NV: Amazon Publishing.
London, J., & Lewin, T. (1997). *Ali, child of the desert*. New York, NY: Lothrop, Lee & Shepard.
Nye, N. S. (2008). *Honeybook: Poems*. New York, NY: Greenwillow Books.
Middle & High School (Grades 6-12)
Marton, E. (2008). *Santa Claus in Baghdad and other stories about teens in the Arab world*. Bloomington, IN: Indiana University Press.
Nye, N. S. (1999). *Habibi*. New York, NY: Aladdin Paperbacks.
Schami, R. (1990). *A hand full of stars*. New York, NY: Dutton.
Stolz, J. (2004). *The shadows of Ghadames*. New York, NY: Delacorte.
David, A. (2006). *Lebanon in the news: Past, present, and future*. Berkeley Heights, NJ: MyReportLinks.com Books.

Adapted from (Morgan, 2012; Mvondo, 2015; Teaching for Change Books, 2016)

APPENDIX B—IDM LESSON PLAN

Inquiry Design Model (IDM) Blueprint		
Compelling Question(s)	Are all Arabs Muslim? Are all Muslims Arabs?	
Staging the Question	Examine the posted image: What are your immediate thoughts? What questions do you have? Where do you think this photo was taken? What is represented in the image? https://upload.wikimedia.org/wikipedia/commons/c/c7/Muslims_praying_in_mosque_in_Srinagar%2C_Kashmir.jpg	
Supporting Question 1	Supporting Question 2	Supporting Question 3
Who are Arabs?	Where are Arab and other Muslim-majority nations located?	How do Arabs and Muslims differ?
Formative Performance Task	Formative Performance Task	Formative Performance Task
Distill from the sources provided key points that describe/define Arabs. Considering these points craft your own definition of Arabs.	Using the world map and sources provided (below) identify/label Arab League nations; then identify/label countries with largest number of Muslims (top ten).	Using the sources provided develop a list of characteristics that distinguish Arabs and Muslims.
Featured Sources	Featured Sources	Featured Sources
Description of Arab history and culture and characteristics of Arab identity: http://arableague.weebly.com/who-are-the-arabs.html Facts about Arabs and the Arab world: http://www.adc.org/2009/11/facts-about-arabs-and-the-arab-world/	BBC Profile of Arab League – source includes geographic information of Arab States along with history and political information concerning est. of Arab League: http://www.bbc.com/news/world-middle-east-15747941 Visual demonstrates global distribution of Muslim population: http://pewresearch.org/files/old-assets/pewforum-muslim-project/weighted-map.htm	Huffington Post blog response that addresses why Muslim and Arab are not synonymous: http://www.huffingtonpost.com/haroon-moghul/even-the-new-york-times-d_b_766658.html Global Connections from PBS dispels common Western perceptions about Islam and the Middle East: http://www.pbs.org/wgbh/globalconnections/mideast/questions/types/
Summative Performance Task	Argument	In groups, students discuss Supporting Questions 1-3 and then develop their argument responding to the compelling question(s): Are all Arabs Muslim? Are all Muslims Arab?

Adapted from http://www.c3teachers.org/inquiry-design-model/

Chapter 5

The Imperative to Teach Marriage Equality in the Social Studies Classroom

A History, Rationale, and Classroom Practice for a More Inclusive Democracy

J. B. Mayo Jr.

On June 26, 2015, the Supreme Court of the United States in *Obergefell v. Hodges* handed down a landmark decision about same-sex marriage. In a 5–4 decision, the Court held that states were required to license the marriage between two people of the same sex under the authority of the Due Process Clause of the Fourteenth Amendment of the U.S. Constitution, which states:

> No State shall make or enforce any law which shall abridge the privileges or immunities of citizens of the United States; nor shall any State deprive any person of life, liberty, or property, without due process of law; nor deny to any person within its jurisdiction the equal protection of the laws.

According to the majority opinion, if states allow people to marry opposite-sex partners of their choice, they must allow people to make the same choice for partners of the same sex (Ford, 2015). In essence, all lesbian, gay, bisexual, transgender, and queer (LGBTQ) people may now legally marry the person of their choice.

Further, the Court held that states must recognize all marriages that were lawfully performed in other jurisdictions. Accordingly, marriage equality became the law of the land in all 50 states, the District of Columbia, and all U.S. territories. Prior to this decision, only 37 states and the District of Columbia had legalized marriage for same-sex couples (Anti-Defamation League, 2015).

A new law of this magnitude, however, does not automatically gain nationwide acceptance. Although the high court made its historic ruling and despite polls showing that 57% of all Americans favored same-sex marriage, while at the same time 72% believed that its legal recognition was "inevitable" (Pew Research Center, 2015), many people do not accept the Supreme Court's decision as the new societal norm. Opposition to the decision continues among loud conservative voices, including some leading Republicans seeking to be the party's 2016 presidential nominee, determined to keep the traditional understanding of marriage – between one man and one woman – as the norm.

On Wednesday, January 6, 2016, the chief justice of the Alabama Supreme Court ordered "probate judges in the state not to issue marriage licenses to same-sex couples" (Blinder, 2016, p. A14). He made this decision, in part, because the Supreme Court's decision is in direct conflict with the State Supreme Court's decision to uphold Alabama's marriage prohibitions, which causes "confusion and uncertainty" among Alabama's probate judges about how to apply the federal court's opinion in *Obergefell v. Hodges*.

In Virginia, Senate Bill 40 would allow clerks of court and their deputies to refrain from issuing marriage licenses to same-sex couples based on their ethical, moral, or religious objections. In such cases, licenses would be issued by Virginia's Department of Motor Vehicles (DMV) offices or by the Registrar of Vital Statistics (Nolan, 2016).

The most well-known opposition to the Supreme Court's ruling for marriage equality, however, came from Kim Davis, the clerk of Rowan County, Kentucky, who famously refused to issue marriage licenses to same-sex couples, "acting under God's authority." This 49-year-old mother of four and worshiper at Solid Rock Apostolic Church proclaimed, "To issue a marriage license which conflicts with God's definition of a marriage, with my name affixed to the certificate, would violate my conscience. It is not a light issue for me. It is a Heaven or Hell decision" (Blinder & Fausset, 2015, p. A15).

Interestingly, the Mormon Church also strongly opposes marriage equality (see Goodstein, 2015), but officials within the church believe that duty to the law on same-sex marriage outweighs faith. Dallin Oaks, a high-ranking apostle in the church, said that public officials like Kim Davis have a duty to follow the law, despite their religious convictions. He says further,

> Office holders remain free to draw upon their personal beliefs and motivations and advocate their positions in the public square. But when acting as public officials, they are not free to apply personal convictions, religious or other, in place of the defined responsibilities of their public offices. All government officers should exercise their civil authority according to the principles and within the limits of civil government. (Healy, 2015, p. A15)

Not only do 70% of White Evangelical Protestants – as exemplified by Kim Davis – remain opposed to same-sex marriage, but so do 51% of African

Americans and 53% of all Americans born between 1928 and 1945 (Pew Research Center, 2015). Sprigg (2011) offers some insight into why these groups may oppose marriage equality. Citing three immediate "negative" impacts of legalizing same-sex marriage, he believes that taxpayers would be forced to subsidize "homosexual relationships" in the form of social security, that same-sex marriage threatens religious liberty, and that schools will teach that homosexual relationships are identical to heterosexual ones.

Given this mindset within opposing groups and individuals and the presence of their children and grandchildren in schools, marriage equality remains an important and controversial topic with which teachers and their students must engage across the United States if the goal is to promote a society that is truly inclusive of same-sex couples, and equality more generally. This may be especially true in those geographic areas where opposing groups tend to be more populous (i.e., in the South, where the Pew Research Center [2015a] reports that 76% of the population identifies as Christian, 34% of whom identify as evangelical Protestant, and which a large proportion of African Americans call home).

It is within these spaces where the traditional understanding of marriage runs deep and where social studies teachers may find the most resistance to teaching about marriage equality. When the number of LGBTQ people living in these areas is low, the resistance to marriage equality may be even more pronounced because "greater LGB population density in a district corresponds with increased support for legal recognition of same-sex couples" (Flores, 2014, p. 296).

THE WINDING PATH TOWARD
MARRIAGE EQUALITY, 1993–2015

Resistance to marriage equality will be decreased with time, but explicit education about how it evolved in the United States must be included in social studies classrooms to bring us closer to this desired outcome. The national discussion began in 1993 when the Hawaii Supreme Court ruled that laws denying same-sex couples from marrying violated state constitutional equal protection rights unless the state could show a "compelling reason" for such discrimination. Prior to this move, only seven states had laws that specifically defined marriage as the union between one man and one woman.

Once the Hawaii decision opened the possibility that same-sex marriage could be adopted, and thus changing the very definition of marriage, state legislatures across the United States took action. Within a few years, "32 state legislatures (including Hawaii) adopted statutory language defining marriage as a relationship between a man and a woman" (National Conference of

State Legislatures [NCSL], 2015). The state of Alaska went as far as adopting the nation's first constitutional provision prohibiting same-sex marriage, and there was growing momentum during this time for a proposed Federal Amendment to the U.S. Constitution banning same-sex marriage.

This momentum was allayed, however, by the passage of the Defense of Marriage Act (DOMA) signed into law by President Bill Clinton in September 1996 (Baker, 2013). This legislation defined marriage for federal purposes as the union of one man and one woman and allowed states to refuse to recognize same-sex marriages granted under the laws of other states. Despite this federal "protection" of marriage, some 40 states had statutory and/or constitutional provisions that limited marriage solely to opposite-sex couples by the end of 2000 (NCSL, 2015).

It was also in 2000, however, that some states began recognizing same-sex couples' relationships. In April of that year, Vermont approved legislation that recognized civil unions between same-sex couples, which granted them virtually all the benefits, protections, and responsibilities that married (opposite-sex) couples enjoyed under state law.

The Vermont legislation resulted from the State Supreme Court ruling in *Baker v. Vermont* that said same-sex couples are entitled, under the state constitution's "Common Benefits Clause," to the same benefits and protections as married opposite-sex couples. In essence, Vermont maintained "marriage" as the union of a man and a woman, while creating a parallel system for same-sex couples that went beyond what had been known as "domestic partnership."

For several years, granting same-sex couples civil unions worked as a viable compromise in many parts of the United States, but in 2003, the landscape began to change once again. In that year, the Massachusetts Supreme Court ruled that barring same-sex couples from civil marriage was unconstitutional. The state Senate then asked the Court for an "advisory opinion" on the constitutionality of a proposed law that would have barred same-sex couples in Massachusetts from civil marriage but would have created civil unions as a parallel institution.

In February 2004 the Supreme Court of Massachusetts answered by stating that "segregating same-sex unions from opposite-sex unions cannot possibly be held rationally to advance or preserve the governmental aim of encouraging stable adult relationships for the good of the individual and of the community, especially its children" (NCSL, 2015). With this decision, the state of Massachusetts began issuing marriage licenses to same-sex couples in May 2004, the first state to take this action.[1]

In the meantime, other states, including Connecticut, New Jersey, and New Hampshire, continued to grant civil unions. It was not until 2008 that California became the second state to grant marriage licenses to same-sex couples, following the decision by the California Supreme Court that same-sex couples should have the right to marry.

A ballot initiative, known as *Proposition 8*, challenged this decision, was passed in November 2008, and was upheld by the California Supreme Court in May 2009, effectively bringing same-sex marriages to a halt in California. It was not until February 2012 that the 9th U.S. Circuit Court of Appeals upheld an earlier district court decision that declared *Proposition 8* invalid, allowing same-sex couples (once again) to be legally wed in California. In the interim, from 2009 to 2011, Connecticut, Iowa, Maine, New Hampshire, Washington, D.C., and New York all passed legislation that allowed same-sex couples to marry.

Over this period of time, public sentiment in favor of same-sex marriage increased, and in 2012 marriage equality supporters witnessed a watershed moment. Until this point, only state legislatures and various courts had upheld the right for same-sex couples to marry, while all decisions left up to popular vote had failed. An initiative in Maine and referenda in Washington and in Maryland, however, witnessed public votes that upheld same-sex marriage laws.

On the very same day, November 6, 2012, voters in Minnesota rejected an amendment to the state Constitution that would have defined marriage as the union between one man and one woman. This marked the first time that *voters* had made such a move, bringing the "Vote No Campaign" to a success-ful conclusion (Baran, Aslanian, & Gilbert, 2012). Six months later, in May 2013, Minnesota became the twelfth state to pass a law allowing same-sex marriage. Momentum for marriage equality was growing at an ever-quicken-ing rate at the state level.

Despite these gains, DOMA still kept same-sex marriages from being rec-ognized at the federal level, and further, any couples legally wed in a state that *did allow* same-sex marriage would *not* be recognized when they crossed the border into a state where same-sex marriage was not allowed. A lesbian couple legally married in Stillwater, Minnesota, on August 1, 2013, for exam-ple, would not have been recognized as a married couple once they crossed the border into Hudson, Wisconsin – a distance of only 8 miles – at that time.

On June 26, 2013, the Supreme Court rendered a decision that struck down part of the DOMA when it held that "the one thousand federal benefits to marriages defined as a relationship between a man and a woman violated equal protection and due process for married same-sex couples" (NCSL, 2015). This decision emphasized that state law reigned supreme when defining marriage and required the federal government to recognize all same-sex marriages that were granted under state law.

For the next two years, a flurry of successful challenges to traditional defi-nitions of marriage took place at the district court level, which saw 37 states adopt marriage equality before the Supreme Court's ultimate ruling on June 26, 2015, that banned DOMA in its entirety. Said Justice Anthony Kennedy who wrote in the majority opinion,

> The federal statute (DOMA) is invalid, for no legitimate purpose overcomes the purpose and effect to disparage and to injure those whom the State, by its marriage laws, sought to protect in personhood and dignity. By seeking to displace this protection and treating those persons as living in marriages less respected than others, the federal statute is in violation of the Fifth Amendment. (Reilly & Siddiqui, 2015)

THE "WHY" OF TEACHING ABOUT MARRIAGE EQUALITY

The historical overview that highlights how marriage equality came to its present state provides social studies teachers with a context from which to launch specific lessons. Because a strong, vocal minority still opposes marriage equality, these lessons take on even more significance because they aim to help students reflect upon what marriage equality means to them and how marriage equality fits into larger issues of inclusion and diversity in a civil society.

Prior to the Supreme Court's decision in June 2015, social studies teachers engaged students in discussions about same-sex marriage with several goals in mind. Hess (2009a) argued that same-sex marriage was an example of an issue that was "in the tip," a place of evolution between open and closed. As she stressed, same-sex marriage was, for years, a closed issue because no one considered it a viable option to traditional marriage. Once societal opinions on same-sex marriage began to shift, in combination with the various court decisions and legislative moves discussed earlier, this issue became more open and thus more controversial.

Though Hess (2009b) recognized the challenges associated with teaching about same-sex marriage, including teachers' fear that parents will object to such lessons because their mere presence is "tantamount to endorsing a particular point of view" (p. 344) and teachers worrying that students' strong religious views impact how they think about the issue, she contended "the time is ripe to engage secondary students in thoughtful, rigorous, well-facilitated deliberations about controversial policy and constitutional questions regarding same-sex marriage" (p. 344).

Hess believed that students must be given the opportunity to participate in the national debate over same-sex marriage, one of the most significant civil rights issues of our time. Further, she believed deliberation on marriage equality had "the potential to teach students essential content and skills that should be at the core of a democratic education curriculum" (p. 344). Others have been very specific, stating that teaching about same-sex marriage increases critical thinking skills, while deepening students' understanding of democratic processes and their awareness that they are "participating in history" (Bailey & Cruz, 2013, p. 298).

Discussing same-sex marriage also sends a clear message that everyone "counts" as a member of society because the very fact that teachers are willing to engage this topic, one that is of particular importance to gay, lesbian, and queer communities, indicates that it is a legitimate part of academic study at school (Thornton, 2009). I contend that even though marriage equality is now the law throughout the United States, it is still controversial and must continue being discussed for all the reasons stated here. Further, I support teachers approaching the discussions on marriage equality as "closed" – settled both legally and morally – a position that "is even more controversial," given the strong advocacy that still exists in many places for the traditional view of marriage (Hess, 2009a, p. 118).

Marriage equality should also be taught as a fundamental topic in social studies classrooms because it is one of many examples of themes that situate lesbian, gay, bisexual, and queer people at the center of the curriculum rather than at the periphery. For far too long, social studies classes have been taught from a perspective that is heteronormative, the idea that everyone is straight without any deviations from this socially constructed norm.

Though there is a long history of achievements – along with moments of infamy – among lesbian, gay, bisexual, and queer people, and a long history of struggle among gay and lesbian teachers to be recognized in public schools (Biegel, 2010), these achievements have too often been overlooked, discounted, erased, and silenced (Mayo, 2012; Thornton, 2009). Marriage equality represents an opportunity to acknowledge a long-time struggle for recognition and equality that is part of the larger American story, not unlike the struggles endured by other under-represented groups of people throughout our history.

Though there is reason to be concerned about the overall well-being of gay, lesbian, and queer youth in classrooms where heated discussions and even more serious conflicts may arise (Beck, 2013), the time has passed for social studies teachers to use fear over what *might* happen as a reason for not acknowledging the full array of diversity that is likely present in their classrooms.

Students may not personally identify as lesbian, gay, bisexual, or queer, but chances are they know someone close to them who is – a family member, a friend, or a favorite character in a book, movie, or television show – and further, they are already fully aware of lesbian- and gay-themed topics that exist explicitly outside of classrooms and implicitly within them (Emery, 2011;

Hawke, 2015; Mayo, 2012, 2013). For all of these reasons, marriage equality and other lesbian-, gay-, or queer-themed materials must be thoughtfully and purposefully engaged in classrooms across the country.

THE "HOW" OF TEACHING ABOUT MARRIAGE EQUALITY

Equipped with a 20-year historical context about the evolution of marriage equality and given the compelling rationale for teaching it in social studies classrooms nationwide, I now turn to some thoughts about *how* marriage equality and other lesbian, gay, bisexual, transgender, and queer rights issues might be taught in K-12 classrooms and in a variety of geographic locations. From the onset, I offer this disclaimer: The ideas presented here are meant as a guide and perhaps a starting point for ongoing exploration and learning. They are not meant to be all inclusive or considered the only ways to approach these topics in the classroom.

As a teacher educator and former middle school social studies teacher who is highly engaged in pre-service teacher preparation, I will begin with a few general thoughts that I believe will result in effective teaching and student learning for any topic that might be considered challenging or controversial. First, teachers would be wise to rely upon and connect marriage equality to standards.

State standards are generally written broadly such that a wide variety of topics and themes may fall within their purview. The National Council for the Social Studies's (2002) ten thematic standards are also helpful at justifying a teacher's choice in presenting various information/themes/topics to students. In particular, theme I (Culture and Cultural Diversity), theme II (Time, Continuity, and Change), theme IV (Individual Development and Identity), theme VI (Power, Authority, and Governance), and theme X (Civic Ideals and Practices) could be used as foundations for lessons on marriage equality.

Next, I suggest that teachers pay close attention to the relationships they form within their social studies departments or teaching teams. As one proceeds, note who allies will be as well as those individuals that might offer the most opposition. Allies will form the support network needed to move forward in teaching about marriage equality, while the opposition will expose the issues and/or reasons why they oppose such teaching so strongly.

Once teachers are aware of that information, it will enable them to defuse some potential fears and myths, while they simultaneously explain more clearly how teaching about marriage equality falls within standard social studies curriculum. In a similar vein, one needs to know the community standards under which you operate in schools. Is the school community generally progressive or conservative? This will make a difference in how teachers proceed because those standards will indicate where they can push against perceived boundaries, many of which are negotiable.

Finally, I suggest that teachers move forward with courage, self-assurance, and optimism. Once teachers have identified allies, located the most likely sources of opposition, and formulated counter-arguments, then they should proceed with excellent teaching that is dynamic, information rich, and relevant to the lives of their students. Once teachers have earned the reputation of being an effective educator, it will be become far more difficult for administrators not to support them and far less likely that parents will question what is happening in their classroom.

Teaching about marriage equality and other issues related to the rights of LGBTQ people supports the larger conversation about civil rights and human rights more generally. These broad topics are strongly attached to an even larger and complex U.S. narrative found within social studies, and exploring/critiquing this narrative is good for all students.

A targeted and purposeful Internet search will yield quite a few sites that offer teaching materials centered on same-sex marriage and/or marriage equality, but two sites stand out for the excellent, student-centered plans they offer. The Anti-Defamation League (2015) in its "Current Events Classroom" series offers a plan called "What Is Marriage Equality?" and Teaching Tolerance (2016) offers "Marriage Equality: Different Strategies for Attaining Equal Rights" and it also presents two lessons for grades pre K-5 that when taught in combination will allow elementary students to grasp the concept and significance of marriage equality. Links to both sites are located in the references section of this chapter so that readers may have direct access to them. Here, I will provide an overview and analysis of what these lessons offer and provide a rationale for choosing these lessons to teach over the others that one may find.

WHAT IS MARRIAGE EQUALITY?

This lesson is designed for students in grades 4–8 and provides information that is accurate and up-to-date, listing national poll results on attitudes toward marriage equality as recent as April 2015. Specific strengths of this lesson are that it provides students with an opportunity to reflect, formulate, and share opinions and to move about the classroom space when they participate in the "here I stand" activity. It also provides teachers with links to other materials that will broaden the learning of both students and teachers once this lesson is complete.

I believe the lesson is adaptable so that high school students would also gain a great deal of knowledge and an expanded perspective upon the lesson's completion. Yet another benefit of this lesson is the sensitivity with which it handles a potential outcome. In a note of caution to teachers, it reads:

> [**NOTE TO TEACHER:** It is important to reflect on and consider that you may have children in your classroom with gay and lesbian parents or who identify as gay or lesbian themselves, so be sensitive to that and prepared. Further, it is possible that if the student has not shared this previously, she or he may disclose it during the course of the lesson. That information should only come from the student directly.] (Anti-Defamation League, 2015, p. 2)

Reminders like these are good for all of us, regardless of how long we have been in the classroom because sometimes we forget the impact our daily lessons may have on students. Predicting students' responses to what we say in class may be difficult, but it is good to be reminded of the possibilities.

This lesson has several strengths, but its learning objectives are less than stellar. Stronger and more measureable outcomes need to be provided by the instructor, and they can be reframed depending upon individual teacher's goals. I am also surprised the lesson does not mention any content area standards within social studies. Whereas this lesson is loaded with material that falls squarely within the realm of the social studies, the chosen content area is reading. I find both of these items to be somewhat limiting, but certainly not anything that a thoughtful social studies teacher cannot tweak.

MARRIAGE EQUALITY: DIFFERENT STRATEGIES FOR ATTAINING EQUAL RIGHTS

This lesson is designed for students in grades 6–8 and for students in grades 9–12. It is specifically meant for reading, language arts, or social studies classes. The lesson introduces students to different pathways toward equal rights and uses marriage equality as the vehicle to achieve this goal. What is most intriguing about this lesson is that marriage equality, in isolation, is not the focal point, and therefore, it flies under the radar. Yet, there is little chance that one could conduct this lesson without diving into details about marriage equality so that students will understand the nuances involved when groups or organizations fight for equal rights.

The lesson's subtlety, I believe, will find acceptance in places that might not normally welcome a lesson about the rights of LGBTQ people. The materials needed to complete the lesson are all provided via embedded Web links, all of which provide information that will enhance the learning of both teachers and students alike. This lesson also provides the teacher with a list of essential questions that will be applicable for lessons that come later so that teachers will be able to demonstrate connections to past learning.

In addition, this lesson contains links to additional resources that may be used in future lessons or that could be used to increase the depth of learning for the lesson provided here. Similar to the previous lesson from the Anti-Defamation League, the learning objectives are written poorly, and there are no stated accommodations for different kinds of learners or learners with special needs. These are items the classroom teacher will have to modify/add before this lesson is executed in class.

WHAT'S FAIR? AND TALKING BACK

These lessons are designed for elementary students from preK through the fifth grade. The concept of fairness is one that children grasp very early and one that is deeply connected to their lived experiences at home and at school. "What's Fair?" will resonate with elementary-aged children because it taps into knowledge and experiences they already have.

When the teacher poses suggested questions like "Should all people be treated the same?" and "What would you do if you saw someone treated unfairly?" students will be able to think back to an experience with a sibling, with a parent or guardian, or with a friend at school and make connections to other issues, including marriage equality. I can imagine a five- or six-year-old student thinking quite deeply about the following question: Should two people who love each other be kept from getting married? Whereas the concept of marriage equality may not be the primary issue at hand, the issue of *fairness* is certainly within the grasp of our youngest students in school.

"Talking Back" allows students to build upon the concept of fairness and grapple with issues like justice and injustice. With connections to media literacy, this lesson introduces students to ideas like bias and stereotypes and allows them to respond in writing to advertisements chosen by their teacher. The act of writing gives young students a sense of agency as they continue reflecting upon fairness and developing their understanding of complex ideas and issues.

CONCLUDING THOUGHTS

The path toward equality for all has been fought repeatedly throughout U.S. history – and continues today. Our students deserve the opportunity to learn about this journey. (Bailey & Cruz, 2013, p. 303)

The above quotation from a former colleague and my doctoral advisor sums up quite nicely what I refer to as the imperative to teach about marriage equality in the social studies classroom. Students need to realize that the freedoms that many enjoy did not come without struggle and that freedoms that are taken for granted by some groups did not come easily or quickly for others. Such is the case with marriage equality. It exemplifies a freedom that was easy, normed, and taken for granted by a large swath of American society, while many others lived and loved their partners without ever enjoying the protections, rights, and responsibilities that come with civil marriage.

The struggle for marriage equality in this country is certainly a part of the larger struggle for equality that many groups have fought and died for throughout our nation's history. It is part of the larger U.S. narrative that must constantly be re-told so that multiple, diverse voices are heard and taken into account. Moreover, it situates the lives of LGBTQ people at the center, rather than at the periphery of our social studies lessons. In addition, marriage equality – and the lessons it teaches – helps us to appreciate the significance and depth of meaning of two simple words – I do.

NOTE

1. In contrast, some Canadian provinces had been recognizing same-sex marriages since 2002 (CBCnews Canada, 2012), followed by the passage of federal legislation legalizing same-sex marriage across all of Canada in 2005 (Schmidt, 2014).

REFERENCES

Anti-Defamation League (2011). Discussing marriage of same-sex couples with students. Unheard Voices: Stories of LGBT History. Retrieved from http://www.adl.org/assets/pdf/education-outreach/discussing-marriage-of-same-sex-couples-with-students-cc-fall-2011.pdf

Anti-Defamation League (2015). What is marriage equality? Retrieved from http://www.adl.org/assets/pdf/education-outreach/What-Is-Marriage-Equality.pdf

Bailey, R. W. & Cruz, B. C. (2013). Teaching about gay civil rights: U.S. courts and the law. *Social Education, 77*, 298–303.

Baker, P. (2013). Now in defense of gay marriage, Bill Clinton. *The New York Times*. Retrieved from http://www.nytimes.com/2013/03/26/us/politics/bill-clintons-decision-and-regret-on-defense-of-marriage-act.html

Baran, M., Aslanian, S., & Gilbert, C. (2012, November 7). Minnesota voters reject marriage amendment. *MPRnews*. Retrieved from http://www.mprnews.org/story/2012/11/06/politics/elex-night-marriage-amendment

Beck, T. A. (2013). Identity, discourse, and safety in a high school discussion of same-sex marriage. *Theory & Research in Social Education, 41*, 1–32.

Biegel, S. (2010). *The right to be out: Sexual orientation and gender identity in America's schools*. Minneapolis, MN: University of Minnesota Press.

Blinder, A. (2016, January 6). Top Alabama judge orders halt to same-sex marriage licenses. *The New York Times*. Retrieved from http://www.nytimes.com/2016/01/07/us/top-alabama-judge-orders-halt-to-same-sex-marriage-licenses.html?ref=topics&_r=2

Blinder, A. & Fausset, R. (2015, September 1). Kim Davis, a local fixture, and now a national symbol. *The New York Times*. Retrieved from http://www.nytimes.com/2015/09/02/us/kentucky-clerk-a-local-fixture-suddenly-becomes-a-national-symbol.html

CBCnews Canada. (2012, January 12). Timeline: Same-sex rights in Canada. *CBC/Radio-Canada*.   Retrieved   from   http://www.cbc.ca/news/canada/timeline-same-sex-rights-in-canada-1.1147516

Emery, L. R. (2011, August 23). When kids bring up same-sex marriage. Retrieved from http://www.cnn.com/2011/LIVING/08/23/kids.explain.samesex.parents/

Flores, A. R. (2014). Reexamining context and same-sex marriage: The effect of demography on public support for same-sex relationship recognition. *International Journal of Public Opinion Research, 26*, 283–300.

Ford, Z. (2015, June 26). Supreme Court brings marriage equality to the entire country. *Think Progress*. Retrieved from http://thinkprogress.org/lgbt/2015/06/26/3672344/supreme-court-brings-marriage-equality-entire-country/

Goodstein, L. (2015, November 6). Mormons sharpen stance against same-sex marriage. *The New York Times*. Retrieved from http://www.nytimes.com/2015/11/07/us/mormons-gay-marriage.html

Hawke, C. E. (2015). Supreme Court term review: Same-sex marriage, healthcare, and redistricting. *Social Education, 79*, 229–233.

Healy, J. (2015, October 22). Mormons say duty to law on same-sex marriage trumps faith. *The New York Times*. Retrieved from http://www.nytimes.com/2015/10/23/us/mormons-still-against-same-sex-unions-take-a-stand-against-kim-davis.html

Hess, D. (2009a). *Controversy in the classroom: The democratic power of discussion*. New York, NY: Routledge.

Hess, D. (2009b). Teaching about same-sex marriage as a policy and constitutional issue. *Social Education, 73*, 344–349.

Mayo Jr., J. B. (2012). GLBTQ issues in the social studies. In W. B. Russell III (Ed.), *Contemporary social studies: An essential reader* (pp. 243–260). Charlotte, NC: Information Age Publishing, Inc.

Mayo, Jr., J. B. (2013). Expanding the meaning of social education: What the social studies can learn from Gay Straight Alliances. *Theory & Research in Social Education, 41*(3), 352–381.

National Conference of State Legislatures (2015, Jue 26). Same-Sex Marriage Laws. Retrieved from http://www.ncsl.org/research/human-services/same-sex-marriage-laws.aspx

National Council for the Social Studies (2002). *National Standards for Social Studies Teachers*. Retrieved from http://www.socialstudies.org/standards/teacherstandards

Nolan, J. (2016, January 28). Gay marriage licenses in jeopardy in Va. *Culpeper Star*Exponent*.   Retrieved   from   http://www.dailyprogress.com/starexponent/

gay-marriage-licenses-in-jeopardy-in-va/article_4465e6fe-c622–11e5–9654-dbe-13fa36d67.html

Pew Research Center. (2015, June 8). *Support for Same-Sex Marriage at Record High, but Key Segments Remain Opposed.* Retrieved from http://www.people-press.org/2015/06/08/support-for-same-sex-marriage-at-record-high-but-key-segments-remain-opposed/

Reilly, R. J. & Siddiqui, S. (2015, June 26). Supreme Court DOMA decision rules federal same-sex marriage ban unconstitutional. *Huffington Post.* Retrieved from http://www.huffingtonpost.com/2013/06/26/supreme-court-doma-decision_n_3454811.html

Schmidt, S. J. (2014). Civil rights continued: How history positions young people to contemplate sexuality (in)justice. *Equity & Excellence in Education, 47,* 353–369.

Sprigg, P. (2011). The top ten harms of same-sex "marriage." The Family Research Council, Washington D.C. Retrieved from http://downloads.frc.org/EF/EF11B30.pdf

Teaching Tolerance (2016). Marriage equality: Different strategies for attaining equal rights. Retrieved from http://www.tolerance.org/lesson/marriage-equality-different-strategies-attaining-equal-right

Teaching Tolerance (2016). What's Fair? [and] Talking Back. Retrieved from http://www.tolerance.org/classroom-resources?keys=&type=lesson&topic=169&grade=3&domain=219&subject=15

Thornton, S. J. (2009). Silence on gays and lesbians in social studies curriculum. In W. C. Parker (Ed.), *Social studies today: Research and practice* (pp. 87–94). New York, NY: Routledge.

Chapter 6

#Black Lives Matter as Critical Patriotism

LaGarrett J. King, Chezare A. Warren, Mariah Bender, and Shakealia Y. Finley

The social movement known as Black Lives Matter has garnered major attention since its creation in 2013 after the acquittal of George Zimmerman, a Sanford, Florida, neighborhood watch volunteer, for the murder of a young African American teenager, Trayvon Martin. After several national events centering on Black death and other transgressions perpetrated by the police within African American communities, the movement has morphed into a chapter-based national organization focusing on a bevy of issues affecting Black communities. As of February 2016, Black Lives Matter has 32 chapters that have participated in over 1,000 demonstrations worldwide (Black Lives Matter, 2015).

Critics have complained that the organization is divisive. They argue that Black Lives Matter is exclusionary to other races, ethnicities, and cultures; promotes antipolice violence; and neglects issues such as voting and Black-on-Black crime. The co-creators of the Black Lives Matter movement, Alicia Garza, Opal Tometi, and Patrisse Cullors, however, reject those sentiments. Garza (2014) notes:

> When we say Black Lives Matter, we are talking about the ways in which Black people are deprived basic human rights and dignity. It is an acknowledgement [that] Black poverty and genocide is state violence. It is an acknowledgment that 1 million Black people are locked in cages in this country – one half of all people in prisons or jails – is an act of state violence. It is an acknowledgment that Black women continue to bear the burden of a relentless assault on our children and our families and that assault is an act of state violence. Black queer and trans folk bearing a unique burden in a hetero-patriarchal society that disposes of us like garbage and simultaneously fetishizes us and profits off of us is state violence. (para. 11)

According to Garza, the notion of the state and its many manifestations (policing, the criminal system, racialized capitalism) rarely acknowledges the humanity of Black people. While police wrongdoings instigated the need for the contemporary recognition of Black Lives Matter, the indictment is the state, which has continually acted hostile toward Black people.

Therefore, Black Lives Matter advocates for the humanity of Black people and desires to transform society through disruption. To achieve this goal, Black Lives Matter chapters possess certain guiding principles including (Black Lives Matter, 2015)

- Anti-Black racism
- Restorative justice
- Black globalism
- Empathy
- Affirming Black queer, transgender, and Black women intersectional identities
- The rebuilding of the Black liberation movement.

In an effort to disrupt the social order, Black Lives Matter activists are willing to force interruptions of everyday life through various mechanisms such as blocking highway traffic, interrupting political events, and overtaking shopping malls, to name a few.

Since Black Lives Matter has ascended within the national lexicon, K-12 as well as college educators have been engaged in creating curricula and enacting instructional activities that attempt to make sense of the movement and the contentious rhetoric that accompanies it (e.g., Edwards & Harris, 2016; San Francisco Public Schools, 2016). Additionally, major educational organizations such as the College and Faculty Assembly of National Council for the Social Studies and the Black caucus for the National Teachers of English have written position statements supporting Black Lives Matter and encouraged teachers not only to critically engage students in the purpose of the movement but to also exercise curricular and pedagogical decisions that promote cultural diversity and antiracism.

We suspect that Black Lives Matter has been explored in nuanced and critical ways in some classrooms, while others may have and continue to ignore its relevance. There are some teachers who probably would like to explore the topic fully but lack the knowledge and curriculum flexibility to do so. This chapter is geared for those teachers and/or teacher educators to provide an additional resource that explores the Black Lives Matter movement and helps with situating the movement with nuance and historical contextualization.

We situate Black Lives Matter as part of a long tradition of Black citizens expressing critical patriotism, a conscious skepticism of the state that recognizes its historic and current deficiencies, and attempts to improve democracy through dissidence and dissent (Tillet, 2012). While this book is focused on social issues that have risen to prominence in the 21st century, we would like the readers to understand that the Black Lives Matter movement and their advocacy is far from a 21st-century problem. Therefore, we briefly contextualize Black Lives Matter within a critical patriotic lens.

In addition, we present two case studies, one high school and one university, of how Black Lives Matter and critical patriotism are shaped in educational spaces. We conclude with curriculum and other resources applicable for understanding the Black Lives Matter movement and critical patriotism. Our goal is to clear misconceptions about what others have deemed a new Civil Rights Movement and help educators begin to conceptualize a praxis that values Black students' lives.

BLACK LIVES MATTER AS CIVIC DISCOURSE AND CRITICAL PATRIOTISM

To fully comprehend Black Lives Matter, we begin by connecting the movement within the oppositional civic discourses that have historically aided Black Americans' struggles for citizenship. While we use critical patriotism as a way to explain counter-hegemonic approaches to citizenship, our theory is grounded within social studies and race research that have explicated how non-White groups understand and situate their place in U.S. society (Brown, Crowley & King, 2011; Howard, 2003; Ladson-Billings, 2003; Tyson, 2003).

Until recently, most of the citizenship discourse in social studies education adopted what Castro and Knowles (in press) have noted as a middle class bias in the way citizenship is taught in schools. This bias often ignores a critical analysis of how race has impacted Black American experiences and how they see themselves as civic actors and agents of social change. Therefore, one has to understand Black Lives Matter in the context of the United States as a racist state (Goldberg, 1993).

If 1619 is our starting point, Black lives in the United States have a longer history of enslavement than freedom, and if adding the 100 years after 1865 of legal discrimination, indeed Black lives have never mattered too much in the United States. Saidiya Hartman's (2008) concept of African Americans suffering from the *afterlife of slavery*, which she described as "the skewed life chances, limited access to health, and education, premature death, incarceration, and impoverishment" (p. 6), is indicative of a contemporary circumstance that has been institutionalized centuries ago.

At every step, however, there has been a class of Black American citizens who challenged and brought awareness that the state and the privileged citizens it protects have historically denied Black people's humanity and their inalienable rights to citizenship. Black American citizens, even before they became "legal citizens," exhibited what Salamishah Tillet (2012) calls a critical patriotism.

Critical patriotism resists what we normally locate as patriotic behavior, blind loyalty, staunch allegiance, and inflexible attachment to the country; instead, patriotism, in this manner, is about critiquing discriminatory systems and critical discourse and holding the country accountable to its egalitarian ideas. In a sense, as Tillet (2012) purports, critical patriotism "enables [one] to become a model citizen, one who does not repudiate but reifies, does not dismantle but reengages the meta-discourse of American democracy" (p. 11).

While some have classified Black Lives Matter as a new Civil Rights Movement, we argue, as do the Black Lives Movement creators, that the movement is not new but instead a reincarnation of a long history of Black citizens exhibiting critical patriotism toward the United States. Like other Black oppositional movements, much of the visible presence of Black Lives Matter has focused on the police state, which has a long oppressive history with the Black community.

Beginning with slave patrols, police policy in Black American communities has historically consisted of social control and geographical containment and has led to what Leonard Moore (2010) posited as an "us versus them" mentality (p. 1). Throughout history, Black communities became resentful of the police based on constant harassment, brutality, and the lack of protection in their communities (Trotter, 1985). Research has shown that police departments often ignored or responded slowly to Black victims and allowed White violators to harass and riot in Black communities (Trotter, 1985; Moore, 2010).

Racial unrest in East Saint Louis in 1917, Chicago in 1919, Harlem in 1935, Detroit in 1942, Watts in 1963, and Miami in 1980 are examples of White police officers inciting violence against Blacks and allowing White mobs to attack, injure, and kill Black people (Cashmore & McLaughlin, 1991). The police, as an institution, has historically served as the enforcer to maintain the racial hierarchy order, protect White privilege, and restrict Black progress.

While not all police participated in aggressive police tactics, they are implicit to a system whose history, demography, training, traditions, and culture is immersed in White supremacy. Black police officers, for example, were heavily indoctrinated in police departments' culture of anti-Black racism and were heavily involved in police brutality (Moore, 2010). It is important, then, to situate police organizations not as independent units but as representatives of the state, the medium to enforced racism and institutional discrimination.

Recent protests against the police are not a result of one police officer killing one Black person. These actions are precipitated through a collective history of the Black community who see the police as an adversary institution, not as protectors or servants.

This new incarnation of Black Lives Matter, however, is more inclusive in its activism as the movement affirms and has given voice to the lives of Black queer and transgender, the disabled, the poor, undocumented Black immigrants, women, and those who are victimized by the legal system, something other mainstream historical movements did not publically recognize or promote. Additionally, because of social media, the Internet, and other technologies, Black Lives Matter's message is more accessible, not fully controlled by mainstream media, and more personal.

Therefore, Black Lives Matter has inspired and given voice and language to many Black people around the globe to take strong stances on the conscious and unconscious ways in which Black lives are neglected. One space has been the education field, both K-12 and higher education. What follows are two case studies, one from Mariah, a social studies pre-service teacher, and the other by Chezare, a teacher educator. They reflect on their experiences situating Black Lives Matter within educational spaces.

MARIAH: A HOLISTIC HISTORIOGRAPHY FRAMEWORK FOR BLACK LIVES MATTER

There is a massive gap between what teacher education prepares pre-service teachers for and the current emotional, political, and social needs of Black youth. This gap has damaging effects and works to further reify the myths of the inferiorities of Blackness and the role of the social studies teacher as apolitical. For Black youth to make sense of the world around them, they must be equipped with the critical tools to change the innumerable societal ills that dehumanize people of color. When social studies teachers distance themselves from creating relevant material to Black students' lives, they also distance themselves from allowing Black students to explore their own racial identities.

By avoiding meaningful and critical historical questions, social studies teachers run the risk of isolating students and ultimately perpetuating racist and hostile school environments founded on the assumption that a "colorblind" framework suits the education of all students. However, in true form to the identity of Black resistance and this conscious skepticism, Black students reject the official one-sided view of Black history within the curriculum, and they dig deeper to uncover the true and full history of Black people within the secondary social studies class.

Black youth deserve a history that is culturally relevant and humanizing that reflects the multitude and complexity of Black identity and history.

As presently constructed, the K-12 social studies curriculum paints a picture that Black people are simply an oppressed and destitute people. As best evidenced through the focus on the atrocities of slavery rather than the innumerable acts of resistance and agitation for freedom, we clearly see the deficit-informed perspectives of Black history.

As an act of critical patriotism, Black youth are resisting official curricula that compartmentalize race and the history of oppressed people to special months and a few events that make up the history of these peoples. However, this "single-story" does not include the complete story of the origins and great achievements of these peoples. The "single-story," as Nigerian novelist Chimamanda Ngozi Adichie (2009) terms this type of perspective, is dangerous, but it also is dehumanizing and oppressive.

Furthermore, it leaves power in the hands of those who only seek to further oppression and impose a second-class citizenship specifically to Black people. Adichie (2009) adds that "power is the ability not just to tell the story of another person, but to make it the definitive story of that person" (para. 29). To deny a people the fullness and richness of their history strips them of their power and space to see a wealth of ideas, perspectives, and events that make up the wholeness of their historical trajectory. Ultimately, this denial of a full history leads to resistance to the study of Black history in schools in general.

Upon the introduction of my slavery unit, for example, my students were visibly disengaged and protested learning about how Black people were only slaves who were abused, lynched, and murdered. Instead, students offered an alternative curriculum and insisted on learning about the Moors, Egyptians, and other African civilizations. This initial resistance was encouraging to my own views of historiography and the alternative viewpoint I had already created. However, it was profoundly significant given that their rejection of the official curriculum, which placed the Black pain and abuse central, came from their prior miseducation of slavery in their former social studies classes.

Rarely do the curriculum or teaching practices exhibit what I term a *humanizing holistic historiography* that expresses the diversity of Black identity. Because of these one-sided views of history, Black students are often resistant to learning about slavery or typical Black History Month type lessons. However, a holistic historiography is best described as one that allows students from under-represented backgrounds to identify with their full history.

Through a holistic historiography framework, students have access to material that allows them to explore their identities and historical experiences as well as allows them to integrate these culturally relevant concepts within the context of the social studies classroom. This type of historiography allows students from oppressed groups to truly immerse themselves in their culture and history. With this centrality, students are the authors and researchers of

Black history and pose their own questions about the construction of history around slavery while openly questioning my instruction at every turn.

Questions such as "When did slavery truly become about race?" drove the discussion from previous histories of slavery as horrible atrocities to understanding the creation and maintenance of White supremacy. Ultimately, these discussions would not have taken place if Black students did not feel safe or validated in the classroom, which began with my own acknowledgment of how race impacts the writing of history, even the history of Black students in schools.

First, to broadly discuss race in ways that are accessible to Black students requires what Skerett (2011) calls sustained and strategic instruction. To demonstrate how a holistic historiography is enacted in a classroom space, I present one lesson from the Ancestor Project in which Black students were able to focus on their own identity in the classroom and also work to define themselves in their own terms, not those of the colonizer. The Ancestor Project is an example of sustained and strategic instruction because the assignment presented opportunities for students to develop a strong racial consciousness.

The activity's purpose centered on remembering one's ancestors. We focused on the Afro-Brazilian religion of *Candomble* within the broader unit on slavery and resistance in the Americas. Candomble is a prime example of the legacy of resistance to oppression and the roots of Africa in Brazil. This dynamic of Black resistance to oppression served as a template for studying similar resistance acts in the Americas and, more closely, in the United States.

Ultimately, *Candomble* represented a holistic historiography given the resistance to the official colonizer religion, which resulted in enslaved Africans retaining their Yoruba gods and their ability to *create* their own religion that paid homage to their African roots. These efforts were all disguised as passive acceptance of the colonizer's beliefs. This example showed students the globalization of Black resistance, and when applied to their own histories in the United States, it allowed them to view resistance more broadly than solely in physical terms.

This specific framing of not only the history of slavery but also the resistance was profoundly significant for Black students whose only knowledge of slavery was from whitewashed and inaccurate perspectives from the official curriculum. Students conducted oral histories of their oldest family member with questions they generated themselves. This project was crucial in the understanding of Black students' historical identities and also the power of knowing one's history.

One student shared how grandparents fled White terrorists on their way to school. The same student explained how her grandmother would have to choose strategic routes to avoid harassment and abuse in Mississippi. Other students shared close similarities between themselves and the relatives they interviewed, such as a passion for protesting and social change. One student recalled her grandmother's stories of protesting in Saint Louis against lunch counter segregation, and these experiences deeply resonated with the student as she fights against police brutality and injustices in present-day Saint Louis.

The connection between a holistic historiography and the Ancestor Project was multifaceted; it allowed students to become researchers of their own history in a way that was meaningful and emotional, and secondly, students were reflective of the experiences with race and oppression of their elders and found overlap in those experiences to the racism and abuses suffered by Black people today. More importantly, it showed that Black students' personal and racial histories are validated in spaces where traditionally Black students have had no connection to their own identities in social studies classrooms.

This project placed the Black experiences at the forefront of the social studies classroom as a reclamation of power, autonomy, and self-awareness. Furthermore, through counterstory experiences of shared ancestry and connection to one's familial history, students placed themselves at the center of the curriculum, honored the classroom space as a home, and developed a strong connection to one's history and family relationships.

It is important to provide spaces for students to explore their identities through reflection on their racialized experiences, gendered identities, and the role of schooling in either oppressing or muting those identities. This space for students to question, critique, and contextualize history gives voice to understanding students' roles in the classroom and acknowledging the power students have within a school structure. The literature on student voice is profound but has even more implications for Black students whose voices have been intentionally silenced.

To bring about a greater dialogue within classrooms, student voice is essential. As Oldfather (1995) writes, "Learning from student voices … requires major shifts on the part of teachers, students, and researchers in relationships and in ways of thinking and feeling about the issues of knowledge, language power, and self" (p. 87). These shifts transform teacher and student interactions, and in the discussion of racial politics, validating student voice is the first step toward authenticity.

Finally, in order to foster a spirit of critical patriotism within our students, we as educators must be just as critical about the complexities of race and White supremacy, sexism and patriarchy, capitalism and imperialism, and how they operate in society. Therefore, the final proposition is to educate preservice teachers to be present and vocal in current issues and to finally abolish the tendency for teachers to be apolitical or neutral. The teacher should be a critical citizen who passes that spirit of critical patriotism on to his/her students as well.

CHEZARE: COURAGEOUS CONVERSATIONS ABOUT BLACK LIVES MATTER

My university was eerily silent in the wake of news that Darren Wilson would not be indicted for his killing of Michael Brown – an unarmed Black male teenager gunned down on August 9, 2014, in Ferguson, Missouri, just outside of Saint Louis. There were no university press releases on the matter. I perceived there to be little movement on our campus.

In late November 2014, however, I received a phone call from a colleague in the Housing Department asking my advice about how the campus community needed to respond to the growing civil unrest happening locally and around the United States. He understood, like I did, that being silent on the issue of extrajudicial murder was morally wrong. It was wrong because it sends the message to those on our campus who are being affected by police brutality, or who have been personally impacted, that their university does not care. As two Black men with an invested interest in students' well-being, our pain underscored our desire to do something, to act.

My colleague and I determined that there needed to be a space to get the conversation moving. Our plan was to host a town hall that would bring together multiple voices in conversation with one another around an issue of grave significance. We wanted to create a space where various institutional actors could be heard at one time. We named it the "Ferguson Town Hall" and advertised it with less than a week's notice using social media as our primary marketing tool.

We designed the town hall to bring Black pain and suffering to the fore and, through the testimony of the town hall's attendees, make the auditorium a site for the development of empathy, discovery, and revelation. The town hall also gave us a moment to identify solutions and to implicate each attendee in the work of racial equity and social justice for a diverse university community.

We held the town hall on the evening of December 4, 2014, the day after a Long Island grand jury decided that there would be no indictment against New York City police officers who choked a Black man to death on camera (i.e., Eric Garner). It was an emotionally draining moment in history to think that one could be filmed murdering a Black man and not even be brought up on charges. The psychological weight of such a proposition was stifling. Nonetheless, we carried on with the program as planned. I opened the event with the following remarks:

On Nov. 24, the St. Louis County prosecutor announced that a grand jury decided not to indict Mr. Wilson. Mike Brown and Ferguson is one very recent case that represents a broader trend in the United States, which is the killing of unarmed Black men and boys at the hands of White police officers. ... Stand out examples in recent history include Sean Bell in New York, Oscar Grant in California (the subject of Fruitvale Station), Tamir Rice in Ohio, Trayvon Martin in Florida, and most recently Eric Garner, who was choked by a New York City police officer, and later died due to complications as a result of the officer's chokehold.

Collectively, these events have had a devastating impact on people of color, Black people and Black men in particular, including myself, as we struggle to make sense of the palpable threats associated with interacting with the police and others in positions of power and authority. Many of us in this community regardless of one's race, gender, socioeconomic status, or other cultural difference are in this moment grappling with notions of justice, fairness, and trust. Given the legacy of oppression experienced by diverse persons in this country and repeated instances of assault against communities of color, we thought it imperative to break the silence and reflect on the implications of Ferguson and all that Ferguson represents, for this community

The room lay silent as I gave my remarks. It was a solemn moment. The space was filled with people of every age and hue. In attendance was university administration, clergy, students, alum, faculty, youth, professional staff, and other interested members from the local community.

It is easy as a person of color to go into an event like this one full of emotion. I knew that the night could be potentially explosive, and rightfully so. Moreover, I am a junior faculty member. I would be dishonest not to admit my concern that an event like this could go awry. The consequences that would have on my professional reputation was an important consideration for my involvement in organizing this event and, ultimately, how the event was structured and executed.

Yet, the risk was necessary to ensure that I was contributing to the improvement of the campus climate for the very students I read and write about. Key to a conversation like this one is to have a strong moderator who has both contextual knowledge and the respect of the audience. This person must manage the conversation in a way that centers (and recenters) the purpose for the gathering, while at the same time routinely communicating and managing expectations for participation.

We developed several guidelines to organize the town hall. Our time was split into two parts. The first 35 minutes was spent discussing our opinions of the impact Ferguson was having, has had, and will have on the university community, from the perspective of individual stakeholders. My colleague audio-recorded the event. Also, as matters of significance related to racial injustice and police abuse came up from those who would choose to speak, my colleague and his assistant noted relevant details of the specific incidences they shared. This was to ensure we had a data catalog we could use in later discussions with campus administrations.

We held the event in a residence hall to ensure its accessibility to students, and we had two microphones assembled on opposite sides of the room for members to speak. In the case that there was a lull in speakers stepping up to the microphone, as a facilitator, we agreed that I would reiterate key ideas and use my expertise as a race scholar to make meaningful interpretations of the speakers' commentary for the audience. I also filled in any dead space between speakers with relevant explanation of complicated concepts important for the comprehensibility of the dialogue.

The final 35 minutes of the town hall were spent discussing how the community felt the university community could respond. More specifically, individuals came to the microphones to make suggestions about the various strategies or approaches needed to guarantee every member of the community felt safe and valued. This was also the time when many of the individual community groups who were organizing at any level could share their initiatives with the larger body. This way, a goal of the event was to help build coalition and collaboration that would spurn collective social action.

The ground rules that we used for this event can provide guidance to others who wish to engage in similar types of discussions. These rules are as follows:

1. Speak your truth and respect the opinions of others
   It is important to have one's voice heard in an authentic way. Participants should not feel coerced to mute themselves or to disregard the impact of an experience for shaping their personal perspective. This ground rule encourages speech that reflects the reality of one's experience. It also holds that participants be aware that it is okay to disagree with others without attacking his or her character, essentializing them, or insisting that someone else's experience, as they describe it, is dishonest or misleading.
2. Seek to understand
   This ground rule maintains that participants should ask more questions and reflect on someone else's ideas before critiquing those ideas. Seeking to understand represents learning to fully comprehend the totality of one's experience before responding. It is sitting in submission and earnestly working to acquire facts so that any response is respectful and well informed.
3. Lean into discomfort
   This ground rule acknowledges that conversations about race are uncomfortable. These conversations may be especially uncomfortable for White people and those who are most aligned with, or constructed as members of, the dominant group. The "leaning" into discomfort is learning how to embrace feelings of angst or insecurity as part of the burden of carrying on such sensitive conversations. This ground rule also encourages participants

not to take claims of oppression or prejudice lodged against culture groups with which they may have personal affiliation, as personal attacks. Rather, leaning into discomfort means listening with intention and diligence without regard to the emotional toll that engaging the problem(s) may produce.

4. Expect and accept a lack of closure

This final ground rule is a reminder that the conversation is just that, a dialogue among stakeholders to spotlight the dimensions of a problem affecting one or more members of a community. These conversations can sometimes carry an emotional weight that is burdensome. As much as participants may want a concrete solution, the one conversation will likely not produce any solutions. The lack of closure reflects the sentiment that a courageous conversation will likely open doors of conflict and contention, not close them. Still, the open door is important for illuminating where the problems exist in the first place, so that they can be exterminated.

These rules are adapted from Singleton and Linton's (2014) *Courageous Conversations*. Anyone who facilitates a "courageous conversation" similar to the one described here must be aware and attentive to the potential challenges such conversations can pose on participants. These ground rules provide a framework for facilitation. The facilitator must be comfortable navigating a tense discussion and providing the necessary affirmation to speakers.

We let the audience know ahead of time that this was not a space to nitpick the details of the Brown case or to argue for one side or another. Also, my colleague and I knew emotions were running high, and while we were in no position to censure anyone, we asked for the sake of the conversation that speakers excuse themselves and rejoin us if they felt they were losing their composure. We aimed to hear from as many persons as possible in a safe, respectful atmosphere.

The event was immensely successful in that there was much truth shared. Faculty and staff, clergy, concerned community members, and students all spoke out against oppression experienced through interactions with those in power and authority. This town hall provided a space for stories to be told and heard in solidarity. Individuals who would likely have never spoken to one another had the chance to talk candidly over mutual pain and discombobulation.

There is no way to predict what can happen in an event like this. The best one can do is be clear about the expectations, model the type of respect and truth telling he or she wants the speakers to emulate, and follow through on any threat of consequence for those who are having difficulty participating in civil discourse.

In closing, it is worth reiterating that a strong facilitator is pivotal for managing a conversation such as this one. It should be an individual who can be perceived by the public as not having specific political allegiances at the institution. It needs to be someone who is critical of the ways structures and systems facilitate and perpetuate oppression. He or she must move the conversation forward by adding the necessary nuance that expands the audience's understanding of complicated concepts such as race, racism, Whiteness, privilege, power, and White supremacy.

It must also be someone with a thorough enough understanding of these constructs who can make the necessary links based on the evidence of life experience as it is described by town hall attendees and broader trends of racial injustice. Recording (or finding some other reliable documentation source) helps to demonstrate that there is a problem to be addressed and that the problem needs the attention of all power brokers on the campus. The facilitator can be a person that helps connect what is learned from the conversation to the priorities of the institution. The work does not happen overnight, but it does provide an opportunity to strategize with those in mind who too often are left out of high-level conversations pertaining to campus climates and culture.

The best thing that any community can do in responding to the broad challenges facing people of color is speaking up and speaking out. We cannot remain silent. There have to be ways that institutions centralize resources to ensure that the collective work/impact is lasting and sustainable.

There are capable individuals on every campus to convene these types of gatherings. There has to be space carved out that includes the voices, perspectives, and stories of multiple stakeholders, *in conversation with another*, around mutual goals, aspirations, and commitments. The work is ongoing, and any initiative aimed at racial justice is the work of an entire community and not the burden of a few designated offices or officers.

CONCLUSION

Mariah's holistic historiography and Chezare's courageous conversations are pedagogical tools that help facilitate the civic aims of social studies education. Their work allows disenchanted voices, those that have experienced what Tillet (2012) proclaims is *civic estrangement*, a chance to be critical patriots and not complicit within a system that would rather have Black apathy and silence.

Mariah's holistic historiography demonstrates a proactive approach toward signaling to students that their lives matter. As she explains, the curriculum, both school and societal, hidden and explicit, relays the message that "people of color are relatively insignificant to the growth and development of our democracy and they represent a drain on the resources and values" (Ladson-Billings, 2003, p. 4). In a similar vein, Carter G. Woodson's (1933) social commentary about violence against Black people in his classic book *Miseducation of the Negro* noted the curriculum is extremely important to understanding Black Lives Matter because "there would be no lynching if it did not start in the schoolroom" (p. 3).

For social studies teachers to be able to approach a holistic historiographical framework in their classes, they need to be able to abstract students' and their own multiple epistemologies through the curriculum and teaching. That means not only being knowledgeable about Black history and how it relates to the subjects considered as social studies but gaining knowledge about the material realities of Black students on micro, meso, and macro levels.

Chezare's courageous conversation represents these teachable moments that are salient in social studies classrooms. As mentioned earlier, we are concerned that in many classrooms, Black Lives Matter has been ignored or silenced in schools in favor of a curriculum that does not support Black voices. When this business-as-usual approach to education is privileged, it signals that teachers, principals, and district-level administrators do not value Black lives.

In addition, Chezare makes a valid point in explaining that courageous conversations about the material conditions of Blackness within a racist society is an uncomfortable and hurtful experience. We are reminded of Zeus Leonardo and Larry Porter's (2010) discussions of safe spaces, where they argue that the safe space is sometimes set up as a tool of Whiteness that is meant to protect the dominant group and not the most vulnerable. They posit, "The term safety acts as a misnomer because it often means that White individuals can be made to feel safe. ... It is a managed health-care version of anti-racism, an insurance against looking racist" (p. 147). Courageous conversations can be an alternative to the notion of safe space where racial spaces are not supposed to be safe but uncomfortable, which breaks a cycle of recurring racist rhetoric and behaviors.

What these case studies promote is a serious dialogue about race and racism in social studies education. For too long, social studies, whose history began as a racist enterprise (Woyshner & Bohan, 2013), has adopted palatable notions of race and racism through national, state, and local policies (Ladson-Billings, 2003). The Black Lives Matter movement within the context of social studies education is about dismantling longstanding beliefs and behaviors based on antiquated ideas about humanity.

The names of Oscar Grant, Amadou Diallo, Tamir Rice, Sean Bell, Freddie Grey, Orlando Barlow, Eric Garner, Michael Brown, John Crawford, Rekia Boyd, Tyisha Miller, Yvette Smith, Aiyanna Jones, Sandra Bland, and Samuel DuBoise were all contemporary instances where Black lives did not matter. As with the thousands of African Americans lynched during the early 20th century, these persons' fates are engrained in the nation's lexical history. Unfortunately,

Textbox 6.1   Resources for Teachers

1. #Ferguson #CrimingWhileWhite – Opinions and perspective on recent events by diverse persons on Twitter, Facebook, and Instagram.
2. www.aclu.org – Real time updates on strategies and work being done around the country and information about rights and privileges pertaining to staging peaceful protests.
3. http://fergusonresponse.tumblr.com – Demonstrations around the country.
4. http://zinnedproject.org/2014/11/teaching-about-ferguson/ – Teaching Ferguson.
5. http://www.micds.libguides.com/ferguson – Reading materials about race that help to contextualize recent events.
6. http://www.whitehouse.gov/blog/2014/12/02/its-not-just-ferguson-problem-its-american-problem-improving-community-policing – Blog that provides an overview of how the White House is responding to recent events.
7. http://www.blacklivesmattersyllabus.com/bio/ – A collection of articles as well as an actual syllabus of a class from NYU entitled Blacklivesmatter.
8. Making Black Lives Matter in Classrooms: The Power of Teachers to Change the World by David E. Kirkland (available at http://www.huffingtonpost.com/david-e-kirkland/making-black-lives-matter_b_7453122.html?utm_source=39749783&utm_medium=Email&utm_campaign=General)
9. Black Students' Lives Matter: Building the School-to-Justice Pipeline by the editors of Rethinking Schools (available at http://www.rethinkingschools.org/archive/29_03/edit293.shtml?utm_source=39749783&utm_medium=Email&utm_campaign=General)
10. From Civil Rights to Black Lives Matter: Lessons for the Classroom, a course offered by the Center for Experiential Learning and Diversity, University of Washington (available at http://expd.washington.edu/pipeline/inner/spring-2015/from-civil-rights-to-black-lives-matter-lessons-for-the-classroom.html?utm_source=39749783&utm_medium=Email&utm_campaign=General)
11. What Educators Can Take from #BlackLivesMatter by Ryan William-Virden (available at http://www.onyxtruth.com/2015/05/13/what-educators-can-take-from-blacklivesmatter/?utm_source=39749783&utm_medium=Email&utm_campaign=General)
12. Teaching about Race and Rights by Beth Fertig (available at http://www.wnyc.org/story/teaching-about-race-and-rights/?utm_source=39749783&utm_medium=Email&utm_campaign=General)
13. How the #FergusonSyllabus Can Help Teachers Talk about Race and Rights on the First Day of School by Liz Pleasant (available at http://www.yesmagazine.org/peace-justice/how-the-ferguson-syllabus-can-help-teachers-talk-race-and-rights?utm_source=39749783&utm_medium=Email&utm_campaign=General)
14. Educators Can Ease Racial Trauma Experienced by Students by Will Morris (available at http://blogs.edweek.org/edweek/the_startup_blog/2015/05/treating_racial_trauma_that_students_experience.html?utm_source=39749783&utm_medium=Email&utm_campaign=General)
15. Teaching "Black Lives Matter" by Kathy Ishizuka (available at http://www.slj.com/2014/12/diversity/teaching-black-lives-matter-slj-talks-to-educator-author-renee-watson/#_)

by the time of the publication of this book, we fear that our collective consciousness will be inundated with new stories detailing the killings of more African Americans under the guise of innocuous policing.

Teaching the Black Lives Matter movement is not about being anti-White, antipolice, or interested in practicing what Audre Lorde (1983) rejects as the *hierarchy of oppressions* or Elizabeth Martinez's (1993) notions of the *oppression olympics*. The purpose is to recognize the humanity of Black people and help the public *see* the invisibleness of racism that continues to plague the United States.

As curriculum gatekeepers (Thornton, 2001), social studies teachers and teacher educators can assist in making Black voices, as well as other historically marginalized voices, heard as a way to begin dialogue and action toward helping society see that Black lives do matter. In other words, Black Lives Matter begins with teachers' curriculum and instructional choices. We conclude with resources that hopefully will lead to some outstanding curriculum and instructional development in our nation's schools and universities.

REFERENCES

Adichie C. N. (2009). *The dangers of a single story*. Retrieved from http://www.ted.com/talks/chimamanda_adichie_the_danger_of_a_single_story/transcript?language=en

Black Lives Matter. (2015). *Black lives matter: Not a moment, a movement*. Retrieved from http://blacklivesmatter.com/about/

Brown, A. L, Crowley, R., and King, L. (2011). Black civitas: An examination of Carter

G. Woodson's contributions to citizenship education. *Theory & Research in Social Education, 39*, 277–299.

Cashmore, E. & McLaughlin, E. (1991). *Out of order?: Policing Black people*. New York, NY: Routledge.

Castro, A. J. & Knowles, R. T. (in press). Democratic citizenship education: Research across multiple landscapes and contexts. In C. M. Bolick & M. M. Manfra (Eds.), *Handbook of research in social studies education*. New York, NY: Wiley-Blackwell.

Edwards, S. B. & Harris, J. (2016). *Special reports: Black Lives Matter*. Minneapolis, MN: Abdo

Garza, A. (2014). *A herstory of the #BlackLivesMatter movement*. Retrieved from http://www.thefeministwire.com/2014/10/blacklivesmatter-2/

Goldberg, D. T. (1993). *Racist culture: Philosophy and the politics of meaning*. Malden, MA: Wiley-Blackwell.

Hartman, S. (2008). *Lose your mother: A journey along the Atlantic slave route*. New York, NY: MacMillan.

Howard, T. (2003). The dis(g)race of the social studies: The need for racial dialogue in the social studies. In G. Ladson-Billings (Ed.), *Critical race theory perspectives on social studies: The profession, policies, and curriculum* (pp. 27–44). Greenwich, CT: Information Age.

Ladson-Billings, G. (2003). *Critical race theory perspectives on social studies: The profession, policies, and curriculum.* Greenwich, CT: Information Age.

Leonardo, Z., & Porter, R. K. (2010). Pedagogy of fear: Toward a Fanonian theory of 'safety' in race dialogue. *Race Ethnicity and Education, 13,* 139-157.

Lorde, A. (1983). *There is no hierarchy of oppressions.* Retrieved from https://lgbt.ucsd.edu/education/oppressions.html

Martinez, E. (1993). Beyond Black/White: The racism of our times. *Social Justice, 20,* 22–34.

Moore, L. N. (2010). *Black rage in New Orleans: Police brutality and African American activism from World War II to Hurricane Katrina.* Baton Rouge, LA: Louisiana State University Press.

Oldfather, P. (1995). Learning from student voices. *Theory into Practice, 43,* 84–87.

San Francisco Public Schools. (2016). *#BlackLivesMatter.* Retrieved from http://sfusd.libguides.com/blacklivesmatter

Singleton, G. E. & Linton, C. (2014). *Courageous conversations about race: A field guide for achieving equity in schools.* Thousand Oaks, CA: Corwin.

Skerrett, A. (2011). English teachers' racial identity knowledge and practice. *Race Ethnicity and Education, 14,* 313-330.

Thornton, S. J. (2001). From content to subject matter. *The Social Studies, 92,* 237–242.

Tillet, S. (2012). *Sites of slavery: Citizenship and racial democracy in the post-civil rights imagination.* Durham, NC: Duke University Press.

Trotter, J. W. (1985). *Black Milwaukee: The making of an industrial proletariat, 1915–45.* Champaign, IL: University of Illinois Press.

Tyson, C. A. (2003). A bridge over troubled water: Social studies, civic education, and critical race theory. In G. Ladson-Billings (Ed.), *Critical race theory perspectives on social studies: The profession, policies, and curriculum* (pp. 15–26). Greenwich, CT: Information Age.

Woodson, G. C. (1933). *The mis-education of the negro.* Washington, DC: The Associated Publishers.

Woyshner, C. & Bohan, C. (2013). *Histories of social studies and race, 1865–2000.* New York, NY: Palgrave.

Chapter 7

Teaching the Gun Control Debate in an Era of Mass Shootings

Bonnie L. Bittman and William B. Russell III

On January 5, 2016, President Obama gave an emotional speech outlining new executive actions to reduce gun violence in American communities. President Obama, through the Bureau of Alcohol, Tobacco, Firearms and Explosives (ATF), is expanding gun seller licensing requirements, background checks for some gun purchases, and the easing of barriers preventing states from reporting mentally ill individuals to the universal background check system (Bradner & Krieg, 2016). Although a majority of Americans believe it is more important to control gun ownership than to protect the right to own a gun, legislation concerning firearms has not been forthcoming from Congress for decades (Pew Research Center, 2015).

The purpose of this chapter is to illustrate two methods for teachers to talk to their students about the gun control debate. The first lesson is a simulation based on Congress. Students create a few bills concerning firearms, debate them, and vote as a class. This lesson, with its focus on the controversial issue itself, is intended for teachers who wish to teach the gun control debate within the political process.

The second lesson provides an overview of campaign financing and the subsequent influence on members of Congress. Focusing on the largest Second Amendment rights and gun control political advocacy groups, this lesson illustrates the influence of money on politics, using the gun control debate as a real-life example.

A BRIEF HISTORY OF GUNS IN UNITED STATES

Gun Control Legislation

Firearms have had a place in the United States since its inception, both as a necessary tool for survival and, later, as a cultural cornerstone. During colonial times, the British embargo of gunpowder at Williamsburg, as well as the attempt to confiscate the cannons of Concord and Lexington, were contributing factors to the American colonists' desire to revolt (Cornell & DeDino, 2004).

As the United States expanded to the West, frontier life required guns for defense and subsistence hunting. Firearms were becoming a part of the new nation's cultural identity. The regional differences continue today, with 63% of people who live in rural areas prioritizing gun rights over controlling gun ownership, compared with 60% of urban dwellers supporting gun control (Pew Research Center, 2015).

The rise of organized crime resulting from Prohibition, including the St. Valentine's Day Massacre of 1929 and the attempted assassination of President Franklin Roosevelt in 1933, prompted Congress to pass the first major piece of gun control legislation, the National Firearms Act (NFA) of 1934. The NFA required machine guns and short barreled rifles to be registered and taxed at $200, a prohibitive amount at the time. The NFA eventually became Title II of the Gun Control Act (GCA) of 1968 (ATF, 2015).

The GCA and the Brady Handgun Violence Prevention Act of 1993 both came about after a series of assassinations and attempted assassinations of politicians and other prominent public figures. The Brady Act created the background check system in which licensed gun sellers review the criminal history background of prospective gun buyers. A person is prohibited from purchasing a firearm from a licensed dealer if they are

- A convicted felon
- Diagnosed as mentally ill
- An undocumented immigrant
- A military veteran with dishonorable discharge
- Someone who has formally renounced their citizenship
- Someone who has been convicted of domestic violence
- Under 18 years of age
- In possession of a medical marijuana card.

However, private sellers who sell guns within the state they reside in are exempt from licensing requirements. This "gun show loophole" allows individuals to sell firearms privately without participating in background checks, but the exact number of guns sold via this process is unknown (Sherman, 2016).

In 1986, the Firearm Owners' Protection Act amended the GCA, and the ATF prosecuted a number of people for technical violations, which was seen by Congress as outside the spirit of the GCA (U.S. Senate, 1982). The act also reopened interstate sales of long guns, legalized the selling of ammunition by mail, and ensured that the transportation across state lines is legal if applicable by state law. The act also banned the sale of machine guns and semiautomatic weapons, except to the military and law enforcement organizations.

Associated with the Federal Assault Weapons Ban of 1994, the ban on semiautomatic weapons ended in 2004 due to Congress not renewing the legislation within the mandated period, and subsequent attempts to renew the assault weapons ban have not been successful. In 1996, Congress restricted funding for the Centers for Disease Control (CDC) from being used to "advocate or promote gun control" after the National Rifle Association (NRA) accused the CDC of advocating for restrictions on gun rights (Frankel, 2015). That year, Congress cut $2.6 million from the CDC's budget, the exact amount of money that was used for gun research the year before.

The CDC was not alone in avoiding gun research. A part of the U.S. Department of Justice, the National Institute of Justice funded over 30 gun-related studies between 1993 and 1998, but none after 2009. The threat of controversy or negative attention from gun rights organizations has prevented research from being conducted regarding gun violence. After the shooting at Sandy Hook Elementary in 2012, President Obama lifted the ban through executive order. Despite the availability of research funding, the controversy surrounding firearm research has continually prevented academics from researching the topic.

Supreme Court Cases

The Supreme Court has also ruled on a number of cases regarding gun rights. The Court ruled in *U.S. v. Cruikshank* (1876) and *Presser v. Illinois* (1886) that the Second Amendment restricted Congress in passing legislation limiting gun rights; however, states were allowed to pass restrictions if they wished. Incorporation, the process by which the Court applies the Bill of Rights to state law, has been an ongoing process, and the Second Amendment was not incorporated until 2010.

The District of Columbia and the city of Chicago, Illinois, in order to curb gun violence, passed legislation requiring all handguns to be registered with the state. The application of this law translated essentially into a ban on all handguns within the cities. The Supreme Court, in 5-4 decisions in both *District of Columbia v. Heller* (2008) and *McDonald v. Chicago* (2010), finally incorporated the Second Amendment to the states.

The Court recognized that the right to self-defense is "fundamental" and "deeply rooted" in American society and that guns play a role in defending the home. These decisions do not, however, claim that the Second Amendment grants unlimited rights; rather, the government can pass legislation in the interests of public safety as long as they do not violate the individual's right to own a gun.

Current Status of Gun Control

The Pew Research Center, in a 2015 poll concerning guns, found that 85% of people favor background checks for gun shows and private sales, with 79% of Republicans and 88% of Democrats holding that view. Further, 85% of Democrats believe there should be a federal database to track gun sales; however, only 55% of Republicans agree with this position. Reinstituting the Federal Assault Weapons Ban is similarly divisive, with 70% of Democrats and 48% of Republicans agreeing.

From 1993 to 2009, a majority of people said it was more important to control ownership, with a peak in 1999 (66% for controlling gun ownership versus 29% protecting gun rights). However, this trend has narrowed since 2009, with 50% of people now saying it is more important to control gun ownership and 47% of people saying that gun rights are more important.

Guns continue to divide people beyond ideology. Racially, Whites say protecting gun rights is more important than gun control (57% to 40%), while majorities of African Americans (72%) and Hispanics (75%) favor gun control. Women favor gun control (55%) more than men (45%). Individuals with a postgraduate degree are almost twice as likely to favor gun control (63% to 32%), but the divide narrows with less education. Urban areas favor gun control over gun rights (60% to 38%), suburban residents are divided (48% to 48%), and rural citizens favor gun rights over gun control (63% to 35%). The nation may support specific pieces of legislation, but the debate concerning guns deeply divides Americans.

The United States is not the only country struggling with the gun debate, but it does occupy a unique place in the world. According to the 2007 Small Arms Survey, private citizens own 270 million guns in the United States, the highest number of firearms per capita in the world. Guns were used in over half the homicides committed in the United States between 2005 and 2012. In comparison, for every one person killed by terrorism worldwide, over a 1,000 were killed by guns inside the United States, including homicides, accidents, and suicides.

Finally, compared with other developed nations, the United States is the leader in mass shootings. Since 1997, the United States has experienced 51 mass shootings, compared with zero in Australia and Japan, one in the United Kingdom, and three each in Germany and Switzerland. The Council on Foreign Relations found that each of the previous nations had stricter gun control laws than the United States, although direct correlations between gun control laws and mass shootings cannot be made.

TEACHING ABOUT GUN CONTROL

The current state of the gun debate has been shaped by the plethora of mass shootings experienced in the United States. Between 1983 and 2012, there were 78 mass shootings, with over 500 deaths and more than 1,000 deaths and injuries (Bjelopera et al., 2013). Currently, the federal government does not have a definition for what constitutes a mass shooting; however, Mark Follman (2012) of *Mother Jones* has developed a database to track mass shootings. To qualify as a mass shooting, the attack must have happened in a public place, a motive of indiscriminate mass murder, and have taken the lives of at least four people.

Table 7.1 shows the number of mass shootings since April 20, 1999, when two shooters stormed into Columbine High School and killed 12 students and a teacher, sparking the gun control debate.

As Table 7.1 shows, mass shootings are occurring more frequently, with places of education the second most likely location (Cohen, Azrael, & Miller, 2014; Bjelopera et al., 2013). Since 1982, 14 mass shootings involved illegal guns, 2 cases are unknown, and 60 involved legally purchased firearms for a total of 76 mass shootings in the United States (Follman, Aronsen, & Pan, 2016).

The perpetrators were overwhelmingly White males, with the remaining shootings committed by Black men (12), Asian men (6), Hispanic men (4), Middle-Eastern men (4), Native American men (2), and women (3; 1 Native American, 1 Middle-Eastern, and 1 White). The increase in mass shootings in the United States is cause for alarm and a necessary topic for teachers to address.

These massacres, of course, are illegal acts. The vast majority of gun owners are responsible citizens. People around the United States grow up with shooting sports, such as trap, skeet, and sporting clay with family members and friends. Handguns are popular in action shooting, where a competitor has to hit multiple targets while on the move, as well as precision shooting, a form of target shooting. Rifles, most commonly used in hunting, can be passed from generation to generation, bonding older and younger members of a family. Gun enthusiasts are a close community, educating future generations in safe handling techniques and passing on their love of shooting sports.

In a recent poll by Gallup, more than 6 in 10 American say guns make homes safer, an argument often repeated by the NRA (McCarthy, 2014). Despite a number of self-defense stories where the possession of a gun prevented violence against a victim, however, the Federal Bureau of Investigation reported in 2012 that of the 8,855 murders committed by firearms in the United States, only 206 were justifiable (United States Department of Justice & Federal Bureau of Investigation, 2013).

A report prepared by the National Research Council (2013) found that "firearm-related suicides significantly outnumbered homicides for all age groups, annually accounting for 61% of the more than 335,600 people who have died from firearm-related violence in the United States" (Leshner et al., 2013, p. 13).

Table 7.1 U.S. Mass Shootings, Since Columbine High School

Case	Location	Date	Victims	Venue	Weapons Obtained Illegally
Excel Industries mass shooting	Hesston, KS	2/25/16	17	Workplace	Unknown
Kalamazoo shooting spree	Kalamazoo County, MI	2/20/16	8	Other	Yes
San Bernardino mass shooting	San Bernardino, CA	12/2/15	35	Workplace	Yes
Umpqua Community College shooting	Roseburg, OR	10/1/15	18	School	Yes
Chattanooga military recruitment center	Chattanooga, TN	7/16/15	7	Military	Yes
Charleston Church shooting	Charleston, SC	6/17/15	10	Religious	Yes
Marysville-Pilchuck High School shooting	Marysville, WA	10/24/14	6	School	No
Alturas tribal shooting	Alturas, CA	2/20/14	6	Other	Unknown
Washington Navy Yard shooting	Washington, DC	9/16/13	21	Military	Yes
Hialeah apartment shooting	Hialeah, FL	7/26/13	7	Other	Yes
Santa Monica rampage	Santa Monica, CA	6/7/13	9	Other	Yes
Pinewood Village Apartment shooting	Federal Way, WA	4/21/13	5	Other	Yes
Mohawk Valley shootings	Herkimer County, NY	3/13/13	7	Other	Yes
Newtown school shooting	Newtown, CT	12/14/12	30	School	No
Accent Signage Systems shooting	Minneapolis, MN	9/27/12	8	Workplace	Yes
Sikh temple shooting	Oak Creek, WI	8/5/12	10	Religious	Yes
Aurora theater shooting	Aurora, CO	7/20/12	70	Other	Yes
Seattle cafe shooting	Seattle, WA	5/20/12	7	Other	Yes
Oikos University killings	Oakland, CA	4/2/12	10	School	Yes
Su Jung Health Sauna shooting	Norcross, GA	2/22/12	5	Other	Yes
Seal Beach shooting	Seal Beach, CA	10/14/11	9	Other	Yes
IHOP shooting	Carson City, NV	9/6/11	12	Other	Yes
Tucson shooting	Tucson, AZ	1/8/11	19	Other	Yes

Hartford Beer Distributor shooting	Manchester, CT	8/3/10	11	Workplace	Yes
Coffee shop police killings	Parkland, WA	11/29/09	5	Other	No
Fort Hood massacre	Fort Hood, TX	11/5/09	43	Military	Yes
Binghamton shootings	Binghamton, NY	4/3/09	18	Other	Yes
Carthage nursing home shooting	Carthage, NC	3/29/09	11	Other	Yes
Atlantis Plastics shooting	Henderson, KY	6/25/08	7	Workplace	Yes
Northern Illinois University shooting	DeKalb, IL	2/14/08	27	School	Yes
Kirkwood City Council shooting	Kirkwood, MO	2/7/08	8	Other	No
Westroads Mall shooting	Omaha, NE	12/5/07	13	Other	No
Crandon shooting	Crandon, WI	10/7/07	7	Other	Yes
Virginia Tech massacre	Blacksburg, VA	4/16/07	56	School	Yes
Trolley Square shooting	Salt Lake City, UT	2/12/07	10	Other	No
Amish school shooting	Lancaster County, PA	10/2/06	11	School	Yes
Capitol Hill massacre	Seattle, WA	3/25/06	9	Other	Yes
Goleta postal shootings	Goleta, CA	1/30/06	8	Workplace	Yes
Red Lake massacre	Red Lake, MN	3/21/05	15	School	No
Living Church of God shooting	Brookfield, WI	3/12/05	11	Religious	Yes
Damageplan show shooting	Columbus, OH	12/8/04	12	Other	Yes
Lockheed Martin shooting	Meridian, MS	7/8/03	15	Workplace	Yes
Navistar shooting	Melrose Park, IL	2/5/01	9	Workplace	Yes
Wakefield massacre	Wakefield, MA	12/26/00	7	Workplace	Yes
Hotel shooting	Tampa, FL	12/30/99	8	Workplace	Yes
Xerox killings	Honolulu, HI	11/2/99	7	Workplace	Yes
Wedgwood Baptist Church shooting	Fort Worth, TX	9/15/99	15	Religious	Yes
Atlanta day trading spree killings	Atlanta, GA	7/29/99	22	Workplace	Yes
Columbine High School massacre	Littleton, CO	4/20/99	39	School	No

Source: Mother Jones (2016).

A meta-analysis of research literature concerning guns in the home found that having a gun in the house is associated with a higher rate of completed suicide and being the victim of a homicide (Anglemyer, Horvath, & Rutherford, 2014). Despite the claim that legal guns make people safer, data show that a gun in the house increases the likelihood of gun violence.

The conflicting experiences between individuals who have been or know the victim of gun violence and those who have participated in shooting sports can cause extraordinary amounts of friction among members of society, which is reflected in the classroom. Teachers and students need to be informed and prepared to discuss this issue using fact-based rationale instead of heated rhetoric.

TEACHING GUNS THROUGH SIMULATION

Oftentimes outside events impact the classroom, and teachers must stop and address concerns of students. These "teachable moments" are often informal and unstructured but can have lasting impact on students. By framing a controversial debate, like the gun control debate, within the context of legislative action, teachers can address controversial issues in the classroom while also addressing national and state standards.

The National Council for the Social Studies (NCSS) *College, Career, and Civic Life (C3) Framework* for social studies state standards, for example, explicitly calls for students to understand the impact of constitutions, how the U.S. Constitution establishes rights, and for students to be able to "evaluate citizens' and institutions' effectiveness in addressing social and political problems" (NCSS, 2013, p. 32). This approach to teaching about gun control in the United States is modeled after a traditional congressional debate. Students create their own gun legislation, debate the merits, and vote as a single body on one bill. It provides a framework for students to discuss this emotionally charged topic in a productive way.

Framework for Debate

When debating the balance between individual rights and the public good as members of Congress, teachers should have students focus on compromise. The ten amendments in the Bill of Rights guarantee a number of individual rights, such as freedom of speech, freedom of religion, and the right of the people to peacefully assemble. However, rights are not unlimited; people cannot slander others, and the police can shut down an assembly if it evolves into a riot.

This protection of the common good ensures that the general conditions of society are to every person's benefit and that the institutions and environments are advancing the social system, rather than harming it. Congress constantly debates and considers this balance, and modeling the process benefits students' understanding of the work of the institution. Furthermore, the increase of mass shootings in the United States has led to renewed focus in Congress on gun control.

For this debate, teachers should first ask students to identify the risks and benefits of guns in society. Students will be sure to mention mass shootings, domestic violence, and gun crimes, and teachers should encourage students to give specifics. They will also provide examples of the benefits guns can have, such as traditional shooting sports and home protection. The role of the teacher at this time is to encourage student participation and to make sure that strong arguments exist for each side. Depending on time, students could continue their research on the Internet or continue solely with the background information.

The teacher should then provide an outline of what legislation looks like. Students, in small groups or individually, will then create a piece of legislation that answers the question "What law should be passed to lower the number of mass shootings in the United States?" Students should be encouraged to decide the type of legislation on their own.

Some students will advocate restrictions on gun sales like the proposed assault weapons ban. Alternatively, some students will argue for increased access to guns, as seen in many states that are lessening open carry restrictions. The class will then act as a congressional subcommittee, passing their legislation around the classroom. The teacher should encourage students to merge similar bills into a single piece of legislation, narrowing the number of bills to two or three. Once the bills have been narrowed down to a few only, the class would come back to their seats.

At this point in the simulation, the debate on gun control should be controlled by the students. In most secondary classes there will be a variety of viewpoints represented, some from students advocating strict gun control laws, some supporting gun rights legislation. The students will then be instructed to write a speech in their groups explaining why their legislation would be the best for the United States.

The teacher should encourage students to prepare their argument using supporting facts and details but should not discourage students from speaking emotionally regarding this topic. After both groups of students deliver their speech to the class, the whole classroom can then begin a traditional debate. Students should be encouraged to criticize and argue against the other pieces of legislation. To help control the classroom, teachers can choose to follow *Robert's Rules of Order*, or structure the debate by time limit.

Once the bills have been debated, the teacher needs to call the class to order. Students, through a roll call, then vote aye or nay. The bill, in order to pass, needs to gain support of over half the students in the class. If there is no majority, the legislation with the fewest votes is then dropped and the debate begins again. Students can become very engaged at this point, attempting to gain supporters to their piece of legislation. This simulation works well with a diversity of opinions, which is necessary for the classroom debate to be lively and engaging. The teacher should refrain from giving their opinion on legislation, encouraging the students to decide on the issue for themselves.

This simulation is intended to provide students with an understanding of the history of gun control in the United States as well assist in developing their opinions regarding gun control laws. By having students create legislation that addresses the spate of mass shootings, students will come to understand the struggle between individual rights and the public safety.

TEACHING GUNS THROUGH THE LEGISLATIVE PROCESS

The second lesson teaches the gun control debate through campaign financing from gun advocacy groups. The following section will introduce the gun rights and gun control lobby, review campaign financing regulations, and explain the implications of money spent by gun advocacy groups. By using this method, teachers will be able to address the gun control debate within the larger context of American politics.

Introduction of Campaign Financing

When introducing campaign financing to students, it is necessary for the teacher to explain the basic regulations. Candidates and political parties have restrictions on the amount of money they can accept from individual or group donors, as outlined by the Federal Election Campaign Act of 1972 and the Bipartisan Campaign Finance Reform Act. However, the Supreme Court decision in *Citizens United v. Federal Elections Commission* (FEC) fundamentally altered the rules governing money in politics.

Independent groups, commonly called SuperPACs, can now accept and spend unlimited amounts of money from corporations and unions as a right guaranteed by the First Amendment. Despite the freedom of speech right granted by *Citizens United v. FEC* decision, SuperPACs cannot coordinate with campaigns, nor can they engage in direct electioneering. Rather, they can spend money on commercials, mailing, and other election materials in support or opposition of a candidate or issue. SuperPACs began spending money on issue-centered advocacy almost immediately, with very few legal restrictions.

Gun Rights Political Action Committees

The NRA, the largest gun rights organization in the United States, was founded in 1871 to improve marksmanship in the armed forces. Evolving as an organization to promote shooting sports and improve gun safety, marksmanship is still promoted heavily by the NRA with marksmanship competitions, gun safety classes, and concealed weapon-permitting classes. In 1990, the organization created the NRA Foundation, a political action committee (PAC), which lobbies federal agencies and donates to campaigns hoping to influence legislation. While regulations state "no substantial part" of the organization's budget can be used for lobbying, the larger the organization, the more money that can be spent in politics (Internal Revenue Service, 2015).

While the NRA is the most prominent gun rights organization, a number of other organizations also support gun rights, such as the Gun Owners of America, Second Amendment Foundation, and Second Amendment Sisters. As a whole, gun rights organizations have donated $36 million in individual, PAC, and soft money contributions to federal campaigns since 1989, with 87% of that money going to Republicans (Center for Responsive Politics, 2015). During the 2014 mid-term elections, the NRA alone spent $14,349,465, with $5.7 million donated to Republicans and $8.1 million spent opposing Democratic candidates (Center for Responsive Politics, 2014).

The amount of money donated to members of Congress, as well as lobbying the bureaucracy, has almost certainly prevented legislation that would restrict gun ownership from passing that would restrict gun ownership, despite public support for certain measures. Gun advocacy groups, particularly after the Columbine Massacre, have used political money to prevent gun control legislation. The increase in mass shootings has only galvanized the gun rights lobby and increased the amount of money spent.

Gun Control Political Action Committees

Gun control organizations have been slower to raise and spend money. The Brady Campaign to Prevent Gun Violence is one of the oldest organizations. Originally founded in 1974 as the National Council to Control Handguns, it was renamed the Brady Campaign in 2001 in honor of Jim Brady, President Reagan's press secretary who was shot during the 1981 assassination attempt on the president. Another organization, Everytown for Gun Safety, boasts a number of mayors and law enforcement officials from large cities on its advisory board.

Lastly, the group Americans for Responsible Solutions, founded by former Representative Gabby Giffords, a victim of an assassination attempt in 2011, has attempted to match the monetary influence of the NRA. In 2012, gun control groups spent $2.2 million on direct lobbying. Even with the massive gap between gun rights and gun control groups, the 2014 mid-term election saw $8 million spent by Americans for Responsible Solutions, and former New York City Mayor Michael Bloomberg's Independence USA PAC (which advocates for gun control as well as other issues) spent $5.6 million promoting the gun control position (Center for Responsive Politics, 2016). The differences in money between gun rights and gun control legislation is stark.

Lesson Overview

To begin the lesson, the teacher should provide students with the overview of gun control legislation provided earlier in this chapter. Students should be aware of previous legislation, the significant Supreme Court decisions, and the increasing number of mass shootings in the United States. Teachers should then ask students if they believe gun control legislation should be passed to address gun violence.

After introducing the polling data that shows Americans are in favor of gun control legislation, the teacher should ask students why no significant gun control laws have been passed. At this point in the lesson, the teacher should provide background information about recent campaign finance legislation and subsequent court decisions.

Teachers should then have students investigate one gun advocacy group and one gun control group through the Center for Responsive Politics' website: www.opensecrets.org. Students can look up the donations from each organization themselves with worksheets provided by the website. To connect the information to students, the teacher should encourage students to investigate their state senators and representatives, looking for donations from either group.

Once students have an understanding of the difference in money provided by gun rights versus gun control PACs, students should be asked if they think the money being donated would change a politician's mind, regardless of public opinion. This line of inquiry segues conveniently into a case study. The teacher would then introduce the Manchin-Toomey amendment, which would have required background checks on all commercially purchased guns, essentially closing the "gun show loophole."

In 2013 and 2015, the Pew Research Center found that 81% and 85% of Americans, respectively, support background checks for private and gun show sales. On April 17, 2013, the Senate voted on the Manchin-Toomey amendment, and gun rights PACs donated $527,970 to the 54 members who voted no on the amendment and $68,330 to senators voting yes. Contributions from gun control PACs totaled $5,000 to 10 senators who all voted yes. Almost every member who voted no to defeat the amendment accepted money from gun rights political organizations.

On December 2, 2015, after 14 people were killed in San Bernardino, California, the Manchin-Toomey amendment was voted on again. The amendment was defeated, 48-50, with pro-gun rights PACs donating $618,090 to senators who voted no and $27,500 to those that voted yes. Gun control PACs donated only $2,500 to a single senator. This stark contrast between gun rights PACs and gun control PACs is the perfect case study to present students. It illustrates the influence of money in politics, beyond public opinion.

Once students understand that the political process is influenced by money, they should be given a writing assignment focused on the gun control debate. Students should gauge the morality of the politician's actions. Students who advocate for gun rights can argue that politicians are protecting the Second Amendment right to bear arms; on the contrary, other students will present arguments that while people are being killed by legally bought guns in mass shootings, the U.S. Congress has done little to halt the spread of guns in the United States because of money. The teacher should encourage students to determine whether the actions of Congress benefit or harm American society.

CONCLUSION

The gun control debate in the United States is currently filled with heated rhetoric and inflamed passions. This chapter provides an overview of guns in the United States as well as two lesson plans for teaching the gun control debate in the classroom. Both lesson plans provide teachers with a structure for teaching the gun control debate within the political process.

The first lesson, a simulation of congressional debate, utilizes the background knowledge provided by this chapter and models the debating style of Congress. The second aims to teach the gun control debate through campaign financing. Both methods focus on how Congress acts (or doesn't) when faced with a controversial topic. Mass shootings are increasing in the United States, and students need to be prepared to argue for rational, sane solutions to the gun control debate. Lives depend on it.

REFERENCES

Alcohol, Tobacco, Firearms, and Explosives. (2015). National firearms act. *U.S. Department of Justice.* Retrieved from https://www.atf.gov/rules-and-regulations/national-firearms-act

Anglemyer, A., Horvath, T., & Rutherford, G. (2014). The accessibility of firearms and risk for suicides and homicide victimization amount household members: A systematic review and meta-analysis. *Annals of Internal Medicine, 160,* 101–110.

Bjelopera, J. P., Bagalman, E., Caldwell, S. W., Finklea, K. M., & McCallion, G. (2013). Public mass shootings in the United States: Selected implications for federal public health and safety policy. *Congressional Research Service.* Retrieved from http://journalistsresource.org/wp-content/uploads/2013/03/MassShootings_CongResServ.pdf

Bradner, E. & Krieg, G. (2016, January 5). Emotional Obama calls for a 'sense of urgency' to fight gun violence. *CNN.* Retrieved from http://www.cnn.com/2016/01/05/politics/obama-executive-action-gun-control/

Center for Responsive Politics. (2014). National Rifle Association. Retrieved from https://www.opensecrets.org/outsidespending/detail.php?cmte=C00053553&cycle=2014

Center for Responsive Politics. (2015). Gun rights. Retrieved from http://www.opensecrets.org/industries/indus.php?ind=q13

Center for Responsive Politics. (2016). Gun control: Background. Retrieved from https://www.opensecrets.org/industries/background.php?cycle=2016&ind=Q12

Cohen, A. P., Azrael, D., & Miller, M. (2014, October 15). Rate of mass shootings has tripled since 2011, Harvard research shows. *Mother Jones.* Retrieved from http://m.motherjones.com/politics/2014/10/mass-shootings-increasing-harvard-research

Cornell, S. & DeDino, N. (2004). A well regulated right: The early American origins of gun control. *Fordham Law Review, 73,* 487–528.

District of Columbia v. Heller. 554 U.S. (2008).

Follman, M. (2012, August 24). What exactly is a mass shooting? *Mother Jones.* Retrieved from http://www.motherjones.com/mojo/2012/08/what-is-a-mass-shooting

Follman, M., Aronsen, G., & Pan, D. (2016, February 25). A guide to mass shootings in America. *Mother Jones.* Retrieved from http://www.motherjones.com/politics/2012/07/mass-shootings-map

Frankel, T. C. (2015, January 14). Why the CDC still isn't researching gun violence, despite the ban being lifted two years ago. *The Washington Post.* Retrieved from https://www.washingtonpost.com/news/storyline/wp/2015/01/14/why-the-cdc-still-isnt-researching-gun-violence-despite-the-ban-being-lifted-two-years-ago/

Internal Revenue Service. (2015, December 15). Exemption requirements- 501(c)(3) organizations. Retrieved from https://www.irs.gov/Charities-&-Non-Profits/Charitable-Organizations/Exemption-Requirements-Section-501(c)(3)-Organizations.

Leshner, A. I., Altevogt, B. M., Lee, A. F., McCoy, M. A., & Kelley, P. W. (Eds.). (2013). *Priorities for research to reduce the threat of firearm-related violence.* Washington, D. C.: Institute of Medicine and National Research Council of the National Academes.

McCarthy, J. (2014, November 7). More than six in 10 Americans say guns make homes safer. *Gallup.* Retrieved from http://www.gallup.com/poll/179213/six-americans-say-guns-homes-safer.aspx

McDonald v. Chicago. 561 U.S. (2010).

Mother Jones. (2016). U.S. mass shootings, 1982-2016: Data from Mother Jones investigation. Retrieved from http://www.motherjones.com/politics/2012/12/mass-shootings-mother-jones-full-data

National Council for the Social Studies. (2013). *The college, career, and civic life (C3) framework for social studies state standards: Guidance for enhancing the rigor of K-12 civics, economics, geography, and history.* Silver Spring, MD: National Council for the Social Studies.

Pew Research Center. (2015). Continued bipartisan support for expanded background checks on gun sales. Retrieved from http://www.people-press.org/2015/08/13/continued-bipartisan-support-for-expanded-background-checks-on-gun-sales/#total

Sherman, A. (2016, January 7). Politifact sheet: 3 things to know about the 'gun show loophole.' *Politifact.* Retrieved from http://www.politifact.com/truth-o-meter/article/2016/jan/07/politifact-sheet-3-things-know-about-gun-show-loop/

United States Department of Justice & Federal Bureau of Investigation. (2013). *Crime in the United States, 2012.* Retrieved from https://www.fbi.gov/about-us/cjis/ucr/crime-in-the-u.s/2012/crime-in-the-u.s.-2012/offenses-known-to-law-enforcement/expanded-homicide/expandhomicidemain.pdf\

United States Senate. (1982). *The right to keep and bear arms: Report of the subcommittee on the Constitution of the committee on the Judiciary* (U.S. Government Publication No. 1042-A). Washington, DC: U.S. Government Printing Office.

Chapter 8

Big Data, Surveillance, and the Unprecedented Conditions of Citizenship

H. James Garrett

Reading the newspapers gives one the sense that media technology, access, and privacy are all in rapid and significant flux. At the time of this writing, the FBI and Apple are in a tense dispute about the degree to which a corporation is required to assist in criminal investigations by providing ways to access locked and encrypted data on products purchased from their company. Moreover, the federal government can legally read any email sent longer than 180 days ago due to an interpretation of a little-known law passed in the 1980s (Wise, 2015).

Other examples exist. In February 2015, for example, *The Daily Beast* called attention to the fact that Samsung warns consumers of its televisions enabled with voice recognition that "personal or other sensitive information" spoken "will be among data captured and transmitted to a third party" (Peralta, 2015 para. 3). The documents made public by Edward Snowden have revealed, and continue to reveal, the extent to which the federal government of the United States operates behind the curtains of secrecy in order to encroach on the privacy of its citizens (Greenwald, 2014).

Volumes have been written in the last five years attesting to the implications of Big Data and the ways in which users of social media networking sites, geolocation services on mobile devices, and Web-based consumers are being tracked and targeted by a wide array of companies and government organizations (e.g., Angwin, 2014). If this all sounds conspiratorial and dramatically thrilling, it may be because so much of this kind of activity has already been represented in fictional literature and blockbuster films. Such is the reality of 21st-century life. It seems as though we are being watched at all times, both in ways we know and simultaneously forget, avoid, or do not know.

These conditions demand attention by social studies educators. Several social studies and curriculum scholars (e.g., Giroux, 2015; Ross 2006) take critical views of the U.S. policies surrounding civil liberties and surveillance. The debate around privacy and security is a compelling and persistent presence in policy discussions and topics of inquiry in civics and history courses. While I find these contributions crucial to social studies education, and they largely inform my thinking, this chapter will take a different entry into this problematic terrain.

The purpose of this chapter is first to discuss these realities and then explore the mismatch between how they are considered in contemporary cultural criticism and how they are treated in social studies research and practice. Throughout the chapter I allude to the implications that these unprecedented developments in information technology have for social studies education and curriculum.

If we are to take seriously any of the visions of social studies education that call for the cultivation of productive and informed citizens (e.g., Brophy & Alleman, 2006; Parker, 1996; Werner, 2000; Westheimer & Kahne, 2004), then addressing the issue of surveillance is a crucial project. While cultural critics and social theorists in popular press and academia are exploring and breaking new ground in understanding these conditions, the social studies education community has not recognized such contributions or lines of thinking in our research literature. Therefore, the questions that guide this inquiry are as follows:

• How is current social thought understanding and responding to the changing conditions related to Big Data and surveillance?
• What are the consequences and implications of these emerging understandings for thinking about citizenship and social studies education in the 21st century?

In this chapter I focus on the ways in which current social thought focuses on the status of disconnection, disruption, and the emotional complexities instantiated by these changing social conditions. The literature from which I draw, my archive, is comprised of long form journalism such as that found in *Harper's* and the *New York Review of Books* combined with an emerging field of cultural theory termed "affect theory" and specifically Berlant's (2011) conceptual term of "crisis ordinariness."

My method for writing this chapter is to use those discourse communities and ideas as devices to provide an alternative conceptualization for a social studies education that reaches beyond disciplinary regimes that currently hold sway in state standards documents as well as the still relatively new *College, Career, and Civic Life (C3) Standards* (National Council for the Social Studies, 2013).

Existing literature in social studies education approaches the status of technology and citizenship by helping students understand how to "safely" use the

Internet and social media so that they do not put themselves in danger (Bradshaw & Keefer, 2007). Another way is to utilize new technologies to enhance student learning. Articles abound about students learning how to blog and use social media applications like Twitter and Facebook (e.g., Berson, Berson, & Manfra, 2012).

These are often exciting and critically oriented pieces that ought to help teachers and students engage in productive conversations. Krutka and Carpenter (2016) lament the fact, though, that while there is vast potential and need for formal pedagogical attention given to social media consumption and production, most schools still avoid and ban social media use in the school building. Krutka and Carpenter conclude that being critically educated about social media is a civic necessity for students' lives outside of classrooms.

Yet another view of social studies education that is consolidated in the research and practice literature is about the ways in which individuals ought to be personally responsible online citizens. This means, among other things, not posting compromising photographs of oneself or one's acquaintances, not sharing passwords, engaging in productive conversation and avoiding cyberbullying, and making sure to keep private information private in order to stave off would-be online predators. All of these are important, to be sure. There are enormous personal dangers associated with the digital lives we lead – credit card and identity theft being primary examples.

These risks, however, are increasingly part of the bargain we make as we participate in the world as it exists. Another stance social studies educators *could* take would be to recommend that we disconnect from social media and information technology altogether, in an attempt to "live off the grid." The implicit curricula of bans on social media and enabled technology in schools would seemingly teach that lesson. However, I am not as interested in that option as I am in exploring the complications of living within the complexity, however ambivalently, of such a media-rich and technologically connected society.

Finally, the issues with which I am concerned are discussed in social studies research and practice outlets within the contexts of a debate between privacy and security. For example, in a search for social studies education literature concerning the Edward Snowden leaks, all I found were a few lessons that allowed students to engage with the actions of Snowden himself – is he a hero or a traitor (e.g., *Education World*, 2015)? That is an interesting question to be sure, but it does not engage the substance of what was revealed through the documents he released: that the National Security Administration (NSA) had secretly and without congressional approval been "collecting everything," from U.S. citizens without their knowledge or consent.

In all of these examples the issues are largely considered to be the domain of an individual and the choices he or she makes. What is not discussed explicitly are the sociopolitical consequences and the stakes of living within this swirling mass of data, including how it is used by private and government agencies.

In other words, while there are lessons about the personal consumption and production of Twitter feeds, for example, there is an absence of a consideration of what it means to have citizenship mediated by such a rapid and rapidly proliferating information landscape. While there are lessons about the personal decisions of a particular figure, there is not an exploration of the broader consequence of what that knowledge does to our understanding of what it means to be a citizen.

The question that might have been asked in these lessons is: How might we think otherwise about privacy and security in an age where our digital lives are tracked in unprecedented ways – ways that we give our explicit or implicit consent to by our simple searching on Google? How might we understand the connections between citizenship and consumption in the economy? These questions would mean that we consider a curriculum that addressed not only the crucial aspects of personal safety and responsibility but also the substance and consequence of what we are coming to know about information, its storage, use, and ubiquity.

CURRENT SOCIAL THINKING

Our time is marked with unprecedented social changes, and so we are obliged to invite students into broader social and political conversations regarding these changes and how people make lives within them. This mode of living within, among, and through crisis is what Berlant (2011) calls "crisis ordinariness" and is used to signify the nonuniqueness of crisis and also to point to the experience of time within it. What is unique about our time, though, is less the existence of crisis (crisis happens all the time) and more the degree to which our mode of relating to the world is given over to this storyline of crisis.

Berlant's claim is that we understand our lives, and thus we contextualize our personal and political decisions in relation to real and perceived crises. Given the enormity and significance of these changing coordinates, and not only within data and surveillance but also climate change, fraying economic security, population/migration shifts, and geopolitical conflict, Berlant wonders:

> What will govern the terms and relations of reliable reciprocity among governments, intimates, workers, owners, churches, citizens, political parties or strangers? What forms of life will secure the sense of affective democracy that people have been educated to expect from their publics? Nobody knows. (p. 225)

Berlant identifies a distance between the expectations and the precarious economic and political realities of a growing segment of the population. She is asking about the most fundamental aspect of social organization: reciprocal relations between people functioning in different capacities.

Berlant's questions provide a way to conceptualize social studies education that focuses on an unfolding present made from histories and particular stories about those histories. As Berlant explains it, the problem is that we seek to mitigate crises and solve problems by investing in the same storylines, devices, and processes that have yielded the very crises we wish to solve.

There is not much realistic hope that our political system can yield a significant change in the ways we relate to the environment, given that our political system has contributed so significantly to those problems, at least up to this point in time. Berlant's investigation focuses on an unfolding present of the ways that people make meaning in the midst of crisis and upheaval. In what follows I will attempt to describe that unfolding present as it relates to the relationships between surveillance, the uses of Big Data, and social studies education.

I begin from the perspective that surveillance is not a novel part of social living nor is it anything new – in all social contexts there are watchers and watched. However, the nature of the watching and the being watched has changed significantly with the rise of Big Data, and so I will define and describe that term. From there I will turn to thinking about what happens when we acknowledge the methods, reach, and blurry legality of surveillance by both government and business (and those often work together) and the consequences to how we think about what we teach students about democracy, the Constitution, and civic life.

Big Data

Big Data is the shorthand term for the massive, unprecedented growth in the production of data and the concurrent ability to find patterns and "mine" that data through complicated computational algorithms. It is not the case, of course, that this is the first time people are using "data" to all sorts of ends. Data existed before the Defense Advanced Research Projects Agency created the Internet in the 1960s.

However, when we talk about Big Data (with those capital letters) we are not talking only about discreet bits of information from which decisions can be made or knowledge can be culled; we are referencing the simultaneous exponential growth in the production of data and the rapidly increasing sophistication with which that data can be analyzed. As Andrejevic and Gates (2014) explained:

> The advent of big data marks the moment when new forms of sense-making can be applied to the accumulated data troves (and, correspondingly, the moment when these troves can be amassed, stored, and shared in forms that are amenable to such techniques). So we take the term big data to refer to a combination of size, storage medium, and analytic capability. To refer to big data is not simply to claim that databases contain more information than ever before (although they do), but also to consider the new uses to which that data is put – the novel forms of "actionable intelligence" that emerge from the analysis of ever-expanding data set. (p. 186)

In other words, we have two processes occurring at the same time. One is we are creating so much data in the form of email, texts, social media, and location-enabled devices. The production of this data is unprecedented. The second process is the ability to make interpretations about it through highly complicated computerized algorithms that are new and increasingly difficult to understand in simple terms. That is also unprecedented.

What happens with this data, "our data," is that it is sold for fractions of a penny in a fraction of a second, and these purchases determine our online experiences. These sales are what make Google and Facebook "free" for us to use. We are the product; advertisers are the customers. What we see online and what messages we receive are largely determined and are largely a product of marketing ploys. What we usually think of as our access portal to information is more accurately (or more primarily) a corporate access portal to profits via our data and search histories. Moreover, there is a high degree of cooperation between those corporate data and the national surveillance state.

There are such extraordinary affordances of such a system, and with that there are also large and imbedded dangers. As these technologies and systems developed, they were used primarily for commercial purposes. However, that purpose changed, as Sue Halpern (2013), writing in the *New York of Review of Books*, explained:

> No longer was the answer to a query solely what was prized; value was now inherent in the search itself, no matter the answer. Google searches, however benign, allowed advertisers and marketers to tailor their efforts: if you sought information on Hawaiian atolls, for example, you'd likely see ads for Hawaiian vacations. (If you search today for backpacks and pressure cookers, you might see an agent from the FBI at your front door.) Though it was not obvious in those early years, the line from commerce to surveillance turned out to be short and straight. (para. 11)

While Big Data is of interest to social studies educators because of the degree to which it forces our hand to revise the practices we use to discuss personal responsibility, protection, safe behavior, and responsible decision-making, it is this close connection to surveillance and the power of government actors that begins to raise more provocative questions. The issue is more than the growth of Big Data; rather, it is the government's increasing ability to render, analyze, and visualize all of this data through complicated, computerized algorithms.

The government does this legally. It also does so surreptitiously. It does so to people both around the world and within the United States. It does so in order to catch terrorist plots before they happen. It also does so in order to intimidate political adversaries (Greenwald, 2014). The private sector and the U.S. government, then, are co-dependent actors in a game that shapes the social and political landscape. These are social studies issues that are crucial in their presentation not only in order to prompt student awareness but to also explore their effects in terms of the stories students tell and want to tell about the various and overlapping communities in which they live.

What I mean to ask here is what kind of implications are there for social studies education when we acknowledge that the data we produce as part of our lives (through transactions in-the-flesh and online) are being collected, parsed, analyzed, and used by corporate and political groups in order to track and influence our behaviors in stores and at the polls. What can we trust of the information we receive from a Google search when our search results are catered to what Google thinks we want to read? What if what our search engine thinks we want is not at all what we need?

Further, what if the picture that our search record paints of us could lead others to think less favorably of us? What if our purchases, locations of our cell phones, content and frequency of our text messages (from where and to whom) make it seem as though we are up to no good? In short, what becomes of a social studies education in an era of unprecedented and near-ubiquitous condition of surveillance?

Surveillance

Many of these concerns, of course, arise in relation to Edward Snowden, who in 2013 downloaded millions of classified documents from NSA servers and fled the country. He eventually was able to contact three journalists to whom he entrusted these files to sort out which ought to be made public and which ought to be kept secret to forestall a risk to national security. Included in these documents were the following revelations:

- The NSA collected mass data mining of U.S. citizens without their consent.
- U.S. corporations were complicit in this effort to "collect everything" without their customers' knowledge or consent.

- These data were used for a wide variety of purposes beyond protecting the country from terrorist threats.

When news broke that Verizon, AT&T, Facebook, and other huge technology companies had secretly given customer data over to the NSA, an enormous media wave followed. In 2014, Glenn Greenwald's book "No Place to Hide" was a national bestseller. In 2015, Laura Poitras's "Citzenfour" won the Academy Award for the best documentary. In other words, we live in a world where we give our explicit or implicit consent to be followed, tracked, and evaluated and where this is public knowledge circulating at all times. We cannot say that we do not know.

We know for verifiable fact that the NSA was running warrantless wiretaps on U.S. citizens under no suspicion of terrorism. Their call, post 9/11, was to "collect everything." To give a broad overview of the patently true conditions of life within this situation, consider that

> today, the government can simply go to the various electronic communications service providers you use and obtain from them detailed information on your every phone call, Web search, e-mail, online chat, or credit card purchase, as well as your physical location whenever you are carrying your cell phone. Under current law, you have no constitutional right to object to the government obtaining the information from the companies that serve you. The government needs no probable cause or warrant to get it. ... And this information tells more about you than your closest family and friends know, more even than you yourself know. I forget what I was doing, where I was going, and what I was thinking about three months ago – but my smartphone, computer, and Internet account have it all recorded, in convenient, computer-searchable form. So it's now possible to obtain a detailed, intimate portrait of anyone at low cost, without any basis for suspicion. (Cole, 2015, para. 11)

In sum, while we must always acknowledge that there has not been a time in history that is free from surveillance, or from "data" for that matter, our current socio-techno-political reality is populated with a persistently functioning system that can track, store, sort, preempt, predict, locate, mine, and distribute personal and collective data in the service of profit, convenience, national security, power consolidation, intimidation, and so many others. It is, in short, an unprecedented situation of citizenship.

THE AFFECTIVE CONSEQUENCES OF
BIG DATA/SURVEILLANCE

As we might imagine, these realizations had a hugely disorganizing function in popular social thought. As commentators, social critics, and theorists began to parse through the implications of these revelations, it became clear that in the United States there was a glaring, impressive problem with the status of privacy and its opposite. Such a disorganizing function is a sticking point for social studies education because it forces us to ask a question about the affective and political conditions of living within this social reality.

When thinking about affective conditions, I am referencing a strain of social inquiry broadly named "affect theory," described by Berlant (2011) as providing

> a way to assess the disciplines of normativity in relation to the disorganized and disorganizing processes of labor, longing, memory, fantasy, grief, acting out, and sheer psychic creativity through which people (consciously, unconsciously, dynamically) renegotiate the terms of reciprocity that contour their historical situations. (p. 53)

I interpret Berlant to mean that a study of affective conditions of living means paying attention to how what passes for "normal" strikes a bargain between the desire for something else (and something better) and the comfort of those "normal" (and often disappointing) ways of being.

In the case of these new coordinates of watching and being watched – or tracking and being tracked – "what's being recorded ... [is] evidence of ... potential intentions, of who they might become. In this sense, every moment of everyday life is now an audition for citizenship, with every potential passerby a culprit" (Berlant, 2011, p. 240). This new way of being monitored disorganizes our experiences of citizenship due to the fact that our every move can be furnished as evidence of who we are and what we are up to.

Consider the reversal of terms of engagement between the citizenry and the government that Greenwald (2014) explains:

> Democracy requires accountability and consent of the governed, which is only possible if citizens know what is being done in their name. The presumption is that, with rare exception, they will know everything their political officials are doing. ... Conversely, the presumption is that the government, with rare exception, will not know anything that law-abiding citizens are doing. Transparency is for those who carry out public duties and exercise public power. Privacy is for everyone else. (p. 209)

Greenwald claims that the direction of scrutiny in a democracy should travel from governed to government. He goes on to write about how what occurs is, in fact, a reversal of these terms. The government knows everything its citizens are doing, transparently opening their lives to scrutiny, and privacy is more and more the domain of the government. Such a condition, according to Greenwald, is not democratic and is unsustainable in a society wishing to be considered as such. Similarly, Cole (2015) comments that "our governments seem to be insisting that our lives be transparent to them, while their policies remain hidden from us" (para. 38).

It is a confusing and unprecedented jumble of familiar terms, thus leading to the disorganizing sensibility Berlant identifies because the elements are both "ever-present and yet absent (unnoticed), material ... and yet ethereal ... and facilitating a safe secure environment and yet facilitating distrust (invading privacy)" (Ellis, Tucker & Harper, 2013, p. 2). These contradictions force consideration of the ways in which surveillance and Big Data operate in simultaneously multidirectional ways. What this simultaneity means is that we can never say for once and for all what the situation "is," because it will always be in flux and tension. Such complicated and ambiguous terrain adds to the sense of disorganization.

This disorganization of the ways in which we can simultaneously "know" and "not know" in relation to all kinds of situations is a process that psychoanalysts call disavowal. Disavowal explains our simultaneous knowing of horrible working conditions for the Chinese workers who produce our computers and our continuing financial support of the companies who create such conditions. Disavowal describes a defense against knowing, a desire not to know, that "leads us to know the world less and promotes conditions where we cannot solve problems that need to be solved" (Alcorn, 2010, p. 353).

Perhaps social studies education is a condition of disavowal. We can "know" that the government has worked in extra-legal ways to mine citizen data and continue to act as though the citizenry holds that government accountable. Consider that one of the "normal" ways of thinking and learning about the United States has to do with, in civics education, the rule of law and representative democracy.

In history curricula, the United States is presented within the rules of separation of powers, popular sovereignty, and the progression toward great freedom and justice for more and more people. Whatever tensions there might be between national security and privacy are considered and actively negotiated through the political process. Of course, teachers of various critical orientations problematize these narratives, but in official curricula these narratives predominate or at the very least are not called in to explicit question.

However, what the Snowden documents confront the American public with is a starkly different picture that is difficult to recognize in the curricula as it exists in national and state standards. These revelations, along with the growing capacities of people to consider what is occurring with the rise of Big Data, have given social critics material for grave concern.

What this dissonance means is that any thinking about citizenship, belonging, and participation in ways that take into account these emerging realities has been disorganized by the tensions between what has counted as "normal" and what is, in fact, no longer a realistic way to account for our social reality. Specifically, we can no longer make the same claims to privacy as we did when surveillance relied on individual agents with eyes on particular individuals or their documents.

We now live within a social fabric in which our actions live on in perpetuity in the form of digitized, identifiable metadata housed on hard drives being used for actions to which our consent is sometimes explicit, implicit, or not even given, but in all cases for which there is no legal precedent or question. In a condition of disavowal, we seem to simultaneously "know" this and proceed as though it were not the case.

Rebecca Solnit (2014) writes helpfully about how citizenship, belonging, and the very nature of our social lives become confused within the situation of surveillance and Big Data. She describes our privacy in the following way, referencing a widely publicized incident in which several celebrities had their personal photographs stolen and leaked to the public via the Web:

> Privacy is part not only of our dignity but also of our power, political and psychological. A technology government cabal that insists on more and more privacy for its own acts and less and less for ours is part and parcel of a society in which power is rapidly being stolen from citizens and the thieves are increasingly unaccountable. Jennifer Lawrence and the rest lost bodily privacy in a very high profile incident; quietly, the privacy of your mind and life – your thoughts, communications, purchases, even our Web searches and movements – has been seeping away, thanks to the collusion of tech and communications corporations with a government intent on violating all of us all the time. (p. 6)

Solnit references the ways in which privacy is a necessity for a healthy democratic life, dependent as it is on the individual's ability to participate in the difficult work of "working things out" both in private and in public as they see fit.

Of course, as we have known for some time, the dichotomy between public and private is never as clean as it may seem at first glance. However, the force of Solnit's point continues with the recognition that any individual ought to be able to research, express thoughts, even photograph her or his naked body, without it being subject to another's unconsented eyes or ears. Further, Solnit's recognition that the need for openness and transparency works unidirectionally (as Snowden claims as well) is another way in which our more traditional sensibilities about democracy no longer work in accordance with reality.

This is all to say, simply, that there is wide agreement that the social and political landscapes are changing. Bauman et al. (2014) key in on these changes following tensions and questions that the Snowden documents bring to light, namely, that they seem to confirm long-term transformations in the politics of states; in relations between states; and in the institutions and norms established in relation to democratic procedures, the rule of law, relations between state and civil society, relations between public policy and corporate or private economic interests, the acceptability of cultural norms and even concepts of subjectivity. (p. 122)

What all of this points to is a disruption of the social and political coordinates of our time and, as such, requires us to rethink our orientation to the project of social studies.

On the one hand, there is an experience of disconnection, and on the other, there is a deep feeling of connection to a sense that the system is broken. How to carry on when politics is "something overheard, encountered indirectly and unsystematically, through a kind of communication more akin to gossip than to cultivated rationality" (Berlant, 2011, p. 227)? It is not, of course, the case that there was ever a golden era of rational political decision-making. However, we do live in an era in which politics is lived and experienced in fragments and sound bites that are marketed through sophisticated targeting vis-à-vis our seemingly nonpolitical lives.

The tangle of an experience of disconnection and the simultaneous feeling of brokenness is a social studies issue for the 21st century. The tangle is an affective, nonrational, political experience. These affective concerns are, I contend, the domain of social studies education. Concretely, there are specific issues of government policy that ought to be taken up in civics class. There are the economic processes involved in the mining of data. There are the constitutional issues, the privacy issues, and the issue of how a citizen "moves" within such conditions and how public opinion is measured, swayed, disseminated, and utilized. Such lessons could likely fit into existing disciplinary ways of teaching social studies.

However, there is another register that my understanding of affect theory provides here, which is the degree to which these realities point to a disjunction between the systems we have adopted as our own and their ability to align our best ideas with reality. The significance of this idea for social studies teachers lies in the idea that citizenship is a mode of relating that is modulated by our personal investments that themselves are shaped by the "affective atmospheres of surveillance" (Ellis et al., 2013, p. 1).

IMPLICATIONS

This is an enormously complicated set of phenomena, the complexity of which I can only begin to describe here. What I hoped to do in this chapter was visit the current social thought related to the realizations of the reach and ubiquity of Big Data and surveillance and comment upon how there is a disjuncture between our current ways of approaching these issues in the curriculum and how cultural critics are understanding them.

Cultural critics and social theorists in and outside of academia are demonstrating the ways that traditional and commonsense versions of citizenship and belonging are no longer adequate ways to represent the experiences of 21st-century citizenship. Yet, these tensions have not been explored in the social studies research and practice literature. Of course, there are critical scholars and teachers who do this work in ways that do not get rendered visible, and there are likely good reasons for that invisibility, given the highly politicized nature of social studies curriculum.

However, in light of this disjuncture, social studies in the 21st century might need to change our terms of engagement in light of the changing coordinates and coordination of democracy, the status of citizenship, participation, relation, agency, and belonging. Focusing on disjuncture as a social studies method necessitates the kinds of problem-posing pedagogies advocated by so many critical scholars in and out of social studies education. Such problem-posing pedagogies must first seek to prolong the engagement with such problems before rapidly moving to "solve" them.

Further, such a view of social studies education would ask the question of not only what knowledge is worth knowing but also how that knowledge comes to have an impact on those who are tasked with the learning. This means not only focusing on what is learned but also devising ways to prompt learners to articulate the myriad ways that new ways of knowing impact already held views.

My sense is that we ought to be careful about moving too quickly to "solve" problems and "apply solutions." Britzman (2000) warns that "knowledge use is strictly defined by its capacity to be externalized and applied to others" (p. 204). In order to counter that view of knowledge, she continues, we must find ways of "turning habituated knowledge back on itself and examine its most unflattering features" (p. 204).

In this case, that means social studies educators should engage in a pedagogy that confronts students with the distance between the habituated knowledge of the dominant narratives of society and the realities of it as they emerge and unfold. Interpretations of society become provocations for students and teachers to think, inviting new modes of relation to each other, to curriculum, and to the world.

CONCLUSION

One cannot talk about Big Data and surveillance without sounding like a conspiracy theorist. The BBC documentary "The Age of Big Data" (Forthergill, 2013) begins with a story of predicting crime before it occurs.

Looking at the transcript, as well as at the scripts for movies such as "Minority Report" (Shusett, 2002), it is difficult to distinguish between the dystopian vision of Hollywood and the reality of the uses of Big Data in the present. Similarly, reading the first chapter of Greenwald's (2014) "No Place to Hide," one cannot be sure whether or not they are reading a crime novel or a recounting of a process of uncovering millions of NSA documents housed by the U.S. government.

We cannot create bogeymen out of the Big Data – we are, of course, the people who tweet, post, like, check in, make dating profiles, search for goods, buy things, watch film, make travel reservations, and sign up on list serves. However, the questions that are raised by acknowledging that things are being disorganized by unprecedented, though present and visible, systems of government and social participation are crucial for teachers and students to broach in their social studies classrooms. If not there, then where?

REFERENCES

Alcorn, M. (2010). "The desire not to know" as a challenge to teaching. *Psychoanalysis, Culture, & Society, 15*, 346–360.

Andrejevic, M. & Gates, K. (2014). Big data surveillance: Introduction. *Surveillance & Society, 12*, 185–196.

Angwin, J. (2014). *Dragnet nation: the quest for privacy, security, and freedom in a world of relentless surveillance.* New York, NY: Times Books, Henry Holt and Company

Bauman, Z., Bigo, D., Esteves, P., Guild, E., Jabri, V., Lyon, D., & Walker, R. B. J. (2014). After Snowden: Rethinking the impact of surveillance. *International Political Sociology, 8*, 121–144.

Berlant, L. G. (2011). *Cruel optimism.* Durham, NC: Duke University Press.

Berson, I., Berson, M., & Manfra, M. M. (2012). Touch, type, and transform: iPads in the social studies classroom. *Social Education, 76*, 88–91.

Bradshaw, D. & Keefer, N. E. (2007). Students and digital privacy: From social control to learned protection and online safety. *Theory & Research in Social Education, 35*, 322–332.

Britzman, D. P. (2000). Teacher education in the confusion of our times. *Journal of Teacher Education, 51*, 200–205.

Brophy, J. & Alleman, J. (2006). A reconceptualized rationale for elementary social studies. *Theory & Research in Social Education, 34*, 428–454.

Cole, D. (2015). Must counterterrorism cancel democracy? *New York Review of Books.* Retrieved from http://www.nybooks.com/articles/archives/2015/jan/08/must-counterterrorism-cancel-democracy/

Ellis, D., Tucker, I., & Harper, D. (2013). The affective atmospheres of surveillance. *Theory & Psychology, 23*, 716–731.

Education World. (2015). How to handle scandal: Edward Snowden. Retrieved from http://www.educationworld.com/a_curr/how-to-handle-scandal/edward-snowden. shtml

Forthergill, J. (Director). (2013). *The age of big data* [Motion picture]. BBC.

Giroux, H. A. (2015). Totalitarian paranoia in the post-Orwellian surveillance state. *Cultural Studies, 29*, 108–140.

Greenwald, G. (2014). *No place to hide*. New York, NY: Metropolitan-Henry Holt.

Halpern, S. (2013). Are we puppets in a wired world? *New York Review of Books*. Retrieved from http://www.nybooks.com/articles/archives/2013/nov/07/ are-we-puppets-wired-world/

Krutka, D. G. & Carpenter, J. P. (2016). Why social media must have a place in schools. *Kappa Delta Pi Record, 52*, 6–10.

National Council for the Social Studies. (2013). *College, career, and civic life C3 framework for social studies state standards*. Silver Spring, MD: National Council for the Social Studies.

Parker, W. (1996). "Advanced" ideas about democracy: Toward a pluralist conception of citizenship education. *The Teachers College Record, 98*, 104–125.

Peralta, E. (2015). Samsung's privacy policy warns customers their smart TVs are listening. Retrieved from http://www.npr.org/blogs/thetwo-way/2015/02/09/385001258/ samsungs-privacy-policy-warns-customers-their-smart-tvs-are-listening

Poitras, L. (Director). (2015). *Citizenfour* [Motion picture]. Praxis films.

Ross, E. W. (Ed.). (2006). *The social studies curriculum: Purposes, problems, and possibilities*. Albany, NY: State University of New York Press.

Solnit, R. (2014, December). Poison apples. *Harper's Monthly*, 5–7.

Shusett, R. (Director). (2002). *Minority report* [Motion picture on DVD]. Dream-Works Pictures.

Werner, W. (2000). Reading authorship into texts. *Theory & Research in Social Education, 28*, 193–219.

Westheimer, J., & Kahne, J. (2004). What kind of citizen? The politics of educating for democracy. *American Educational Research Journal, 41*, 237–269.

Wise, L (2015). Government wonders: What's in your old emails? *McLatchy Washington Bureau*. Retrieved from http://www.mcclatchydc.com/2015/02/11/256304/ government-wonders-whats-in-your.html#storylink=cpy

Chapter 9

Digital Citizenship

Social Media Discourses within Social Studies

Eric D. Moffa, Carolyn J. Brejwo, and Robert A. Waterson

During the 21st century, the innovation of social media has radically changed the way in which information is collected and disseminated. New websites offer platforms that allow individuals from around the world, or around the block, to interact in ways not possible twenty years ago. Facebook, for example, was launched in February 2004, Twitter in March 2006, Instagram in October 2010, and Snapchat in July 2011. These dates were confirmed via Wikipedia, which was launched on January 15, 2001.

In 2014 and 2015, it was estimated that more words were published via Twitter than had been published in the entire history of printed text ("Is Twitter Bad," 2014). Moreover, we discovered this estimation in a 2014 Huffington Post article rather than in the book in which it was originally published (see Rudder, 2014), demonstrating the new reality that information is often shared electronically. ~~_omnipresent_~~

As social space has moved, so too must the component of schooling that is concerned with society. The social studies curriculum must expand to address these new and ubiquitous social media discourses. This need is pressing as research suggests there are dangers in assuming that all teenagers are "digital natives" that possess innate skills and knowledge to make the most of their online experiences (boyd, 2014, p. 176).

Teenagers create media and share online content, but they do not "inherently have the knowledge or perspective to critically examine what they consume" (boyd, 2014, p. 177). In fulfillment of citizenship aims, social studies teachers should help teenagers become conscientious social media users.

This chapter examines digital citizenship via social media discourses as a critical component of social studies education. Support is provided for the inclusion of digital citizenship into the social studies curriculum by analyzing how it fulfills the goals of citizenship education, including media literacy. Emerging research on online political discourse informs the analysis. This chapter contextualizes social media by examining the polarized nature of 21st-century politics and the current online behaviors of teens and young adults. Five classroom activities are introduced to assist teachers with the inclusion of social media discourses into their classrooms.

THE IMPORTANCE OF SOCIAL MEDIA IN SOCIAL STUDIES

"Social media" describes websites that allow users to create and share content with other users. Social media, also known as online social networking, create new domains and therein new ways for people to share political knowledge and opinions. While social media holds great democratic potential, such as witnessed during the Arab Spring (Wolfsfeld, Segev, & Sheafer, 2013), some scholars suggest political discourse shared through social media may actually produce insularity and promote polarization (Himelboim, McCreery, & Smith, 2013).   *an island, alone*

In the United States post-9/11 political discourse is often anger filled and partisan (Journell, 2011); however, the intensity of these political messages matters greatly because messages are broadcasted to a much larger audience than in the pre-Internet era. Adolescents step into this polarized online environment through their engagement with social media and receive messages that likely influence their opinions about specific social issues and the nature of political discourse (Levy, Journell, He, & Towns, 2015). Perhaps most significantly, the messages adolescents receive through social media contribute to an understanding of their society's political culture. In this way, social media acts as an agent of political socialization.

Due to the power of social media discourses to transmit political culture (including its polarized ideologies) and its ability to simultaneously promote democratic engagement and insularity, educators must learn how to best incorporate this new space into the curriculum. In turn, social studies students should learn to confront bias and political discourse in de-polarizing ways (Hess & McAvoy, 2015).

Since democratic life is played out in the everyday actions of citizens, students should see their contributions to online social networks as a democratic activity. Teaching how to discuss political issues face-to-face is already an important part of the social studies curriculum (Parker & Hess, 2001), but now the curriculum must be expanded to address online discussions and the interpretation of online political messages. The modern citizen is, in part, a *digital citizen.*

DIGITAL CITIZENSHIP AND THE SOCIAL STUDIES CURRICULUM

Collier (2009) defines digital citizenship as, "critical thinking and ethical choices about the content and impact on oneself, others, and one's community of what one sees, says, and produces with media, devices and technologies" (para. 2). Simply stated, digital citizenship involves considering how one uses online mediums to execute their social and political roles. Every time a person engages with others on the Internet, they are responsible for what they say and do in that community. Teenagers need guidance negotiating this new space (boyd, 2014).

Since citizenship is a contested concept with multiple dimensions (Groen, 2014), the roles and expectations manifested through people's online activity are diverse and unsettled. Yet, the convergence of people's identities, values, and behaviors on social media websites recreates democratic relationships. Through the recreation of these relationships, online mediums simultaneously redefine citizenship and restructure the political landscape by providing a new arena for political thought and a greater audience for sociopolitical messages and actions.

The Internet provides new ways to execute traditional citizenship roles while also enabling innovative citizenship actions and interactions. To ensure democracy is enhanced and not diminished through online mediums requires that people possess egalitarian dispositions that respect others' political voices. Respectful online discourse should be the norm, not the exception. Teaching students expectations for digital citizenship is the responsibility of social studies teachers as they are charged with the mission of educating society's youth to be "component and responsible" citizens (National Council for the Social Studies [NCSS], 2013).

Many schools and schools districts presently teach constructive online behavior in the form of character education, such as anticyberbullying campaigns (see STOMP Out Bullying, 2016; StopBullying.gov, 2016). These campaigns instruct students to be thoughtful in their online interactions with one another, but they fail to address political talk. Because political talk is contentious, we posit students be taught skills to use social media for democratic deliberations.

Specifically, students must learn how to engage in constructive political conversations and how to interpret biased messages. Also, students should know how to use the Internet to research candidates, find information to clarify their positions on controversial social issues, and share their informed and reasoned opinions on social media websites in respectful ways. Executing these skills exemplify the actions of a responsible digital citizen.

NCSS's (2013) *College, Career, and Civic (C3) Framework* provides implicit support for incorporating social media discourses into the curriculum by recommending each student be able to gather and evaluate information from multiple types of sources. Since information is often shared online in the 21st century, today's citizens must be prepared with critical thinking skills to effectively participate in online arenas of civic life. Furthermore, scholars suggest that practice in sharing political thoughts is a critical part of social studies education (Levy et al., 2015).

In many ways, teaching about political discourses on social networking sites extends upon the already established premise of teaching media literacy through the social studies curriculum (Mason & Metzger, 2012). Stein and Prewett (2009) recommend social studies teachers incorporate media literacy "to hone students' abilities to evaluate media as evidentiary sources, to identify bias in mediated constructions of history and society, to understand how media frame issues, to separate fact from opinion and to assess the credibility of media sources" (p. 132). We theorize that the increase in content created and shared by individuals on social media websites means conceptions of media literacy must broaden to include social media discourses.

Several social studies scholars recognize the potential of social media to act as a new arena for democratic dialogue. Journell, Ayers, and Beeson (2013), for example, studied students using Twitter to actively comment during a televised vice presidential debate. The researchers suggest that using social media as a learning tool can eliminate geographic boundaries and encourage otherwise reticent students to join in political discussions; however, they also found students tweeted politically intolerant commentary during the debate by making fun of candidates.

Furthermore, students tweeted generalities without providing any support or reasons for their comments. In this aspect, Twitter failed to foster substantive political dialogue. The authors suggest "Tweeting for academic purposes is a skill that needs to be taught, similar to the way academic face-to-face discussions require different skills than casual conversations" (p. 477).

Teaching the specific skill of tweeting induces the need for students to possess a larger understanding of political interactions in online social networks. Students hold potential to both contribute to online political discourse by creating media and consume messages produced by others. This dual role as media makers and media consumers requires discernment, which demands a deep knowledge of politics and government, media messages, political ideologies, and political discourse. As Journell (2011) wrote:

> Students run the risk of being inundated with political information every time they turn on a television or log onto the Internet, and if schools are truly responsible for preparing students for life in the 21st century, then a critical understanding of politics and political media is needed. (p. 11)

Due to the presence and power of online political messages converging with the goals of media literacy and citizenship education, we believe it is essential in this evolving digital era to make social media and digital citizenship part of the 21st-century social studies curriculum.

SOCIAL MEDIA AND THE 21ST-CENTURY POLITICAL CLIMATE

The terrorist attacks of September 11, 2001, altered political discourse in the United States. After the attacks, patriotism soared in the Unites States and support increased for unilateral foreign policy actions (Pew Research Center, 2002). Apple (2002) raised concerns about the dangerous effects of educating students within a culture of enforced nationalism that emerged in the wake of 9/11. Though patriotic fervor increased, the nation simultaneously developed a bellicose partisanship and polarization (Baum & Groeling, 2008; Journell, 2011).

Increased partisanship can be seen in Congress, yet more relevantly, an ideological divide is seen among millennials nationwide (Harvard University Institute of Politics, 2013). A national survey of 18- to 29-year-olds found at no time have young Democrats and Republicans been more divided on President Obama's job performance. Results show 85% of Democrats approve of the job the president is doing, while only 11% of Republicans say the same. Also relevant to understanding millennials' political beliefs, only one quarter of millennials say that the nation is headed in the right direction, suggesting the group entrusted with carrying the nation's political culture forward holds a pessimistic view about the future.

Increased partisanship and polarized ideologies appear to exacerbate in online arenas. While online, many Americans do not seek out perspectives that differ from their own (Messing & Westwood, 2014). Some people block friends on social media sites so they will not have to see opposing political views (Rainie & Smith, 2012). Also, when political conversations do occur on social media sites, a majority of the comments are supportive of the original post (Kushin & Kitchener, 2009).

The insular-enabling nature of online access to political information, paired with the post-9/11 heightened sense of patriotism, may result in the belief that individuals' personal views make them the "right" kind of citizen, and people opposed to their views are the "wrong" kind of citizen. Polarization of this sort may be harmful to democratic processes as constructive dialogue and compromise are unlikely. Additionally, this online insularity parallels actual life trends as research suggests Americans are self-selecting where to live, clustering by ideological similarities (Bishop, 2008).

Students step into a polarized political environment via social media where they encounter ideological-driven rhetoric, powerful images and symbols, and misleading texts – and no direct assistance in making sense of this onslaught of information. This is unlike traditional political socialization where parents guide children through the political landscape during dinner table conversations.

While perhaps ideologically homogenous, information and beliefs learned around the dinner table are tied deeply to associations with specific people. Children know their family members and can recognize their foibles. On the Internet, information and beliefs are depersonalized. They are often presented as "truth" without the corresponding experience of having close associations with the person behind the opinion or the benefit of interacting in a shared physical space over time.

If children are not equipped with deep knowledge of politics and thinking skills to evaluate biased messages, their experiences on social media may negatively affect attitudes toward their political community or understandings of their society's political culture. Every student needs to learn to search out different perspectives to moderate the negative aspects of hyper-partisanship, yet some teachers may be afraid of having students with divergent views engage in political discourse (Levy et al., 2015).

While the literature on best practices is clear that discussion of controversial public issues is a valuable classroom activity, the practice seems to be rare. For example, Kahne, Rodriguez, Smith, and Thiede (2000) found that in 80% of social studies classrooms in Chicago, no social problems were discussed, and more recent studies on schools in other parts of the United States have generated similar findings (e.g., Kahne & Middaugh, 2009).

Another relevant component of the 21st-century political climate is the "civic opportunity gap" that exists between people with college experience and people without any college experience (Levine, 2009). From 2000 to 2008 there was an increase in youth voters in the United States, but almost all were college graduates or young adults with some college experience.

Approximately half of all young people in the nation have never been to college, and these individuals are less likely to vote, volunteer, belong to civic groups, and join unions than their college-educated peers (Flanagan, Levine, & Settersten, 2009). Yet, these individuals are still likely to participate in social media discourses as both consumers and creators of content. In this case, social media acts as a prominent medium for individuals that lack traditional efficacy in politics. Social media holds potential to inform (or misinform) noncollege-educated citizens about politics, therefore increasing the importance that K-12 educators place on it.

Since social studies teachers are already charged with development of civic ideas in students (NCSS, 2010), tackling new platforms for political messages and sources of political ideology becomes vital to fulfilling the mission of citizenship education. Today's students must learn how to evaluate information, identify bias, and prepare for (physical and digital) life as citizens in their community, nation, and world. The role of the "digital citizen" requires as much consideration as the traditional role of the "civic actor."

SOCIAL MEDIA AND YOUNG PEOPLE

Examining the ways teens and young adults use social media strengthens the case for including it in the social studies curriculum. A Pew Research Center study revealed 81% of American teens use some kind of social media, and of those teens, 94% had a Facebook account. Also, teens frequently engage with social media with 75% checking a social media site every day (Madden et al., 2013), and due to mobile phone technology, 24% report being on the Internet "almost constantly" (Lenhart, 2015, p. 2). This level of involvement with social media suggests teens are exposed to online content, produced and/ or shared by others in their networks, on a regular basis.

boyd (2014) suggests teens "create their own publics" online. Using social media, they form communities with their peers that act as new public spaces instead of competing with adults in preexisting ones. "Teens want access to publics to see and be seen, to socialize, and to feel as if they have the freedom to explore a world beyond the heavily constrained one shaped by parents and school" (boyd, 2014, pp. 201–202). While not normally political, at times, teenagers use social media to make political commentary and organize acts of protest that adults may deem unacceptable (boyd, 2014).

One study examined the most common sources that people access for news on government and politics (Mitchell, Gottfried, & Matsa, 2015). When asked to select from a list of 42 common news sources, Facebook came in at the top of the list for millennials (61%). The next closest news source for their age group was CNN (44%). However, prior to selecting from the list of 42 sources, participants were asked to separately name their main source for news on government and politics and only 3% of millennials stated Facebook.

This suggests getting news on Facebook is largely an incidental experience. Users do not directly associate Facebook with the acquisition of political news. Also relevant, 24% of millennials reported that over half of the posts they see on Facebook are related to government and politics, and many of these posts are not in line with their views.

The way young people encounter news today is drastically different than previous generations. Young people encounter online information produced by a variety of news agencies and websites, trustworthy or untrustworthy, as well as created and/or shared by friends, family, and other acquaintances. Placing this type of information-sharing in a historic context, Demby (2015) suggests that social media makes the redistribution of current events more immediate than past decades, in essence, instantly producing a historical record that informs citizens.

To exemplify this phenomenon, Demby states that very few people remember the 1985 MOVE bombing. The Philadelphia-based MOVE organization is a radical, largely African American group that fuses religious and political themes, including deep commitment to ecology and Black power. Its name is not an acronym, but signifies the organization's commitment to radical change (Wall, 2002). In 1985, police dropped explosives into a West Philadelphia house occupied by members of MOVE, killing 11 people and starting a fire that destroyed 65 homes. If social media existed then, it would have made the event immediately known with information shared and discussed online and accessible to the nation's teachers. Demby (2015) writes:

> If the MOVE bombing were to happen today, bystanders would be furiously uploading videos to YouTube, spawning Twitter hashtags and interconnected protests in cities around the country. CNN would be camped out in West Philly for weeks, to say nothing of the countless think-pieces. If MOVE happened today, it might be quickly folded into the classroom, as has happened with other recent incidents of police violence. Teachers have all the materials at their fingertips: clips from livestreams, links to mainstream news articles and personal blogs, embeddable tweets, and so on. Back in the mid-80s, you'd have to wait around for the inevitable Frontline documentary or for an academic to publish a book. History gets commodified and redistributed much more quickly today. (para. 10–11)

This change in how people disseminate and access news requires teachers to be facile and aware of social media chatter so that they can be prepared to have critical conversations in their classrooms. Unfortunately, the quickness of this commodified historical record creates misinformation as messages get politically spun or taken out of context. When young people encounter this type of news via social media, they are frequently exposed to biased messages in the forms of political-based memes.

Memes are photos, videos, or texts, often photoshopped or edited, shared rapidly by Internet users. They are a phenomenon made possible by the interconnectivity produced in social media platforms. Yet, memes and other online snippets are often shallow and misleading. Even presidential candidates in the 2016 primary election campaign have taken to Twitter and Instagram to share short videos and photoshopped images that degrade their opponents (Sanders, 2015). The nature of political information young people receive through social media websites begs for educators to assist them in developing intelligence to select, interpret, and challenge these messages.

For social studies teachers, the overriding concern is that students not isolate their opinions before exploring contradictory and challenging viewpoints.

Unfortunately, much of online political information comes in messages that lack depth. Political posts on social media are shared from "friends" or people with whom users may have exclusively digital relationships. Thirty-three percent of teens, for example, report being friends on Facebook with someone they have never met face-to-face (Madden et al., 2013).

The veracity of information received on social media may be secondary to the acceptance of it based on its relational presentation. Additionally, the very presentation of it may lead students to select or deselect relationships based on agreement with individuals rather than the presentation of different perspectives.

Research shows 24% of Facebook users have hidden, blocked, "defriended," or stopped following someone because they disagree with their online political statements (Mitchell, Gottfried, Kiley, & Matsa, 2014). Online relationships.become defined by agreement with a smaller set of political beliefs, narrowing the discussion into a personal echo-chamber.

LEARNING OBJECTIVES FOR DIGITAL CITIZENSHIP

Competent participation in social media discourses requires students possess specific skills, knowledge, and dispositions. Since digital citizenship expands upon critical thinking and ethical choices that are already part of traditional citizenship (Ribble, 2012), existing citizenship aims can be surveyed and adapted for their use in digital spaces. For example, to develop students' abilities for democratic deliberations, Hess and McAvoy (2015) suggest teachers should aim to teach students political equality, tolerance, autonomy, fairness, engagement, and political literacy. These aims provide the basis to craft new learning objectives for improved online interactions.

Yet, online interactions generate several additional considerations. First, anonymity and/or physical distance between political discussants may obfuscate the human element of political discourse, leading to reduced civility or misinterpretations of meaning. Second, the visual presentation of online messages presents the need for competency in the analysis and critique of varied media sources. Third, being media creators with the power to contribute more broadly to public dialogue heightens the importance of students' commitment to and displays of democratic principles like tolerance and equality.

Building on Hess and McAvoy's (2015) aims for the political classroom, Table 9.1 provides a summary list of learning objectives for digital citizenship. Also, the corresponding activity for each objective is listed. The next section of this chapter describes the activities in full.

Table 9.1   Learning Objectives for Digital Citizenship

Learning Objectives	Corresponding Activity
Think critically and analytically to uncover bias in online political messages.	Truth behind the memes
When creating social media posts, display substance that contributes to shared understandings of the issue and adheres to the principles of tolerance and political equality.	Class blogs/discussion forums
Show fairness when discussing controversial political issues online and a willingness to seek solutions that promote the common good.	Script creation
Recognize limitations of online mediums such as the effects of creating and consuming short snippets of information and the lack of shared physical space.	Historic Twitter debates
When creating visual images or other social media posts, demonstrate knowledge of the issues and commitments to use reasons and evidence to back up your claims.	Instagram images

TEACHING FOR DIGITAL CITIZENSHIP

This section shares five learning activities that help student become digital citizens who recreate positive democratic life in online spaces. The activities strive to deepen learning of both social studies content and knowledge of the nature of political discourse and social media. The activities demonstrate how to discuss political controversies in productive ways online by clearly stating positions, supporting positions with evidence, and working to extend understanding of social issues and the values underlying them. Through these activities, students will be better prepared to interpret the political messages they encounter and engage in media creation that produces constructive democratic relationships.

The learning activities are best implemented in secondary classrooms where students are more likely to be of the age where they are exposed to online political messages via social media sites. Each activity could stand on its own as a lesson on digital citizenship or it could be infused into a lesson on another social issue. Teachers can likely implement each activity in one to two class meetings. Also, due to some classrooms' lack of access to technology, as well as schools that block social media sites on their Internet servers, considerations are made about how these activities can be adapted into traditional classrooms.

The five learning activities for digital citizenship include:

The Truth Behind the Memes – This activity teaches students to thoughtfully interpret misleading online political messages. Teachers should select political memes or other viral online content that depict a specific political issue in a simplistic, biased, or partisan manner, and electronically project the meme or print and distribute the meme to students.

Teachers can find political memes by searching Google images or websites (e.g., facebook.com/ThePoliticalMemes, PolitcalMemes.com, MemeCenter.com), but they should be aware that some of the content of these sites are not suitable for students. Teachers should use their discretion to select appropriate memes that deal with a relevant political issue. Teachers can then guide students as they research the hidden sides of the issue. Teachers should ask students:

- What information does the meme provide?
- How can we discover if this information is accurate?
- What questions does this meme raise but not answer?
- What was the intention of the author of this meme?
- What information may challenge this meme's message?
- How does this meme (mis)represent the issue?
- What is the opposite position from this meme?
- What position does the author not want us to consider as valid?

Students can use fact-checking websites (e.g., FactCheck.org, PolitiFact.com, Snopes.com) in their research, in addition to other relevant source material (e.g., textbooks, news articles, op-eds, video clips).

Class Blogs or Discussion Forums – To assist students in positive and intelligent online media creation, teachers can construct password-protected blogs or discussion forums for class use. On these sites, teachers can prompt students to answer open-ended questions about commonly consumed materials (e.g., news articles, document excerpts, video clips). For example, teachers can post a link to a news clip about the Syrian refugee crisis and ask students to respond to the clip with their opinions about whether or not the United States should accept refugees.

Students may complete their responses during a class meeting or outside of class time. Since students' divergent political opinions are likely to be exposed, teachers should provide guidelines and expectations for online discussion prior to this activity. These guidelines should emphasize civility, tolerance, and political equality. Students should adhere to these guidelines by deliberating with respect for differing opinions and values.

The teacher works as a moderator, focusing on the development of democratic deliberation. Under the teacher's guidance, students can engage in thoughtful online dialogue, sharing multiple perspectives on issues and backing up their claims with support from the document or other sources. This activity allows students to practice digital citizenship in a friendly, authentic online environment. Students can display substantive knowledge in their posts and work toward shared understandings of the issue. Furthermore, research suggests online discussions may encourage the involvement of vocally reticent students (Flynn, 2009).

Script Creation – Teachers can assign students to groups and assign them the task of creating a script that displays several online characters discussing a controversial political issue. The script could be created electronically or on paper designed to resemble the layout of a social media site. The teacher may choose for students to portray themselves, contemporary political figures, or generalized citizens (e.g., a struggling farmer, a retired person, a college student). For example, the teacher may ask students to develop a script where characters discuss a state legislative proposal to adopt or reject "right to work" laws.

Students should research the issue to gather information on opposing viewpoints to utilize in their scripts. This activity encourages students to think deeply about an issue, take on a perspective that differs from their own, and model civil online discourse. Students' scripts should demonstrate fairness by seeking a solution that promotes the common good. This requires students to "habitually weigh self-interest against the interest of others and seriously consider who is being asked to sacrifice within each policy option" (Hess & McAvoy, 2015, p. 156).

Since political insularity is present in online environments (Messing & Westwood, 2014), this activity acts to diversify viewpoints while simultaneously advancing the practice of online civil discourse. Also, students receive the added benefit of working cooperatively on the project – something that inherently builds democratic dispositions (Hendrix, 1996).

Historic Twitter Debates – Teachers can quickly turn any history lesson into a lesson on modern social media by asking students to encapsulate viewpoints on historic controversies into 140-character tweets. Using paper and pencil, students can write period-accurate tweets to answer a historic question, such as "Should the United States enter the Great War?" Tweets can be physically exchanged between students, and they can read and respond to one another using the "@" and "#" symbols that are commonly used on real Twitter exchanges. The "@" symbol is used to reply or tag a specific person in a post. The "#" symbol, called a hashtag by online users, is used to identify a message for a particular topic.

For an additional challenge, students can fulfill the role of a historical figure during the Twitter debate. This activity enables students to engage in political dialogue using the framework of a social networking site, but carry out the dialogue in an offline academic setting. After several rounds of tweets, students can reflect on their exchanges, including the difficulty encountered when attempting to discuss complex issues in short snippets. Other scholars have been successful when implementing similar history-based Twitter lessons (see Krutka & Milton, 2013; Lee et al., 2012).

Instagram Images – Mimicking Instagram images, teachers can ask students to develop persuasive memes that address issues and use facts rather than hyperbole or extrapolation. The facts should be sourced to teach students the responsibility of using evidence to support their claims. Students can use their artistic abilities, in print or by means of photo-editing software, to teach each other about political issues or personas.

By using the Instagram form, students learn how to responsibly engage in social media discourse using words and images to convey political opinions without resorting to bias and misinformation. In this activity, it is important for students to display their knowledge of an issue and an awareness of how the issue fits into competing ideologies. Accompanying their development of memes, teachers should ask students to explain their creative choices, orally or in writing, to produce student contemplation about the roles and responsibilities of being media creators.

CONCLUSION

Social media has changed the way citizens relate to each other as members of a political community. Young people come to understand their society's political culture by the messages encountered through social media. These messages are often negative, shallow, and polarizing. Social studies educators have the responsibility to prepare students to confront, question, and challenge unhealthy political communication wherever it may be encountered.

The advent of social media in the 21st century demands social studies educators explicitly address it as a new and powerful medium for citizens' thoughts and actions. The social studies curriculum must better prepare students with the skills and knowledge to interpret misleading Internet messages, participate in respectful and thoughtful online political dialogue, and create social media content that enhances, and does not diminish, democratic relationships.

REFERENCES

Apple, M. (2002). Patriotism, pedagogy, and freedom: On the educational meanings of September 11. *Teachers College Record, 104*, 1760–1772.

Baum, M. A. & Groeling, T. (2008). New media and the polarization of American political discourse. *Political Communication, 25*, 345–365.

Bishop, B. (2008). *The big sort: Why the clustering of like-minded America is tearing us apart.* Boston, MA: Houghton Mifflin.

boyd, d. (2014). *It's complicated: The social lives of networked teens.* New Haven, CT: Yale University Press. Retrieved from http://www.danah.org/books/ItsComplicated.pdf

Collier, A. (2009, September 15). A definition of digital literacy & citizenship. ConnectSafely. Retrieved from http://www.connectsafely. org/a-definition-of-digital-literacy-a-citizenship-571/

Demby, G. (2015, May 13). I'm from Philly. 30 years later I'm still trying to make sense of the MOVE bombing. *National Public Radio.* Retrieved from http://www.npr.org/sections/codeswitch/2015/05/13/406243272/im-from-philly-30-years-later-im-still-trying-to-make-sense-of-the-move-bombing

Flanagan, C., Levine, P., & Settersten, R. (2009). Civic engagement and the changing transition to adulthood. Medford, MA: CIRCLE. Retrieved from http://www.civicyouth.org/PopUps/ChangingTransition.pdf

Flynn, N. K. (2009). Toward democratic discourse: Scaffolding student-led discussions in the social studies. *Teachers College Record, 111,* 2021–2054.

Groen, M. (2014). Literacy and the meaning of citizenship in American education. *American Educational History Journal, 41,* 77–91.

Harvard University Institute of Politics. (2013, April 30). Survey of young American's attitudes towards politics and public service: 23rd edition. Retrieved from http://www.iop.harvard.edu/sites/default/files_new/spring_poll_13_Exec_Summary.pdf

Hendrix, J. C. (1996). Cooperative learning: Building a democratic community. *Clearing House, 69,* 333–336.

Hess, D. E. & McAvoy, P. (2015). *The political classroom: Evidence and ethics in democratic education.* New York, NY: Routledge.

Himelboim, I., McCreery, S., & Smith, M. (2013). Birds of a feather tweet together: Integrating network and content analyses to examine cross-ideology exposure on twitter. *Journal of Computer-Mediated Communication, 18,* 40–60.

Is Twitter Bad for Language? Statistical Analysis Says No (New Book). (2014, September 10). *Huffington Post.* Retrieved from http://www.huffingtonpost.com/2014/09/10/twitter-language-book_n_5786556.html

Journell, W. (2011). The challenges of political instruction in a post-9/11 United States. *The High School Journal, 95,* 3–14.

Journell, W., Ayers, C. A., & Beeson, M. W. (2013). Joining the conversation: Twitter as a tool for student political engagement. *The Educational Forum, 77,* 466–480.

Kahne, J. & Middaugh, E. (2009). Democracy for some: The civic opportunity gap in high school. In J. Youniss & P. Levine (Eds.), *Engaging young people in civic life* (pp. 29–58). Nashville, TN: Vanderbilt University Press.

Kahne, J., Rodriguez, M., Smith, B., & Thiede, K. (2000). Developing citizens for democracy? Assessing opportunities to learn in Chicago's social studies classrooms. *Theory & Research in Social Education, 28,* 311–338.

Krutka, D. G. & Milton, M. K. (2013). The Enlightenment meets Twitter: Using social media in the social studies classroom. *Ohio Social Studies Review, 50*(2), 22–29.

Kushin, M. J. & Kitchener, K. (2009). Getting political on social network sites: Exploring online political discourse on Facebook. *First Monday, 14*(11). Retrieved from http://firstmonday.org/article/view/2645/2350

Lenhart, A. (2015). Teens, social media, technology overview 2015. *Pew Research Center*. Retrieved from http://www.pewinternet.org/2015/04/09/teens-social-media-technology-2015/

Lee, V. R., Shelton, B. R., Walker, A., Caswell, T., & Jensen, M. (2012). Retweeting history: Exploring the intersection of microblogging and problem-based learning for historical reenactments. In K. K. Seo & D. A. Pellegrino (Eds.) *Designing problem-driven instruction with online social media* (pp. 23–40). Charlotte, NC: Information Age Publishing.

Levine, P. (2009). The civic opportunity gap. *Educational Leadership, 66*, 20–25.

Levy, B., Journell, W., He, Y., & Towns, B. (2015). Students blogging about politics: A study of students' political engagement and a teacher's pedagogy during a semester-long political blog assignment. *Computers and Education, 88*, 64–71.

Madden, M., Lenhart, A., Cortesi, S., Gasser, U., Duggan, M., Smith, A. & Beaton, M. (2013). Teens, social media, and privacy. *Pew Research Center*. Retrieved from http://www.pewinternet.org/2013/05/21/teens-social-media-and-privacy/

Mason, L. & Metzger, S. (2012). Reconceptualizing media literacy in the social studies: A pragmatist critique of the NCSS position statement on media literacy. *Theory & Research in Social Education, 40*, 436–455.

Messing, S. & Westwood, S. (2014). Selective exposure in the age of social media: Endorsements trump partisan source affiliation when selecting news online. *Communication Research, 41*, 1042–1063.

Mitchell, A., Gottfried, J., Kiley, J., & Matsa, K. E. (2014). Political polarization & media habits. *Pew Research Center*. Retrieved from http://www.journalism.org/2014/10/21/political-polarization-media-habits/

Mitchell, A., Gottfried, J., & Matsa, K. E. (2015). Millennials and political news: Social media - the local tv for the next generation? *Pew Research Center*. Retrieved from http://www.journalism.org/2015/06/01/millennials-political-news/

National Council for the Social Studies (2010). *National curriculum standards for social studies: A framework for teaching, learning, and assessment*. Silver Spring, MD: NCSS.

National Council for the Social Studies (2013). *The college, career, and civic life (c3) framework for social studies state standards: Guidance for enhancing the rigor of k-12 civics, economics, geography, and history*. Silver Spring, MD: NCSS.

Parker, W. C. & Hess, D. (2001). Teaching with and for discussion. *Teaching and Teacher Education, 17*, 273–289.

Pew Research Center. (2002). One year later: New Yorkers more troubled, Washingtonians more on edge. Retrieved from http://www.people-press.org/2002/09/05/one-year-later-new-yorkers-more-troubled-washingtonians-more-on-edge/

Rainie, L. & Smith, A. (2012). Social networking sites and politics. *Pew Research Center*. Retrieved from http://www.pewinternet.org/2012/03/12/social-networking-sites-and-politics/

Rudder, C. (2014). *Dataclysm: Love, sex, race and identity- What our online lives tell us about our offline selves*. New York, NY: Broadway Books.

Sanders, S. (2015, September 3). Instagram: The new political war room?. *National Public Radio*. Retrieved from http://www.npr.org/sections/itsallpolitics/2015/09/03/436923997/instagram-the-new-political-war-room

Stein, L. & Prewett, A. (2009). Media literacy education in the social studies: Teacher perceptions and curricular challenges. *Teacher Education Quarterly, 36*, 131–148.

STOMP Out Bullying. (2016). About STOMP out bullying. Retrieved from http://www.stompoutbullying.org/index.php/about/

StopBullying.gov. (2016). About us. Retrieved from http://www.stopbullying.gov/about-us/index.html

Wall, D. (2002). Move. In J. Barry & E. Frankland (Eds.), *International encyclopedia of environmental politics* (pp. 324–325). London, United Kingdom: Routledge.

Wolfsfeld, G., Segev, E., & Sheafer, T. (2013). Social media and the Arab spring: Politics comes first. *The International Journal of Press/Politics, 18*, 115–137.

Chapter 10

Financial Literacy in the Wake of the Great Recession

Thomas A. Lucey, Mary Frances Agnello,
and James D. Laney

Nearly a decade and a half into the 21st century, the United States, the most affluent country in the history of the world, continues to experience a widening gap between rich and poor. According to the U.S. Census Bureau (2014), between 2000 and 2011 the median household net worth between the highest quintile and the second lowest quintile widened from 39.8 to 86.8 times. This wealth gap portends social challenges given correlations between the degree of wealth disparities and social wellness (Wilkinson & Pickett, 2011). The greater the differences between rich and poor in a country or state, the less the population experiences personal security and life satisfaction in general.

In this chapter, we observe that philosophies that undergird financial literacy teaching reinforce a system of control and judgment, and we present another way of thinking about financial literacy based on principles of compassion. We acknowledge that this interpretation of a compassionate approach to financial literacy raises potential objections from many financial education scholars; however, we think it necessary to provide balance to existing financial literacy endeavors that employ a focus on financial wealth.

Through an approach that balances this structure through principles of care and compassion, we believe it possible to educate a critically thinking citizenry that interprets financial decisions through a humanitarian lens and resists lifestyles controlled by corporate executives. In classrooms we may acknowledge that through the presentation of "commonsense" economic notions, the individual stories of those exploited for economic gain become lost in what have come to be accepted as success stories justified in the name of manifest destiny and national development (Bell, 2010).

The arguments presented here build from literature (e.g., Arthur, 2012; Lucey, 2012; Lucey, Agnello, & Laney, 2015; McGregor, 2010) that challenges conventional wealth accumulation conceptions of financial literacy founded upon notions of choice. It considers recent psychological and child development literature (e.g., LeDoux, 2002; Narvaez, Panksepp, Schore, & Gleason, 2013; Panksepp & Biven, 2012) that associates affect and cognition to posit that all financial decisions involve emotional foundations unaddressed by the existing repertoire of financial literacy approaches.

For example, a person may consider the patterns of emotional influences that prompt one to purchase a can of Coke or to purchase a car. Rather than considering such transactions solely as activities toward personal fulfillment, he or she may consider whether he or she may truly benefit from the purchase of consumer goods that corporately defined personal lifestyles.

Because financial decision-making relates to an emotionally rooted process, social studies educators may consider how to build financial education efforts from these care-based pedagogies. Such efforts may use various art forms, case studies, and class discussions to prompt students to consider how selflessness represents an element of sound financial practice. These types of instructional strategies seek to balance existing wealth accumulation approaches with strategies for management of financial resources informed by stewardship and care.

The basis for this balanced approach lies within literature that concerns foundations of child psychology, moral development, and citizenship. We encourage the tempering of a choice-based framework for economic and financial literacy by reconsidering the causes of individuals' and groups' poor financial decisions. Finally, we describe possible points of contention regarding contextual and compassionate views of financial literacy, offering them as grounds for classroom discussions.

ECONOMIC THEORY

We begin with the claim that two foundational notions to economic theory (as conceptualized by some industrialized countries) relate to the ideas of choice and incentives (Agnello & Lucey, 2008). According to these precepts, people make economic choices that affect their life conditions, and every decision involves an evaluation of its costs and benefits. If classrooms are to view choice and incentives from the perspective of the decision-maker, they need to consider the perspectives of other parties to the decision. This position relates to the equal human value of each person.

We would argue that a balanced accounting of choice and incentives includes the following ideas:

- An economic-based rationale provides a limited decision-making perspective.

- Economic choices develop beyond decision-makers' control.
- Other parties may manipulate the availability or knowledge of costs and benefits.

The economic-based rationale holds that individuals make economic decisions that provide them with the most benefit. The *Prudent Man Rule*, which guides financiers in making choices, requires making decisions based on the preservation of capital. This philosophy implies that money has more value than people. It signifies further that even if people are harmed by the investment decision, one should avoid the loss of money in making financial choices because one's economic wherewithal is the basis upon which all decisions flow.

A balance for these views may be found in those described by Adam Smith in his *Theory of Moral Sentiments*. Smith (1976) observed the necessity of social interaction in supporting one's personal welfare and claims that through socialization people learn to empathize with each other, sharing in their successes and challenges. Smith recognized the value of caring for others more than controlling financial resources:

> The person who has lost his whole fortune, if he is in health, feels nothing in his body. What he suffers is from the imagination only, which represents to him the loss of his dignity, neglect of his friends, contempt from his enemies, dependence, want and misery, coming fast upon him. (p. 28)

For Smith, financial loss, although it may present a challenge to one's social status, does not change the nature of the person. Smith observed that when society becomes too obsessed with financial accumulation, it loses sight of the importance of compassion for others, making it necessary to examine its social values. The *Prudent Man Rule* provides a rationale for behavior that prioritizes money over people. It attempts to separate the emotion of care for others' points of view from financial decision-making to instill a principle of control or self-interest.

Our second idea holds that patterns of economic choices relate to the social and economic environments and that one does not select these conditions in which one originates. To put it differently, one does not merit his or her social origin. This idea undergirds an alternative explanation of costs and benefits for indentured servants in colonial America as presented by Schug and Wood (2011).

Their presentation describes the incentives for servanthood as relating to prospects for future land ownership. The ownership of land for the indentured servants represented an incentive for fulfillment of employment obligations. Servants would earn or merit the land as a consequence for their performing the tasks assigned by their employer. In other words, the employer controlled the conditions under which indentured servants could access the land.

The alternative explanation could interpret the arrangement through a different lens, that of social conditioning through manipulation of resource access. Interpreting the environment as a matter of choice and incentive presumes the right of landowners to make land access conditional. A broader vision of the indentured servant arrangement interprets the relationship as a matter of selfishness in which those with prior access contextualize the value of their servants in terms of the work performed rather than the individual stories of who they are. It also observes the perspective of the indigenous cultures, who lost control of the land, in part, through massive smallpox epidemics caused by immune systems insufficient to offer protection from the European diseases (Loewen, 2007).

Another assumption of traditional economics education is that of choice. A question of choice intimates the freedom to decide which economic action to take. The employment of a choice-based explanation for economic/financial decision-making relies upon the premise that every decision made in one's life involves contexts of one's own selection. While the reader of this chapter may readily acknowledge that

- She or he chose the institution that she or he attends or in which he or she practices
- She or he chose to work hard to earn her or his grades in school
- She or he even chose whether or not to read this chapter, the environments that provided the resources for these decisions were not of her or his choosing.

We also think it likely that the reader of this chapter did not choose her or his parents or the time and place of conception or birth. These events, which are not of one's choosing, have a great influence on one's developmental contexts and the patterns of choices that one makes.

Rather than living lives earned by "good" decisions, people live existences based on the conditions constructed in a larger social context and encountered at a certain place and time. This notion of "habitus" interprets being as temporary placements in our global environment (Bourdieu & Passeron, 1977). Life decisions relate to the extent this experience involves developing personal control of resources and those of our companions and familial descendants. Yet, perhaps more importantly, life decisions also depend on the extent to which an encountered experience involves compassionate management of resources grounded in empathy for others whose circumstances are less fortunate.

The field of economics represents a study that concerns both individual behavior and patterns of group interaction (Hudick, 2011). When classrooms do not provide a complete accounting of all factors that influence decisions, they distort the conditions under which choices occur, offering limited explanations for economic decisions and predicaments of those individuals making decisions within those systems. Regardless of the instructional strategy employed, classrooms may offer alternative explanations for the bases of economic decisions.

We need not look further than Paulo Freire's (1970) *Pedagogy of the Oppressed* to make sense of financial literacy as an exchange between those who control the economy and those who are controlled by it. With regard to financial literacy, the matter of how to accumulate resources represents one that emphasizes control. The matter of compassion involves a development of inner sense of appreciation to create the long-term self-discipline to resist the temptation to purchase material goods that produce temporary fulfillment. As Freire tells us, even when those who have little attain assets, they emulate the oppressor because that is the model that they have seen.

This is not to say that poor financial decisions depend on the greed of the affluent. Each person has the potential to be selfish and selfless. Rather, it is to say that an environment that teaches about financial decision-making purely on the basis of amassing financial assets, such as stocks and bonds, without regard for the welfare of others less fortunate reinforces an unjust system founded on principles of resource control and manipulation.

It is a complex proposition for those of us who have seen few compassionate models to imagine ourselves somewhere between the opposite poles of "controller" and "the controlled." Educational discourses about personal finance emphasize the mathematical processes for building financial wealth without discussing the social injustices that relate to consumer decisions that reinforce corporate profitability through global exploitation (Arthur, 2012). In economic systems that define critical thinking within a box of profit maximization, economic global exploitation is likely to occur.

NOTIONS OF CITIZENSHIP

Westheimer (2015) expands upon the three types of citizens explored in his (Westheimer & Kahne, 2004) seminal work, which are displayed in Table 10.1. This typology identifies personally responsible and participatory citizens as acting in ways to solve social problems that maintain and reinforce existing social structures. The justice-oriented citizen, on the other hand, seeks solutions by challenging the principles of the system. Social education construes personal finance and economics through lenses of personally responsible and participatory citizenship. In this view, financial literacy represents knowledge of how to account for and control material resources.

Table 10.1   Financial Education Conceptions and Westheimer and Kahne's (2004) Types of Citizens

Citizen Types	Characteristics	Focus for Financial Education
Responsible	Follows rules	Wealth accumulation and control
Participatory	Leads for change within system	Changes of standards to make education of wealth and control more efficient
Justice Oriented	Seeks change in assumptions and structures	Democratic focus that values ideas based on social stewardship, rather than wealth control

When financial education includes a compassionate element, the structures for citizenship change from a vision in which responsible conduct reinforces the agenda of a wealthy minority to a framework in which all parties have compassionate respect for each other and for who they are. This compassionate approach to financial education remains open to alternative explanations for financial circumstances and advocates care for those whose contexts limit the opportunities for sound decision-making or financial choices.

When citizenship education is relegated to the margins of the curriculum, it becomes a voter registration activity or a visit to the local courthouse. Citizenship education, optimally taught, is enacted in classrooms and schools engaging students in service to each other and their local, state, national, and international communities.

ENVISIONING A MORE COMPASSIONATE APPROACH TO TEACHING FINANCIAL LITERACY

In the wake of the Great Recession, we encourage social studies educators' consideration of a balanced approach to financial literacy that includes principles of compassion. In this view, one's personal worth relates to a compassionate sense of oneself, regardless of the resources with which one is associated in comparison to others. We argue that in realizing this sense of compassionate personal self-worth, students develop the ability to self-regulate themselves such that they have the emotional stability to discipline their financial behaviors.

In the following sections, we provide suggestions for viewing existing financial literacy themes in a more compassionate manner. As stated earlier, our interpretation of a compassionate approach to financial literacy raises potential objections from many financial education scholars who advocate choice-based frameworks that support the merits of wealth accumulation. We organize our suggestions based on the generally accepted areas of financial literacy.

Income

In the conventional view of personal finance, a person earns income when he or she develops the set of job skills necessary to perform the tasks expected of those who control resources. The ability to develop wealth relates to completion of tasks desired by those who control financial resources. Income represents a conditional amount or stream of money that depends on performing a task or other form of work for someone willing to pay the money. This view involves elements of merit because one uses his or her opportunities to develop the skills necessary to satisfactorily perform the required tasks.

Balancing this perspective with a compassionate approach to financial literacy recognizes that self-worth does not depend on accumulation of resources. One only needs to enter into an employment agreement if he or she views the prospective work environment as compassionate and/or considers any related manufacturing process or service as compassionate.

In a compassionate employment relationship, the employee and employer enter into a caring agreement based on trust and respect for each other. The hiring process involves conversations about mutual needs and how each party may contribute to their fulfillment. Regular interactions allow for candid communications about each party's welfare. Manufacturing processes emphasize employee safety.

Money Management

Some existing financial literacy approaches are based on the principle of wealth accumulation. A compassionate approach to money management recognizes that one's worth does not depend on the accumulation of goods and services. As a matter of clarification, this is not to say that people who control vast amounts of resources have poor images of themselves. Nor are we saying that people who are in poverty have great images of themselves. A positive sense of oneself based on care and compassion does not and should not depend on material objects or people for that awareness. It involves a sense of trust founded on associations with people and environments that are safe and mutually respectful.

Balancing this perspective with a compassionate approach to financial management involves principles that relate to social outcomes in a broad sense. This perspective differs from Maier, Figart, and Nelson's (2014) proposed augmentation of financial literacy standards, which advocates for content that informs students about the influences of institutions and social structures on financial choices and the knowledge of how individual decisions require awareness of these institutional complexity coupled with social process. Rather than considering choices that involve the greatest amount of income or the least amount of financial outlay, compassionate money management relates to the outcomes of these decisions on those affected by the choices.

For example, a compassionate consumer may be willing to sacrifice money for higher prices to purchase goods and services from local suppliers rather than corporate sources that exploit resources and harm the community and its environment. Such a decision rests on care for supporting the local community instead of international corporations that may provide jobs but that may not support local infrastructure because its loyalties lie with stockholders, boards of trustees, and/or other nonlocal entities.

Credit and Debt

Within existing frameworks, conditions for debt favor those who control financial resources by providing them with compensation for the use of their funds. The system of debt represents a process for social control that maintains the financial disparities between those with financial resources and those without.

For example, credit cards represent high interest and unsecured forms of lending to compensate lenders for higher risk while creating a financial noose for those who cannot discipline their spending. While credit cards were originally intended as tools for business travelers to receive temporary credit for their travel expenses until receiving employer reimbursement, current environments exploit youth, and the public in general, and dubiously influence lifestyles by marketing credit cards as spending tools for consumer goods and services.

A compassionately balanced view of credit and debt recognizes that creditors create financial needs through the marketing of credit for the purchase of goods and services and that the building of community does not depend on the acquisition of luxury items. Credit represents a convenient service because it increases opportunities for purchasing goods and services that one might not be able to purchase otherwise.

For example, one may use a credit card to purchase a new wardrobe of clothes for which he or she lacks the necessary cash. Instead of viewing credit as an opportunity to acquire goods and services, a compassionate approach questions whether the potential to acquire goods or services improves the worth of the individual. In the final analysis, compassion for oneself does not depend on the goods or services that he or she controls but in the psychological security the individual has for him or her.

Risk and Insurance

The underlying principle with purchasing insurance concerns the transfer of financial risk to the insurance company. Our criticism of existing conceptions of risk and insurance resides within the notion that insurance presents a consumer good that may be purchased to compensate the policyholder in the case of financial losses. However, because insurance companies have the resources to determine the probabilities of policyholders incurring insurable events and the ability to adjust their premiums accordingly, the act of purchasing insurance preserves practices that maintain the gap between rich and poor.

The balanced view of risk and insurance illuminates difficulties with the purchase of insurance based on the following beliefs:

- The potential for social bias and corporate control of criteria associated with determinations of insurability
- The perpetuation of economic class disparities that arise from mathematical approaches to determining insurance coverage amounts with maximum benefits for those who need financial resources the least and vice versa
- The imposition of a belief among social participants that financial insurance represents a necessity service
- The influence on social valuing of particular social commodities through the availability of insurance products.

A truth of worth and insurability becomes unchallenged as corporate interests drive the ideology that the commodity of insurance is an absolute necessity. While one may construe the Affordable Healthcare Act as a justice-oriented solution, the act plays into the corporate ideology by requiring that citizens purchase healthcare insurance through a number of competing firms. These challenges relate to a neo-classical wealth assumption and approach to financial literacy. Such an assumption asserts that personal needs are satisfied through what is presented to the buyer as the neutral consumption of goods and services provided by holders of wealth.

The psychological-moral reasons for our challenge to these assumptions relate to a process of social control that fosters a competitive framework advocating for self-fulfillment through accumulation of goods and services. The belief that consumers have choice in the matter of purchasing insurance or not provides a rational explanation for differences in resource control that undoubtedly benefits the insurance company rather than the masses of consumers that purchase insurance. Such widespread economic practices ignore the points by which one enters the social environment as an economic imperative and the sources of control exerted by policymakers and special on financial decision-making.

In keeping with Foucault's (1972) theory of discourse, the economic power of insurance discourse obligates consumers as both individuals and broad-based influencers of socioeconomic behavioral control. Because consumers think they need insurance (or are required to purchase it), they purchase coverage but hope they will never need to use it. They are willing to pay the insurance company because they have been conditioned to believe in the need for coverage.

It might be more beneficial to those with few monetary resources to find other ways to support each other in case of emergencies and economic exigencies. Through the formation of credit unions, cooperatives, and other mutually helpful collaborations, the insured may realize a more personable sense of security.

Savings and Investing

Savings and investing represent processes for accumulating additional resources by using one's money to fund business operations, through either ownership or learning. A choice-based financial system that emphasizes investing for financial accumulation reinforces an inherent bias for those who control more resources than others.

Consider, for example, voting laws for shareholders in which a shareholder is represented by the number of shares that he or she owns. In a meeting of 200 shareholders, a minority of wealthy shareholders (often executive officers or directors of the corporation) control their own corporate fates by voting on their own policies. The outcomes may be significantly different from an environment in which one person receives a vote simply because of his or her stockholder status.

A compassionate approach to financial literacy contemplates the socially just nature of the companies with which one considers investing. Because investing provides businesses with financial capital to support their operations, a compassionate investor possesses a caring for himself or herself to capitalize those businesses that practice socially compassionate principles rather than seeking investment opportunities based on the amount of anticipated profit.

OPPORTUNITIES FOR CONVERSATION

Classrooms may facilitate opportunities for students to discuss these views of financial literacy and the citizenship conceptions that they may support. Teachers may ground these discussions on the psychological assumptions that support these approaches to financial literacy.

For example, one scenario may consider claims that profit represents the outcome of merit by good choices with regard to resources, and they may contend that the framework described in this chapter positions profitability as malevolent. The responding discussion may assert a claim that foundations of choice-based arguments lack consideration of habitus, restrictions on peoples' doing and becoming (Bourdieu & Passeron, 1977)—all of the things in their lives and environment over which they have little or no control.

People do not choose to be born into their social family contexts. Rather, those situations relate to the decisions made by others. One could argue whether profitability relates to good choices by entrepreneurs and oversimplifies notions of business and profit. Such discussions may question the moral integrity of a business that becomes so profit focused that it ignores or discounts the quality of human life sacrificed for the products produced, the conditions under which its workers labor, or the environmental destruction that their business may cause.

Another basis for consideration would claim that current financial literacy efforts are founded on efforts to improve the quality of life through ownership of financial accounts, which allow for participation in a global economy. The response could argue that quality of life based on resource control represents a contrived notion that relates to manipulation of material resources, including people, for personal gain. A society based on principles of control, anger, and fear leads to uneasy tensions between individuals and institutions, which creates community based on possession of resources rather than respect for individuals. The compassionate person accepts himself or herself, regardless of his or her circumstances.

A third possible discussion could consider claims that there are rules in society that need to be learned for all to be participating citizens in society. The response could suggest that social rules relate to context and those controlling resources often guide their allocation to maintain an order that reinforces their social view. Technical aspects of social interworking are necessary parts of education; however, citizens need to become compassionate to develop the openness to realize the benefits of alternative interpretations and ways of being or transforming societies.

Current approaches to economic/financial literacy provide limited account of bases for decision-making. For example, Schug and Wood's (2011) attribution of English colonial successes (versus French and Spanish failures) to mercantilism provides a limited account of social behavior because it ignores the perspectives of Indigenous American and West African cultures.

From a European perspective, the colonization represented the ingenious use of available resources. The complete picture conveys a process of human exploitation for manual labor rated to crop production and human eradication for land control. In either case, the process of mercantilism was designed to control resources through entrepreneurship. It lacks compassion because it sets a standard for human worth based on control of resources, as well as exploitation of nature and people, rather than on an individual as a community member.

The definition of normative lies in the context of one culture (i.e., European). It ignores the effects of disease and global placement that provided the condition for cultural domination. It discounts the emotional framings that guided patterns of thinking and the conditions prompting development of technological sophistication.

In a balanced vision, Europeans in the late 15th century experienced overpopulation and limited resources that prompted the necessity for social rules (Diamond, 1999). A select few families whose ancestors fought to control resources in vast amounts created these rules. On the North American continent, various nations of indigenous people worked with plentiful resources. These nations met their European contacts with various degrees of receptivity.

The broader version indicates that European expansion to the American continent related to placement on an east-west landmass that experienced temperature fluctuations (Diamond, 1999). A psychology of control resulted from a preoccupation with needs for natural resources that were rare in that part of the world.

Another basis for deliberation could relate to a claim that disparities between rich and poor always exist. Why is the present such an important time to address this situation? The response could interpret rich and poor as a matter of wealth ownership. A rich person owns much wealth. A poor person owns little wealth.

The discussion could consider that interpretations of rich and poor represent expressions of patterns of compassion and control. One could argue that people experience different degrees of psychological trauma that may challenge their willingness or ability to be compassionate and, thus, lack empathy for another's social context and financial position.

For example, a person with a drinking addiction experiences an alcoholically induced trauma that increases the revenues and potential profit of the alcohol producer. This individual is poor in the sense that she or he possesses limited compassion for himself or herself to stop the habit or escape the conditions that prompt it to occur. Because the alcohol corporation makes a profit by controlling the supply of the resource that traumatizes the individual, it has little compassion for the individual aside from encouraging the individual to seek professional assistance. A compassionate approach to financial literacy interprets richness and poorness as relating to the extent of one's sense of being, independent of perceived control of goods or services.

Willis (1983) describes disruptive school behaviors, such as overt criticisms of authority figures, of high school seniors in the United Kingdom, which represent responses to the rigid efforts of school officials to maintain civil educational settings. While one might label such behaviors as subversive or disrespectful, such descriptors are based on cultural norms established by the economically fortunate. From the perspective of these working-class youths, these behaviors represent forms of expression that occur as manifestations of frustration with struggles within an education system that values obedience and cultural conformity.

Such patterns of low esteem from marginalization relate to research findings that trace the origin of these attitudes to lower grade struggles to perform simple tasks (e.g., Hatt, 2012). When youth have lost hope in institutions of schooling as being relevant to them, they move to the margins of the community where they and others like them do not feel valued or significant, and therefore, their values are not concerned with the apparatus that might take them elsewhere in the economic hierarchy.

On the other hand, elite youth may feel community with others like them who know that their families have resources and power, take for granted that they are privileged, and therefore, do not develop compassion for those around them. Financial literacy that develops an individual sense of compassionate personal worth such that he or she conducts himself or herself in a manner respectful to himself and to others could alleviate these environments.

One final basis for discussion could consider that economic and financial theory already includes compassionate principles in that they offer information about processes for developing financial success within existing capitalist systems. It is up to citizens to make the decision to adapt these principles within their own lifestyles. Further, societal institutions satisfy the compassionate needs of its members, and participants can volunteer or provide financial support to those institutions as compassionate gestures for social needs.

The counter-view would be that financial contributions to compassionate institutions represent forms of financial transfer (as is used with insurance) to compassionate specialists. These financial transfers represent efforts to control one's compassion by providing resources to the institution that provides compassionate services; however, they do not represent compassionate actions, but are behaviors of convenience. This reasoning is analogous to that used by critics of markets for pollution credits, in which one corporation that does not wish to relax its environmental policies can purchase pollution credits from another corporation.

These actions represent efforts to transfer responsibility of one's moral obligations to another party. The analogy would be a schoolyard where a bully pays money to a mild-mannered individual to receive credit for being polite to other children so that she or he can use her or his time to traumatize other persons without fear of consequence. The use of financial transactions as mechanisms to excuse oneself from social responsibility represents an uncompassionate process of control.

CONCLUSION AND IMPLICATIONS
FOR SOCIAL EDUCATION

In this chapter, we claimed that existing approaches to citizenship, economic, and social studies teaching often developed on economic principles rooted in notions of control and oppression. We have asserted an argument for financial literacy education grounded in principles of compassion that challenge principles of wealth accumulation and advocate for care of one's social community within the macrocosm of the global community.

Social education should consider the value of a compassionate approach to balance financial literacy and its relevance to citizenship education. When considering the nature of responsible citizenship, social educators should recognize the relevance of balancing perspectives of economic and financial control with compassionate stewardship. When defining social concepts in terms of economic outcomes and markets of exchange, the ideas become objects of a locus of control that lacks capacity to respect alternative perspectives based upon different sets of principles.

We encourage social education experiences that employ critical dialogue to integrate the patterns of economic control at local, regional, national, and global levels and consider alternative approaches to decision-making that value contributions from all participants.

The final illustration of this compassionate perspective lies within our global environment and the extinction processes for which humankind is responsible. When considering the extent to which financial literacy presents an issue of compassion and control, we should ask ourselves the extent to which a fraction of humankind is so superior to the majority of others and to other species on this planet that it has the right to control a lifestyle of convenience that imposes patterns of actions and thinking that lack any justifiable merit.

When, in the final analysis, we consider that our compassionate responsibilities extend to all members of this earth community, perhaps we need to realize the little time we have left to let go our trivial grandeurs of status. Such visions promote accumulation, overuse, and abuse of finite resources to engorge the pocketbooks of the wealthy who have not acknowledged their responsibility to the welfare of the many, rather than of the few or one (Slater & Boyd, 1999).

Inconsistent with dominant discourses of education to prepare global workers, we must shift gears to educate globally minded citizens who do not view their personal financial success as an end or a laudable goal in life. Financial literacy entails engaging us all in taking stock of the state of the planet and asserting ourselves in sustainable, moral, and ethical ways of doing and being in the world.

REFERENCES

Agnello, M. F. & Lucey, T. A. (2008). Toward a critical economic literacy: Preparing K-12 learners to be economically literate adults. In D. E. Lund & P. R. Carr (Eds.), *Doing democracy. Striving for political literacy and social justice* (pp. 247–266). New York, NY: Peter Lang.

Arthur, C. (2012). *Neoliberalism, the consumer, and the citizen.* Rotterdam, The Netherlands: Sense Publishers.

Bell, L. A. (2010). *Storytelling for social justice. Connecting narrative and the arts in antiracist teaching.* New York, NY: Routledge.

Bourdieu, P. & Passeron, J.C. (1977). *Reproduction in education, society and culture.* Thousand Oaks, CA: Sage Publications.

Diamond, J. (1999). *Guns, germs, and steel. The fates of human society.* New York, NY: W. W. Norton & Company.

Foucault, M. (1972). *The archaeology of knowledge and the discourse on language* (A. M. Sheridan Smith, Trans.). New York, NY: Pantheon Books.

Freire, P. (1970). *Pedagogy of the oppressed.* New York, NY: Seabury Press.

Hatt, B. (2012). Smartness as a cultural practice in schools. *American Educational Research Journal, 49,* 438-460.

Hudick, M. (2011). Why economics is not a science of behaviour. *Journal of Economic Methodology, 18,* 147-162.

LeDoux, J. (2002). *The synaptic self: How our brains become who we are.* New York, NY: Penguin Books.

Loewen, J. W. (2007). *Lies my teacher told me. Everything your American history textbook got wrong.* New York, NY: Touchstone.

Lucey, T. A. (2012). Conceptualizing financial morality. In T. A. Lucey & J. D. Laney (Eds.), *Reframing financial literacy: Exploring the value of social currency* (pp. 47-63). Charlotte, NC: Information Age Publishing.

Lucey, T. A., Agnello, M. F., & Laney, J. D. (2015). *A critically compassionate approach to financial literacy.* Rotterdam, The Netherlands: Sense Publishers.

Maier, M. H., Figart, D. M., & Nelson, J. A. (2014). Proposed national standards for financial literacy: What's in? What's out? *Social Education, 78,* 77-79.

McGregor, S. L. T. (2010). *Consumer moral leadership.* Rotterdam, The Netherlands: Sense Publishers.

Narvaez, D., Panksepp, J., Schore, A. N., & Gleason, T. R. (Eds.). (2013). *Evolution, early experience, and human development. From research to practice and policy.* Oxford, UK: Oxford University Press.

Panksepp, J. & Biven, L. (2012). *The archeology of the mind. Neuroevoluntionary origins of human emotions.* New York, NY: W. W. Norton.

Schug, M. C. & Wood, W. C. (2011). *Economic episodes in American History.* Morristown, NJ: Wohl Publishing.

Slater, R. O. & Boyd, W. L. (1999). Schools as polities. In J. Murphy & K. S. Louis (Eds.), *Handbook of research on education administration. A project of the American Educational Research Association* (pp. 323–336). San Francisco, CA: Jossey Bass.

Smith, A. (1976). *Theory of moral sentiments* (D. D. Raphael & A. L. MacFee, Eds.). Oxford, Clarendon Press. (Original work published 1759).

Westheimer, J. (2015). *What kind of citizen? Educating our children for the common good.* New York, NY: Teachers College Press.

Westheimer, J. & Kahne, J. (2004). What kind of citizen? The politics of educating for democracy. *American Educational Research Journal, 41*(2), 237-269.

Willis, P.E. (1983). *Learning to labor. How working class kids get working class jobs.* Aldershot, England: Gower Publishing Company.

Wilkinson, R. & Pickett, K. (2011). The *spirit level: Why greater equality makes societies stronger.* New York, NY: Penguin Books.

About the Editor and Contributors

ABOUT THE EDITOR

Wayne Journell is an associate professor of secondary social studies education and coordinator of the secondary teacher education program at the University of North Carolina at Greensboro. A former high school social studies teacher, his research focuses on the teaching of politics and political processes in secondary education. He has published over fifty peer-reviewed publications, including articles in leading journals such as *Teachers College Record, Theory & Research in Social Education, Educational Studies, Phi Delta Kappan, Educational Leadership,* and *Social Education.* He currently serves as the editor for *Theory & Research in Social Education,* which is the premier research journal in the field of social studies education. In 2014, he received the Exemplary Research in Social Studies Award from the National Council for the Social Studies and the Early Career Award from the College and University Faculty Assembly of the National Council for the Social Studies. He is also the editor of *Reassessing the Social Studies Curriculum: Promoting Critical Civic Engagement in a Politically Polarized, Post-9/11 World* (2016, Rowman & Littlefield).

ABOUT THE CONTRIBUTORS

Mary Frances Agnello is an associate professor at Akita International University in Japan. Her research focuses on critical analyses of education, particularly the teaching of economics and financial literacy.

Jeannette Balantic is the social studies curriculum coordinator in the Garden City School District. She has been a social studies teacher for twenty-five years and has taught social studies methods classes at Hofstra University and Teachers College. She is currently co-editor (with Andrea S. Libresco) of *Social Studies and the Young Learner*.

Mariah Bender is a secondary social studies educator working in the Chicago Public Schools. Her research is centered on creating youth-centered spaces for Black youth, understanding positive racial identity through performative pedagogy, and interrogating the proliferation of charter schools and limited school choice in Chicago and Saint Louis.

Bonnie L. Bittman is a doctoral student of social science education at the University of Central Florida. She teaches social studies education courses and serves as the communications coordinator for the International Society for the Social Studies. She taught high school for seven years in a rural county in Florida, including AP U.S. Government and Politics, civics, economics, and world history. Her research interests include civics education, teacher instruction, and instructional strategies.

Carolyn J. Brejwo received her doctorate from the University of West Virginia in 2012 and is currently an adjunct faculty member in the Department of Curriculum and Instruction. Her research focuses on civic education in rural environments and the impact of rural poverty on social studies education as well as the role that educational standards play in the classroom.

Shakealia Y. Finley is a Gus T. Ridgel Fellow in the learning, teaching, and curriculum social studies education PhD program at the University of Missouri – Columbia. Her research interest is pre-college economic education. She taught high school economics in Atlanta, Georgia, and New York, New York, as well as online at Georgia Perimeter College.

H. James (Jim) Garrett is an assistant professor in the Department of Educational Theory and Practice at the University of Georgia. His research focuses on the ways in which learning and learning to teach, while rewarding and exciting, are also home to difficulty and burdensome complexity. His work has been published in the *Journal of Teacher Education*, *Curriculum Inquiry*, and *Theory & Research in Social Education*.

Jeremy Hilburn is an assistant professor at the University of North Carolina Wilmington. His primary research interest is social studies curriculum and pedagogy specific to immigration and immigrant students in new gateway states. A second strand relates to the spatial dimension of citizenship education, specifically the ways teachers conceptualize and teach civic action at the local, national, and global levels. The final strand focuses on social studies pedagogy in multiple contexts – middle level, secondary, and teacher education.

Aaron P. Johnson is an assistant professor of social studies education at the University of Nebraska-Lincoln. His research interests include technology integration, global education, citizenship education, and the pedagogical locations of convergence that link these areas in the context of social studies education.

Fares J. Karam is a doctoral candidate in the English education program at the University of Virginia. He has taught English in Lebanon and the United Arab Emirates in K-12 contexts and taught graduate and undergraduate courses at the University of Virginia. His research interests include refugee education, language and identity, and classroom interaction and ELs/ELLs.

LaGarett J. King is an assistant professor of social studies education at the University of Missouri, Columbia. His research focuses on Black history education, critical theories on race, social studies history, and critical multiculturalism. He has work published in *Theory & Research in Social Education*, *Teaching Education*, *Journal of Negro Education*, and *Race, Ethnicity, and Education*.

Andrea S. Libresco is a professor of social studies education, director of elementary education and of the minor in civic education at Hofstra University. She was a high school social studies teacher and lead teacher for elementary social studies in the public schools for nineteen years. She is currently co-editor (with Jeannette Balantic) of *Social Studies and the Young Learner*.

James D. Laney is a professor and chair of the Department of Teacher Education and Administration at the University of North Texas. His research interests include generative teaching-learning theory, general social studies education, economic education, aging education, and arts integration.

Thomas A. Lucey is an associate professor in the School of Teaching of Learning at Illinois State University. His current research project concerns intersections of spirituality, citizenship, and financial literacy.

J.B. Mayo Jr. is an associate professor in social studies education in the College of Education and Human Development at the University of Minnesota. He researches how to incorporate LGBTQ topics/themes in the standard social studies curriculum. In addition, Mayo has written about how gay-straight alliances, in both high schools and middle schools, affect the individuals who participate in them and the larger (school) communities in which they are located.

Paula McAvoy is a philosopher of education and program director for the Center for Ethics and Education at UW-Madison. Her research interests include democratic education, cultural and religious accommodations, and the ethics of teaching about politics. Paula has also worked as an assistant professor at Illinois State University and as an associate program officer for the Spencer Foundation. She is the co-author, with Diana Hess, of the book *The Political Classroom: Evidence and Ethics in Democratic Education* (2015, Routledge Press).

Eric D. Moffa is a doctoral student in curriculum and instruction/social studies education at West Virginia University, where he also assists the Center for Democracy and Citizenship Education. His research has been published in the *Journal of International Social Studies* and has been presented at multiple national conferences. Eric's research interests are in citizenship education, rural education, and John Dewey.

William B. Russell III is an associate professor of social science education at the University of Central Florida. He also serves as the director for the International Society for the Social Studies and is the editor-in-chief of the most widely read research journal in the field, *The Journal of Social Studies Research*. Dr. Russell has authored over fifty-five peer-reviewed journal articles related to social studies education and has published two of the most notable social studies methods textbooks in the field, *Essentials of Elementary Social Studies*, 4th ed., and *Essentials of Middle and Secondary Social Studies* (co-authors T. Turner and S. Waters; Routledge).

Ashley Taylor Jaffee is an assistant professor of social studies education at James Madison University. She is a former middle and high school social studies teacher and taught world geography, civics, and world history in San Juan, Puerto Rico. Her research focuses on social studies and citizenship education, culturally and linguistically relevant pedagogy, immigrant youth, and pre-service social studies teacher education.

Chezare A. Warren is an assistant professor in the Department of Teacher Education at Michigan State University. He has over a decade of professional experience as a public school math teacher and school administrator in Chicago, Houston, and Philadelphia. Dr. Warren's research interests include urban teacher education, culturally responsive teaching, and critical race theory in education. He is vice president of the critical race studies in education association, and his work has been published in several peer-reviewed journals, including *Urban Education, The Urban Review, The Interdisciplinary Journal of Teaching and Learning, Teachers College Record,* and *Race, Ethnicity, and Education.*

Robert A. Waterson is an associate professor at West Virginia University, with research and teaching interests in social studies and citizenship education. He also serves as the director of the WVU Center for Democracy and Citizenship Education, which offers many experiential learning opportunities for social studies methodology students.

Paul J. Yoder is a doctoral candidate and instructor in the secondary social studies education program at the University of Virginia. A former middle school social studies teacher in a culturally diverse school system, his primary research interests focus on the teaching and learning of history and social studies among English language learners. Additionally, his work explores the complex relationships between language, identity, and the enacted curriculum.